# TO FEAST ON US AS THEIR PREY

FOOD AND FOODWAYS

SERIES EDITORS:
JENNIFER JENSEN WALLACH
AND MICHAEL WISE

OTHER BOOKS IN THIS SERIES

*Inventing Authenticity: How Cookbook Writers Redefine Southern Identity*

*Chop Suey and Sushi from Sea to Shining Sea: Chinese and Japanese Restaurants in the United States*

*Forging Communities: Food and Representation in Medieval and Early Modern Southwestern Europe*

*Aunt Sammy's Radio Recipes: The Original 1927 Cookbook and Housekeeper's Chat*

*Mexican-Origin Foods, Foodways, and Social Movements: Decolonial Perspectives*

*The Taste of Art: Food, Cooking, and Counterculture in Contemporary Practices*

*Devouring Cultures: Perspectives on Food, Power, and Identity from the Zombie Apocalypse to Downton Abbey*

*Latin@s' Presence in the Food Industry: Changing How We Think about Food*

*Dethroning the Deceitful Pork Chop: Rethinking African American Foodways from Slavery to Obama*

*American Appetites: A Documentary Reader*

# To Feast on Us as Their Prey

## CANNIBALISM AND THE EARLY MODERN ATLANTIC

EDITED BY
RACHEL B. HERRMANN

The University of Arkansas
Fayetteville
2019

Manufactured in the United States of America

ISBN: 978-1-68226-081-4 (cloth)
ISBN: 978-1-68226-082-1 (paper)
eISBN: 978-1-61075-656-3

23 22 21 20 19 5 4 3 2 1

♾ The paper used in this publication meets the minimum requirements of the American National Standard for Permanence of Paper for Printed Library Materials Z39.48-1984.

Library of Congress Cataloging-in-Publication Data

Names: Herrmann, Rachel B., author.
Title: To feast on us as their prey : cannibalism and the early modern Atlantic / edited by Rachel B. Herrmann.
Description: Fayetteville : University of Arkansas Press, 2019. | Includes bibliographical references and index. |
Identifiers: LCCN 2018017414 (print) | LCCN 2018031014 (ebook) | ISBN 9781610756563 (electronic) | ISBN 9781682260814 (cloth : alk. paper) | ISBN 9781682260821 (pbk. : alk. paper)
Subjects: LCSH: Cannibalism—Atlantic Ocean Region. | Atlantic Ocean Region—Social conditions.
Classification: LCC GN409 (ebook) | LCC GN409 .T6 2019 (print) | DDC 394/.9091821—dc23
LC record available at https://lccn.loc.gov/2018017414

# CONTENTS

# SERIES EDITORS' PREFACE

The University of Arkansas Press Series on Food and Foodways explores historical and contemporary issues in global food studies. We are committed to representing a diverse set of voices that tell lesser-known food stories and to provoking new avenues of interdisciplinary research. Our strengths are works in the humanities and social sciences that use food as a critical lens to examine broader cultural, environmental, and ethical issues.

Feeding ourselves has long entangled human beings within complicated moral puzzles of social injustice and environmental destruction. When we eat, we consume not only food on the plate, but also the lives and labors of innumerable plants, animals, and people. This process distributes its costs unevenly across race, class, gender, and other social categories. The production and distribution of food often obscures these material and cultural connections, impeding honest assessments of our impact on the world around us. By taking these relationships seriously, Food and Foodways provides a new series of critical studies that analyze the cultural and environmental relationships that have sustained human societies.

In *To Feast on Us as Their Prey: Cannibalism and the Early Modern Atlantic* Rachel B. Herrmann has assembled a group of extraordinary interdisciplinary essays written by ten scholars at various stages in their careers. In her deft introduction, Herrmann gives a useful overview of the scholarly literature on the subject and uses the ongoing debate about whether or not cannibalism occurred and with what frequency during the 1609–1610 Starving Time in Jamestown, Virginia to elucidate one of the major claims of the collection. She argues that although much scholarship on the subject has focused on ascertaining whether or not cannibalism took place, answering this question is a far less revealing exercise than endeavoring to understand what stories about the consumption of human flesh reveal about the people who first circulated and interpreted them. Together the contributors examine how various Native American, European, and African peoples defined themselves or were defined by others in relation to this enduring taboo. Throughout the text the idea of hunger is used both as a metaphor and to describe a physical sensation. Hunger to dominate, to explore, to understand, to explain, and to eat undergirded the cross-cultural encounters discussed in this volume, a fact that makes this important collection a vital contribution to the food studies canon.

—JENNIFER JENSEN WALLACH AND MICHAEL WISE

# ACKNOWLEDGMENTS

I was unknowingly working on the ideas in this volume long before I envisioned it as a book and have subsequently accrued a large number of people to thank. Gratitude goes first to Marc Palen: had he not set an example of graduate student publishing when we were both working on our PhDs at the University of Texas at Austin, I might have waited much longer to turn my master's thesis into an article. Other graduate students offered crucial feedback and support; thanks go especially to Rachel Ozanne (the best Other Rachel I know), Benjamin Breen, Felipe Cruz, Chris Heaney, Cameron Strang, and Alexis Harasemovitch Truax. I am grateful to Carolyn Eastman for encouraging me to publish, for her help in convening Erika Bsumek and James Sidbury to workshop my essay, and for their comments on that piece of work.

That essay landed at the *William and Mary Quarterly*, where observations from anonymous peer reviewers, editor Christopher Grasso, and managing editor Erin Bendiner and careful work by the journal's editorial apprentices taught me an enormous amount about framing an argument and writing for a scholarly audience. Thank you to everyone who has taught that article, especially the people who recognized that it was intended as a piece of historical research as well as a lesson plan for teaching students about reading primary sources. E-mails about and discussions over that piece have made me a better—and I hope more generous—historian.

I was thrilled when Jennifer Jensen Wallach approached me about editing a cannibalism volume for the University of Arkansas Press, and I thank her for her guidance on cannibalism and food history in this volume and elsewhere. After securing a contract from the press, a generous grant from the Wellcome Trust (grant number 105351/Z/14/Z) made possible a conference on cannibalism in the early modern Atlantic. Thanks go to keynote speaker William Kelso and to conference participants for beginning the discussion that resulted in these essays and to Kelly Watson for her comments on this book's introduction. The two anonymous reviewers made suggestions that helped contributors undertake revisions to improve their chapters. I am grateful to Kate Babbitt for her copyedits, to Molly Rector for her work as project editor, and to David Scott Cunningham for his editorial support for this volume.

I am particularly appreciative of my colleagues at the University of Southampton. Julie Gammon, Maria Hayward, and Claire Jowitt attended the conference and offered support throughout it and Mark Stoyle offered a useful sounding board as I gathered my thoughts about cannibals. Eve Colpus became a fierce friend after I moved to the university, and I could not have put together the conference, run it, or completed this book without her cheering me on. I thank Kendrick Oliver and Chris Woolgar for their mentorship and Niamh Cullen, Chris Fuller, George Gilbert, Jonathan Hunt, Nick Karn, Claire Le Foll, Matt Kelly, Priti Mishra, Chris Prior, Charlotte Riley, and Helen Spurling for the dinnertime talks out in Southampton that gave me the stamina to pull this volume together. I am additionally grateful to my new colleagues at Cardiff University, particularly to David Doddington for listening to my thoughts as I completed the edits on this volume.

Finally, thanks go to my mother, Marilyn Herrmann, and my sister, Amy Coppernoll. They may never share my interest in cannibalism, but our interest in and love of food were products of the Herrmann table.

# TO FEAST ON US AS THEIR PREY

INTRODUCTION

# "Cannibalism and . . ."

RACHEL B. HERRMANN

A 1780 print cartoon titled *The Allies—par nobile fratrûm* depicts a cannibal feast in the middle of the American War for Independence (1775–1783).[1] At this gruesome meal, two Native American warriors from an unidentified, caricatured tribe crouch on the ground while another man stands to drain the blood from a dismembered corpse. The blood trickles down from the torso and into a skull that has been fashioned into a drinking cup. One of the Indian men gnaws one end of a long bone. Alongside him lounges a bewigged, non-Native figure—perhaps King George III or perhaps his prime minister, Lord North, whose name is scrawled faintly next to the man's head.[2] This gentleman sucks the marrow from the bone's other end, while holding another blood-filled skull. The blood is still fresh; hot steam wafts toward his face. The fluid has come in all likelihood from the chubby, curly-haired child whose decapitated head lies at the Briton's foot. Behind him, a Holy Bible stands upside down, its binding on the wrong side of the book, and beside him, a starving dog vomits up this feast, his skeletal frame rejecting the fare that the Indians and the non-Native man readily consume.

The scene is divided by a flagpole topped with a cross; it supports a disintegrating flag that proclaims the king's role as "Defender of the Faith." On the right side of the flag stand a corpulent bishop and a sailor. They approach the eaters, bearing scalping knives, tomahawks, and crucifixes as presents for the Indians, proclaiming "we are hellish good Christians." The caption of the scene reads, "The Party of Savages went out with Orders not to spare Man, Woman, or Child. To this cruel Mandate even some of the Savages made an Objection, respecting the butchering the Women & Children, but they were told the Children would make Soldiers, & the Women would keep up the Stock."

*Image 1.* John Almon, *The Allies—par nobile fratrûm!*, London, February 3, 1780. Prints and Photographs Division, Library of Congress. *Courtesy of the Library of Congress.*

This image encapsulates the state of cannibalism studies today while hinting at the new questions the contributors to this volume answer. Currently, three overlapping strains of cannibalism scholarship exist. The first contends with the question of whether or not cannibalism took place at various times and in myriad locations around the globe. The second instead asks what representations of cannibalism meant at the time when those representations appeared. The third studies individual cases of cannibalism with the aim of categorizing peoples' practical, religious, symbolic, and gendered ways of and motivations for consuming other people or for levying accusations of cannibalism. Each of these approaches might profitably be applied to this political cartoon.

People in the past and the historians who have written about them have debated the veracity of accounts that suggest that men and women ate each other. Using this frame of analysis, it seems reasonable to interpret this image as a rebel American argument that British soldiers and their Indian allies committed "atrocities" during the War for Independence. Because American newspapers circulated stories of Indian and British war crimes—accounts of rape, attacks against civilian women and children, and mutilated corpses—it would not be surprising if an American artist had tried to claim that their enemies also cannibalized young toddlers.[3] Nor would it be surprising if Britons levied similar charges against the American soldiers and *their* Indian allies, who fought against Great Britain. There was scope for both sides to accuse each other of what they called "savagery." But the publisher of this cartoon was not American. John Almon was British, and he printed this cartoon in London.

Cannibalism scholars have also drawn conclusions about what cannibal representations meant to the people who produced, read, and viewed them. This approach to writing about cannibalism might suggest that a political cartoonist in the late eighteenth century showed the king or his prime minister eating non-Native children because he wanted to persuade the viewer that the act of allying with Indians had debased the country and its inhabitants. The Christians become "hellish," Bibles get turned upside down, the king ceases to defend the faith, and the Crown spends too much money on maintaining destructive alliances. In some Englishmen's eyes, Indian-Anglo military alliances ran the risk of corrupting white men by turning them into metaphorical cannibals. This interpretive angle is less interested in asking whether people at the time believed that the British ate babies and more concerned with how depictions of baby-eating reflected contemporary anxieties about real events.

A scholar invested in the third and last type of scholarship might be interested in classifying the types of cannibalism taking place in this scene. Endocannibalism, or the consumption of members of one's own group, and exocannibalism, or the eating of enemies or outsiders, are both evidenced in the print, depending on how one interprets it. If the artist wanted to suggest that Indians and Englishmen were different, then either the Indians or the British are practicing exocannibalism. If the non-Native people in the print—the gentleman, the bishop, the sailor, and the dead toddler—belong to the same group, then the king or his prime minister is an endocannibalist. Both of these behaviors might also be considered warfare cannibalism.[4] Further readings along these lines might suggest that people cannibalized each other for the practical necessity of dealing with hunger, the strategic reason that it made them more fearsome to their enemies, or because they believed that God wanted them to do so. An analysis like this might also undertake a survey of the people represented in the image, asking why women, children, and men are referenced but women left out of the print itself. These scholars might suggest that military conflicts exposed civilian women to traumatic sexual violence and that the documents produced by military leaders often glossed over women's participation in war efforts.

All of these approaches have something to add to our understanding of "the allies," but they miss an additional point that would interest food historians. The men in this print are cannibalizing a corpse, but they are also sharing it equally between them. If we consider this cannibal feast as an actual meal, it becomes clear that this alliance demanded specific food etiquette. And indeed, during the War for Independence, Indians expected their British and American allies to feast them at key moments, and while the combined forces of Natives and Britons were on their campaigns and took stores of food as plunder, Indians expected a fair share of the edible spoils.[5] In considering cannibalism *and* histories of food and hunger, this interpretation makes an argument for the value of combining studies of cannibalism more seriously with other disciplinary questions. It is this volume's main contention that cannibalism can no longer be studied on its own terms; incidents of cannibalism must instead be placed in conversation with broader questions about how we delimit the chronology of the early modern period and how we conceive of the geography of the Atlantic world.

▪ ▪ ▪

In the summer of 2015, a group of scholars gathered at the University of Southampton for a conference called "Cannibalism in the Early Modern Atlantic," which was generously funded with a grant from the Wellcome Trust.[6] William Kelso, director of Jamestown Rediscovery, delivered the keynote address, in which he discussed his team's recent archaeological findings about the seventeenth-century Jamestown colony, including a particularly controversial case of cannibalism during the Starving Time of 1609–1610. Conference attendees then linked cannibalism to Europeans' quests for food, to stories about colonization, to Europeans' interactions with Native Americans and Africans, to maritime famine, and to the Atlantic world paradigm. The most salient point that emerged from the conference was that analyses of cannibalism now nearly always appear in combination with analyses of something else. In shifting from asking whether cannibalism occurred to querying why it mattered, scholars placed the study of cannibalism in conversation with other topics such as literary theory, imperialism, the history of science, gender relations, and settler colonialism. Cannibalism scholarship is now scholarship on cannibalism and something additional. This volume's contributors take important steps in discussing cannibalism's implications for the wider Atlantic world and, in some cases, even beyond it.

In order to understand how contributors have approached the question of what mattered to people in the past, in addition to cannibalism, it is first necessary to examine what has been written on the subject thus far. It is important to differentiate cannibalism from anthropophagy, although most scholars—including many of the writers in this volume—use the two terms interchangeably. Anthropophagy connotes eating people, but during the early modern period the term cannibal came to mean someone who ate people and was also perceived as "savage." Early modern observers who spoke of anthropophagites thought of mythical man-eaters during the classical period, but they came to associate cannibals with Caribbean peoples during their own time.[7]

Anthropologists have traced actual and perceived instances of cannibalism among Australian Aboriginals, the Ashanti of Africa, Aztecs in Mexico, the Maoris of New Zealand, the Hurons and Iroquois of North America, the Uscochi of the Balkans, the Tupinamba in Brazil, and the Foré of Papua New Guinea, among others.[8] Such work tends to fall on a spectrum between those who argue that people cannibalized other people for symbolic reasons (structuralists) and those who suggest that people ate each other for practical reasons (cultural materialists). The structuralists are perhaps best exemplified by Claude Lévi-Strauss, who discussed the different modes of preparing bodies, from boiling to roasting. He suggested that boiling was a more primitive form of cookery than roasting and that methods for food preparation could thus demarcate the line between civilization and savagery.[9] At the other end of this continuum, cultural materialists such as Marvin Harris interpreted cannibalism as a reaction to the physical need for protein. Harris contended that human flesh was little different from the flesh of other animals and eventually became "bad to eat" for economic reasons similar to those that explain taboos about eating pigs, cows, and horses.[10]

We thus return to the three intersecting types of scholarship on cannibalism. The anthropologist William Arens sparked debate during the first wave of work that argued over whether or not cannibalism had occurred. The 1979 publication of his book *The Man-Eating Myth* examined a number of well-studied episodes of cannibalism and refuted their existence.[11] Since then, numerous scholars have engaged with Arens's conclusions. Marvin Harris went through all of Arens's cases and re-examined each one of them in his 1985 book, *Good to Eat.*[12] Peggy Reeves Sanday's *Divine Hunger* argued for the existence of cannibalism in all of the Americas, Africa, and Oceania; its rarity in the Mediterranean; and its absence in East Eurasia.[13] In 1997, Frank Lestringant's *Cannibals: The Discovery and Representation of the Cannibal from Columbus to Jules Verne* also contradicted Arens by mapping incidents of cannibalism from Columbus to the nineteenth century while also explaining how cannibalism discourses changed over time.[14] George Franklin Feldman's 2008 *Cannibalism, Headhunting and Human Sacrifice in North America* reemphasized the practice of cannibalism among North American Indians.[15] Thomas Abler made a similar point in an article about Iroquois cannibalism.[16] Gananath Obeyesekere's 2005 *Cannibal Talk* revealed a return to Arens's original argument.[17]

Situated within this work is Jamestown, the most recent topic of debate. In 2012, the Jamestown Rediscovery project uncovered human remains—a partial skull and tibia. A team of forensic anthropologists at the Smithsonian's National Museum of Natural History analyzed them, and in 2013 various media outlets broke the news that Jamestown's early colonists had cannibalized each other during Virginia's Starving Time of 1609–1610.[18] Later in 2013, the Colonial Williamsburg Foundation and Preservation Virginia published their findings in a short book based on an exhibition on the same topic.[19] In 2017, William Kelso published a longer monograph on this subject and on archaeological developments at Jamestown more broadly.[20]

These two works chart the struggles of Jamestown's colonists; their inability to establish peaceful diplomatic relations with the region's Native peoples, on whom they depended for food; the deterioration of those already tense relationships; and the colonists' shrinking food supplies.[21] They quote the written sources describing the subsequent cannibalization of Englishmen and women and explain how the Jamestown Rediscovery team uncovered and analyzed the physical evidence of a female body bearing signs of butchering. Researchers performed a facial reconstruction of the skull and named the partial remains of this young woman "Jane." The analysis of Jane's bones echoed many of the written primary sources that historians have known about and analyzed for many decades.[22] Numerous historians had written that Jamestown colonists cannibalized each other, but before 2012 no physical evidence existed to confirm this assertion. Kelso's most recent book calls these findings "incontrovertible evidence that a girl, whom we came to call Jane, had been cannibalized" during the Starving Time.[23]

In 2011—before the discovery of Jane's bones and before this conference—I published an article in the *William and Mary Quarterly* that made two arguments about cannibalism and abundance.[24] First, I voiced skepticism about some of the accounts of cannibalism in the written records of Jamestown, given the conflicting nature of the primary sources and the biases of the self-promoting men who penned them. Second, and more important, I argued that proving whether or not cannibalism occurred was less helpful than understanding what cannibalism stories meant to people at the time. The tales of English cannibals that circulated, first in 1610 and again in the 1620s, were crucial in pushing Virginia's government to enact famine-preventing food laws and in reassuring colonial investors that the Virginia colony would not become a failure. The Starving Time encouraged colonists to secure the colony's abundance, often to the detriment of the region's Native inhabitants. For what my opinion is worth, I think that some cannibalism occurred but that understanding the meanings of cannibalism to people during the early seventeenth century is a far more important aim than conclusively proving that English colonists ate each other during the early years of Jamestown's existence.

With these caveats in mind, I feel compelled to lay out a few reasons for remaining skeptical that Jane's bones offer conclusive proof of cannibalism.[25] To be sure, Jamestown Rediscovery's team offers some convincing evidence. The fact that archaeologists uncovered Jane's bones in a trash pit along with the bones of snakes and horses is a point in support of cannibalism because the remains are the first human bones to appear alongside the refuse of other items that colonial observers recorded eating during the Starving Time.[26] The Smithsonian's analysis suggests that Jane's remains, which made it into the trash pit during the winter of 1609–1610, were butchered postmortem.[27] These pieces of evidence constitute a convincing argument that a woman was killed and butchered in early Jamestown. My main concern is that it is difficult to make the jump from proving that someone was murdered and dismembered to proving that someone else consumed her remains. It is troubling that the only scholarly publication to share these findings has been William Kelso's most recent book, which references the forensic report produced by Douglas Owsley at the Smithsonian, but does not cite it—it cites the 43-page book produced by Colonial Williamsburg and Jamestown Rediscovery.[28] To my knowledge, the forensic report and its findings have been neither peer-reviewed nor published. This lack of access to evidence makes it impossible for other scholars to assess the results, which makes suspect the claim about irrefutable truth. At the cannibalism conference, furthermore, other participants, such as Kelly Watson, cautioned against giving more weight to forensic evidence than to textual evidence. Forensic anthropology and history are different fields, neither of which should be considered more important than the other.

John Smith and George Percy, contemporaries who wrote about the Starving Time, did describe colonists eating each other. Percy charged men with drinking fellow colonists' blood and digging up corpses and eating them. Smith said that one of these bodies belonged to a Native American that they had murdered, buried, and then disinterred. Smith and Percy both wrote about a woman who was killed, butchered, and then cannibalized.[29] Yet the way they wrote about this woman should encourage some cynicism. Their stories diverged at significant points. To the butchering and cannibalization of this woman, Percy added an unborn fetus who was ripped from the mother's womb and thrown into a river uneaten. If the situation in Jamestown was so desperate, why did the man cannibalize the mother and not the child? This part of Percy's story seemed calculated to invoke outrage. Although this craftiness does not prove the story false, it should encourage a cautious reading. John Smith was not physically present during the Starving Time, when cannibalism supposedly took place, so his account also lacks some credibility. He wrote jokingly about the woman's fate, speculating about whether boiled, roasted, grilled ("carbonado'd"), or salted ("powdered") corpse tasted better.[30] He might even have told this story as a type of sailor's sea yarn, knowing that people would not believe it all.[31] A third writer, Thomas Gates, went out of his way to refute the cannibalized wife story. He argued that the husband only claimed to have eaten his wife because he hoped to avoid a hanging; in reality, Gates suggested, the man had murdered his wife to avoid sharing food with her. Gates supported this assertion by pointing out that when the community discovered her butchered body they also found food stores hidden throughout the man's house.[32]

Even if one believes Percy and Smith and discounts Gates, the question that arises is whether Jane is the same person as the wife that Gates, Percy, and Smith mentioned in their narratives. The Jamestown Rediscovery research suggests that Jane was about fourteen years old.[33] Although young, she might have been the wife in these tales. If so, it seems just as plausible to suggest that Jane was killed, decapitated, and dismembered—but not cannibalized—so her husband could eat her share of stored food, as Gates suggested, and so her killer could make the mutilated corpse that much harder to identify. And if Jane is not the same person as the murdered wife, it seems odd that both Smith and Percy passed up the opportunity to sensationalize this additional death. The future of the colony rested on the capacity of Jane and other women to bear children, and Jamestown's female population was disproportionately small. Both Smith and Percy had much to gain by making the whole winter seem as lamentable as possible.[34] Consequently, I think that the research conclusively shows that a young woman was killed and dismembered, but I find it more difficult to be certain that Jane was cannibalized. I will be especially interested in seeing whether evidence emerges that can confirm whether Jane had ever been pregnant. It would also be of particular significance if archaeologists were to uncover remains of Native American and non-Native male bodies bearing signs of cannibalism, because the sources seem to concur that colonists ate Indians. And I continue to believe that ultimately, it is less fruitful to prove that cannibalism did or did not occur than it is to ask why it mattered so deeply to people at the time.

Gananath Obeyesekere tended to agree that most writers exaggerated cases of cannibalism and that stories about cannibalism proliferated because early modern Westerners who arrived in South America, Africa, Asia, and the Pacific assumed that most of the peoples they encountered engaged in the practice. When they returned home, their writings institutionalized these assumptions. Obeyesekere's monograph thus straddled two approaches; he reassessed whether cannibalism occurred while also asking what it meant to the people who wrote about it.[35] His work was preceded by a monograph and two edited volumes—Peter Hulme's *Colonial Encounters* (1986); Francis Barker, Peter Hulme, and Margaret Iversen's *Cannibalism and the Colonial World* (1998); and Laurence Goldman's *The Anthropology of Cannibalism* (1999)—all of which heralded this second shift in analyses of man-eating.[36] Hulme's book was organized around the idea of encounters and was interested in the structure of the narratives that portrayed them, the meanings of single words in those narratives, and the repetitions that appeared over the course of three centuries. These encounters produced a colonial discourse that became an ideology.[37] The writers who followed him, many of whom were postcolonial scholars of anthropology, art history, history, and literature, argued that early modern Europeans' writings about cannibalism revealed more about Europeans than about the Natives they encountered. Accusations of cannibalism were intricately connected to broader imperial goals and anxieties.[38] Other writers, such as Merrall Llewelyn Price and Heather Burton, have suggested that representations of monstrous, sexualized cannibals in the early modern and medieval periods were meant as political metaphors that became important in the creation of a cultural and national English identity.[39] Cătălin

Avramescu's *An Intellectual History of Cannibalism* (2009) asked comparable questions about political theorists' and philosophers' takes on cannibalism during the early modern period.[40] Jennifer Brown's *Cannibalism in Literature and Film* (2012) jumped forward in time to map representations of cannibalism in both the colonial novel and in Italian films and serial killer novels, concluding that representations of cannibals expose contemporary fears.[41] Most recently, Kelly Watson's *Insatiable Appetites* (2015) puts gender and sexuality at the forefront. Watson states that Europeans levied charges of cannibalism because it strengthened claims of patriarchy and masculinity in the Americas.[42]

The last category of scholarship contains works that delineate various reasons why people practiced cannibalism. In cannibalism scholarship, work on medicinal cannibalism usually seems to be the odd topic out, but it fits in neatly when placed in conversation with other works that reckon with the contexts in which people deemed cannibalism appropriate. Richard Sugg's *Mummies, Cannibals, and Vampires* (2011) and Christine Louise Noble's *Medicinal Cannibalism in Early Modern English Literature and Culture* (2011) trace the practical reasons why people thought it was beneficial to their health to consume pieces of mummified humans, powdered skull, and blood.[43] Karen Gordon-Grube and P. Kenneth Himmelman have looked at corpse medicine in New England and medieval Europe, respectively.[44] Frank Lestringant's work, while predominantly engaged with refuting Arens, did so by suggesting some of the reasons why people saw cannibalism as a viable practice. Hans Askenasy described cannibalistic practices such as famine cannibalism, survival cannibalism, magic, ritual, and madness cannibalism. Later works expanded on these forms.[45] Nicholas Constantine's *A History of Cannibalism* (2006) added to these justifications with examples of cultural and disaster cannibalism.[46] Daniel Diehl and Mark Donnelly's *Eat Thy Neighbour* (2006), in addition to talking about some of these other practices, also discussed warfare cannibalism.[47]

This survey of the extant literature should suggest some prevailing trends while also elucidating the problems that have yet to be solved. Earlier work spent time debating the existence of cannibalism. Thereafter, much scholarship homed in on violence and misunderstandings arising from European encounters with people they assumed to be cannibals. This work revealed more about bellicose Europeans than it did about indigenous peoples. Efforts at classifying forms of cannibalism also became frequent. For the most part, observations about cannibalism continue to center on Latin America and the Caribbean. Much remains to be done on North America—especially British North America—and Africa and on what cannibal representations by Native Americans and Africans tell us about these peoples. Other areas for exploration include investigations of cannibalism and cooperation, or at least the absence of aggression. Finally, more written works would benefit from efforts to link histories of cannibalism with histories of food, histories of eating, and histories of hunger. In their treatment of different time periods and locations, the scholars in this volume bear these observations out while taking up some of these newer themes.

We begin by trying to understand how Native Americans conceived of cannibalism rather than how Europeans understood it. Gregory Smithers reads cannibalism tales as evidence of how Native peoples in Southeastern North America used oral traditions to define ritual and ceremonial eating practices. Such customs were shaped by a combination of syncretic food cultures wrought by settler colonialism and the epistemological and spiritual connections between living and inanimate beings. From there, three contributors revisit the most familiar accounts of New World cannibalism: the reports associated with Columbus, the writers who described his voyage, and the Spanish colonists who followed him. Elena Daniele examines how Italian merchants and diplomats were the first to generate, receive, read, and revise early reports of New World cannibalism. Her work provocatively shows that the information circulated in Italian mercantile networks tended to discount initial news of cannibals rather than reproduce such stories. Kelly Watson's chapter places discourses of cannibalism in conversation with ideas about sexual partners, eating taboos, modesty, chastity, and power. Watson suggests that Europeans practiced what she calls "sexual diplomacy" with non-anthropophagite partners but felt few qualms about raping Indigenous women, some of whom were supposedly cannibals. Rebecca Earle argues that scholars who want to more profitably analyze the two tropes of drunken Amerindians and cannibal Amerindians would do well to consider the additional context of the Christian sacrament of communion.[48] Her focus on the significance of wheat bread and wine within Spanish religious and dietary regimes charts how these substances distinguished (and sometimes failed to distinguish) Amerindians from Spaniards.

We return to familiar Anglophone territory with chapters by Jessica Hower, Matt Williamson, and Julie Gammon, but these authors challenge our notions of cannibalism in the British Atlantic by exploring earlier and later chronologies and lesser-studied sources. Hower analyzes the connections between cannibal reports and British imperialism. Going back farther in time than most studies of the British Atlantic, she interprets cannibalism discourses formed abroad as evidence of political upheaval at the Tudor court, finding evidence of continuity over more than a century of early modern British history. Williamson performs a close reading of the play *The Sea Voyage* and links cannibalism to political debates, unruly European appetites, and an emerging capitalist system. The play's authors, he suggests, figured cannibalism as the product of the New World *and* a reflection of excessive English appetites. Gammon reexamines the oft-told tale of Sawney Bean, demonstrating how English people used cannibal stories over time. In the early eighteenth century, representations of cannibals in English writing and print implied the savagery of non-English Celts, Irish, and Scots, but by the late eighteenth and early nineteenth centuries the English were using cannibal stories to promote the supremacy of the British Empire. Taken together, their chapters suggest the need to analyze cannibalism's domestic meanings alongside its applicability to foreign and imperial affairs.

The last set of contributors engage with the Atlantic world paradigm. Their work implicitly seeks to broaden our understanding of cannibalism discourses, the geography of the Atlantic world, and histories of food and hunger. Robert Appelbaum goes back to Lestringant's work to theorize a new form of cannibalism that he calls honor eating, or the use of cannibalism to move beyond biology while participating in a timocratic system of symbolic exchange. Jared Staller's chapter picks up on this theme of symbolic acts of eating. He takes a look at cannibalism and conspicuous consumptions in Andrew Battell's travels in late sixteenth-century South America, Angola, and Loango, interpreting cannibalism in Africa as a public, deliberate, and wasteful demonstration of wealth. My chapter explores the ties between cannibalism and hunger on sea voyages, showing that hunger held multiple meanings to the enslaved peoples, sailors, and slave captains who crossed oceans in the eighteenth and nineteenth centuries. Sailors and slaves fought over food but also shared it, and at times the refusal of food could be an act of asserting power.

These contributions suggest a few ideas for the future of scholarship on cannibalism. The first, and I think most significant, is that the field has moved on from debates over whether or not cannibalism occurred. Although scholars will doubtless continue to ask this question, I would urge them to consider it in tandem with other lines of inquiry. The second point is that although the Caribbean has received the most attention, there is much to say about English cannibalism before and after Jamestown, about North American Indians, the African and Spanish Atlantics, and about bondpeople who were forced to cross the Atlantic Ocean before becoming embroiled in New World systems of slavery. The third point is that cannibalism studies continue to rely on interdisciplinary contributions: history matters, but so too do literature, theatre, anthropology, art history, and archaeology.

Finally, I would like to emphasize that studies of cannibalism have the potential to refine and develop our understandings of food history, histories of eating, and studies of hunger during the early modern period. Cannibalism studies have changed over time. Similarly, as the field of food studies has matured, scholars have reworked their approaches to food history, studies of eating, and histories of hunger. Culinary microhistories, or books on single commodities such as sugar or milk, have been joined by broader histories of food that pay special attention to gender, trade, power, race, and change over time.[49] Recent work on hunger has explored state-sponsored attempts to prevent hunger in the nineteenth and twentieth centuries.[50] This book's authors, in pinning down the specifics of cannibalism in each of their case studies, offer scholars the opportunity to sharpen definitions of hunger, of food deprivation, and of food's myriad meanings in the early modern Atlantic world.

By considering cannibalism *and* topics including the British, African, and Native American Atlantics; the early modern period; imperialism; cooperation; food history; diplomatic networks; and theatre, new answers emerge in response to the question of why and how cannibalism mattered. Connecting cannibalism to the British Atlantic and to imperialism demonstrates that cannibalism concerned British people well before Jamestown and continued to inflect colonial thinking long after 1610. Looking at the topic alongside the African and Native American Atlantics shows how Indians and Africans pushed back against the assumption that they cannibalized peoples unlike them and used these discourses to critique European imperialism, settler colonialism, and the slave trade. Examining man-eating in tandem with cooperation makes power relations seem much more contingent than previously supposed. Studying it in conversation with food history makes scholars' definitions of early modern hunger more precise. Analyzing cannibalism and diplomatic networks offers insight into the ways that people constructed knowledge, and looking at it in the context of theatre reveals early modern peoples' economic anxieties in an ever-expanding world. In sum, the act of studying cannibalism and these other interdisciplinary questions has the effect of making the topic itself less odd and titillating and more relevant to adjacent and important fields of study.

CHAPTER 1

# Rituals of Consumption

## Cannibalism and Native American Oral Traditions in Southeastern North America

GREGORY D. SMITHERS

There was once a man who left his home every day to hunt deer. Each morning the man said goodbye to his pregnant wife. He also made sure that the couple's home was secure because "many strange creatures" kept visiting their home when he was out hunting. These "strange creatures" made regular attempts to convince the pregnant woman to let them in her home so they could dance with her. Their true intentions, however, were far more sinister: these creatures "ate people [who] lived in the neighborhood." During one of these visits, the "strange creatures" danced outside the pregnant woman's house and coaxed her into joining them. "A short time afterwards they caught her and devoured her."[1]

This tale, known in Natchez oral tradition as the "Lodge Boy and Thrown-Away," had many forms. It was also common among other tribal polities; ethnologists recorded different versions of the tale across North America. It was a violent story, but in the version above the focus remained on the demise of the woman and the fate of her unborn twins. Once the "strange creatures" consumed the woman, they deposited one of the newborns in the "lodge" and the other was "thrown away."[2]

The Natchez, who resided in the Lower Mississippi Valley, shared these types of oral traditions with family and community members. Such narratives described how people acquired game while they also prescribed what were and were not acceptable sources of flesh for human consumption. Eating human flesh was generally a forbidden way of obtaining nourishment.[3] In one of the Natchez versions of "Lodge Boy and Thrown-Away," the woman's husband returned home after his hunt and heard only the sound of a crying baby. The man located the baby lying beside a blood-spattered leaf, the only sign of his deceased wife. The man gathered up the bloodstained leaf, fed it deer soup, and locked it in the house. He then discovered the umbilical cord that had once connected mother and child. The umbilical cord transformed into a child slightly bigger than the crying baby. Although this larger child was wild and quite strong, the man determined to capture him so that his baby might have a playmate.

After a period of time, the father "tamed" both of the boys. The brothers subsequently embarked on a number of adventures before one day encountering "a house where cannibals lived." Curious, the boys edged closer to the house and heard the "cannibals laughing, feasting, and playing inside." Suddenly, a number of cannibals rushed out of the house, one "carrying a baby which they set in a bowl on the fire." The boys reacted angrily, throwing something into the bowl and cracking it. This infuriated the cannibals, who proceeded to "roast" the baby over the hot coals. Once the baby was fully cooked, the cannibals feasted and then fell asleep. Seeing the sleeping cannibals, the twins acted on their anger by tying all of the sleeping cannibals together by their hair and setting their house on fire. The house burned, and the boys fled.

These types of oral traditions attempted to illuminate socially acceptable behavior in relation to the consumption of flesh within Native communities. Oral traditions of a similar nature existed among other Native southerners, such as the Cherokees, Creeks, Choctaws, and Chickasaws and smaller polities such as the Yuchi, Apalachee, and Miccosukee. As a general rule, Indigenous people in the Southeast viewed the consumption of human flesh as taboo. But while the Natchez narratives provide us with a small historical window into Native American attitudes about cannibalism, they also inform us about the importance of oral traditions among Native peoples in the Southeast and how those traditions helped define ritual and ceremonial practices related to acceptable food sources for human consumption.

This chapter explores the connections between cannibalism, consumption, and oral tradition among southeastern Native Americans from the late seventeenth to the early nineteenth centuries. Focusing especially on the articulation of Indigenous food consumption amid colonial encounters involving Native Americans and Europeans, my analysis reveals how Indigenous oral traditions about food items and consumption were defined by both the syncretism of the different food cultures of the ever-changing settler colonial context during this period and by a spiritual and epistemological understanding of the interconnectedness of all animate and inanimate beings.

## Savages, Cannibals, and the European Imagination

If Native American oral traditions such as "Lodge Boy and Thrown-Away" highlight prohibitions on the eating of human flesh, where, then, did the pervasive belief that Native Americans routinely engaged in cannibalistic activities come from? Answers to this question are not hard to find in the writings of early modern Europeans. For example, the sixteenth-century Italian explorer Christopher Columbus linked the Carib Indians of the Lesser Antilles to cannibalism.[4] Over the ensuing decades, European authors routinely referred to the "*men-eaters in the West-Indyes*" and the "homely" diet of Native people on the mainland Americas.[5] The association of Indigenous people with the practice of eating human flesh had a clear purpose: to highlight what European writers imagined was the vast gulf between Christian Europeans and the "savage" peoples of the Caribbean and Americas.

Tales of flesh-eating Native peoples in the Caribbean, the mainland Americas, and ultimately throughout the Pacific also informed broader Eurocentric stories about how Indigenous people were impediments to the European quest for gold and riches and about how they threatened the establishment of settler societies after the late sixteenth century.[6] Such narratives tell us more about how Europeans incorporated their cultural preoccupation with necrophagia/cannibalism and superimposed those anxieties onto their perceptions of Indigenous

Brazilians cook human flesh. Arnoldus Montanus, *De Nieuwe en onbekende weereld . . .* (Amsterdam: J. Meurs, 1671), 370. *Courtesy of the Library of Congress.*

American, Polynesian, Micronesian, and Australian Aboriginal culinary and cultural traditions.[7]

When Europeans traveled across the Atlantic Ocean and began exploring and settling the Americas in the sixteenth century, they brought a treasury of cultural images about cannibalism. In the early sixteenth century, Western Europeans routinely associated "savages," "wild men," and "barbarians" with cannibalistic practices. Such people appeared in Lorenz Fries' *Carta Marina* (1525) and in the writings of explorers such as Sir Walter Ralegh. "Savages" and "wild men" threatened European-based sociocultural order. In Europe, for instance, heretics and witches were routinely accused of indulging in cannibalism. In the European imaginary, "wild men" were also thought to live in the woods, far from the civilized life of the town. These "wild men" allegedly took captives—usually infant children—who would later be consumed. Eating babies was perceived as a particularly debased manifestation of their savage lifestyle in the Christian European imagination.[8]

Despite these European antecedents, it is the association between Native Americans and cannibalism that continues to shape how millions of Americans perceive the history of Indigenous people in the United States.[9] The historian Jack Forbes (Powhatan) attacked such associations during his career by inverting the racial mythologies associated with cannibalism. In one instance, Forbes argued that the ancient Greeks and Turkish sultans castrated boys who "were equally consumed by cannibals whose high degree of derangement cannot be denied."[10]

Forbes was writing against the grain of multiple centuries of racial stereotypes and cultural assumptions about Native people. Indeed, the trope of the white civilizer and the savage Indian—which the narrative of Native cannibalism served so well—continued throughout the twentieth century and persists into our own time. These powerful racial stereotypes have filtered into Native oral traditions.

Federal employees recorded just such a story in the 1930s. In an interview with a Works Project Administration employee, T. C. Carriger recalled how his wife, Pearl, believed that cannibals existed among some Native tribes. Carriger, who traced his family lineage back to the Cherokee homelands in Tennessee, was born in Kansas in 1868.

Pearl, however, wasn't Native. She arrived in Kansas at the age of eight with her father, a white man appointed as the federal agent to the Tonkawa Indian Reservation in 1894. Pearl grew up playing with Native children and hearing Indigenous stories. Despite seeing the Tonkawa as "the truest friends," she continued to filter stories about them through a racial imagination shaped by popular media images of "savage" Indians and "treacherous" warriors. T. C. recalled that his wife often remembered the stories and gossip of the old-time Tonkawa women that convinced her that "they were once a cannibal tribe of people."[11]

In the twenty-first century, racial slurs designed to denigrate and dismiss Native Americans persist. From the "Indian squaw" to the "Savage cannibal," these terms remain part of public discourse in the United States. An example of such racial vilification emerged in December 2015 when a fourteen-year-old Choctaw girl was verbally attacked—grown men shouted abuse at her and called her a "squaw"—for protesting the use of Native American mascots.[12] And on October 10, 2017, conservative media pundit Ben Shapiro was forced to issue a public apology after he posted a social media video depicting Native Americans engaged in cannibalism.[13]

The deployment of cannibalism to vilify twenty-first-century Native people is by no means a new phenomenon. Europeans and Euroamericans accused Native Americans of cannibalistic practices to justify colonial attempts to extinguish Indigenous communities and to objectify Native people. Such savages, the trope went, were so far removed from European Christianity and settler colonial civilization that the only effective way to deal with Indigenous cannibals was to annihilate the problem.[14] Europeans and, later, Euroamericans imagined Indigenous communities who engaged in cannibalism to be so far beyond the pale of civilization as to be unredeemable human beings.[15]

This logic was circular: Native Americans were savages because they ate human flesh and people who ate human flesh were clearly savages. Significantly, the circulation of such formulations helped give meaning to the racial taxonomies that ultimately naturalized perceptions of Native Americans as "savages" and decontextualized Indian chiefdoms, tribes, and nations. In Eurocentric hands, the diversity and dynamism of Native American cultures was homogenized, reduced to a singularity: the "savage."[16]

## Cannibalism and Colonialism

If cultural and religious assumptions informed (and continue to inform) European and Euroamerican perceptions of cannibalistic acts among Native Americans, so too did the sensation of hunger. Hunger influenced how Europeans perceived what they called the New World, especially during the formative years of exploration and settler colonialism. All sorts of creatures, not just humans, reportedly acted on feelings of hunger and the primal urge to sustain life. In the Floridian wilderness, for example, the sixteenth-century French explorer and artist Jacques le Moyne de Morgues observed that in the sweltering tropical climate all living creatures preyed on and fed on the flesh of others. Local "crocodiles" (alligators), le Moyne wrote, were "driven by hunger, they come out of the rivers and crawl about on the islands after prey."[17]

The uncomfortable sensation of hunger played havoc with the thought processes of the newly arrived Europeans. Le Moyne's account recalled the fear of hunger that pervaded among the French in North America.[18] Those fears and an inability to supply their own reliable sources of food meant that the French relied on Native peoples for food if they hoped to avoid the "extremity of hunger."[19]

The shadow of hunger meant that death stalked these early European invaders in North America. In truth, though, no people—European, African, or Native American—were free from hunger's grip. And where hungry people wasted away, rumors about cannibalism followed. Historian Bernard Bailyn observes that starvation among English colonists in the Chesapeake during the early seventeenth century gave rise to reports about settlers engaging in acts of cannibalism.[20] Bailyn describes the early decades of English settler colonialism as the "barbarous years." It was not long before the English began to accuse Native people up and down the Atlantic coast of cannibalism.[21]

The English were not the first to develop and refine their narratives about Native American cannibalism. The Spanish made reports of Indian cannibalism decades before the English arrived in the Chesapeake and New England. Spanish explorers, such as Cortés in the early 1500s, identified Native peoples as perpetrators of sins of the flesh that ranged from cannibalism to sodomy. Framing Native Americans as savages who were given to excesses of the flesh proved that they simply weren't equipped to live in civil societies governed by laws and political structures. Such arguments were fictions, to be sure, but they served Spanish colonizers well as they refined their legal and cultural arguments for Native dispossession and colonial expansion.[22]

Sixteenth- and seventeenth-century Spanish explorers, missionaries, and colonial officials began building an archive of colonial knowledge that informed the logics of Christian conversion (or Hispanicization), labor exploitation, or territorial dispossession. Woven into this archive were dramatic accounts of cannibalistic practices among the Indigenous people. In Florida, for example, accounts of the Apalachee engaging in practices such as ritual sacrifice and cannibalism, especially during times of war, became a mainstay of Spanish ethnographic knowledge.[23]

Similarly, French explorers and missionaries insisted that they had repeatedly heard stories of Native people engaging in cannibalism on ceremonial occasions.[24] For example, Jesuit missionaries took great interest in Algonkian folklore pertaining to Kiwakwe, the "Cannibal Giant."[25] Although Algonkian narratives about cannibalism reflect a concern about social order, just as they did in Native American oral traditions throughout the Southeast, missionaries often viewed such

DELL'HISTORIE DEL

Come gl'Indiani colauano l'oro in bocca à gli Spagnuoli, & dell'habito che lor portano in diuersi lochi di terra ferma.

QVEGLI, *che pigliauano viui, spetialmente i Capitani, legategli le mani & i piedi, gettatigli in terra, colauano loro dell'oro in bocca, dicendo, mangia, mangia oro Cristiano, et per più stratio, & vituperio, con çortelli di pietra Focaia, chi gli tagliaua vn braccio, chi d'vna spalla, chi d'vna gamba, & arrostitola sopra i carboni, cantando*

An image from Girolamo Benzoni's *La Historia del Mondo Nuovo* (Venetia, 1572) depicts Native people pouring molten gold into the mouth of Spaniards. Such grisly practices were common during the Spanish inquisition and often accompanied descriptions of bursting organs. The above image attempts to set this Christian European punishment apart from Native culture by adding Indigenous people cutting up and consuming the flesh of the recently deceased.

LC-USZ62-71987, Prints and Photographs Division, Library of Congress. *Courtesy of the Library of Congress.*

stories as reminders of the urgency of their work and the need to save Indian "souls."[26]

Europeans' curiosity about Native cultures and their desire to convert souls all too often turned to suspicion about the meaning of those cultures and the intentions of Indigenous chiefs and warriors. Such feelings were magnified by colonial anxieties about the urgent need to establish something approximating social order in the Southeast. This urgency fueled perceptions of Indians as bloodthirsty savages. In southern Florida, for example, seventeenth-century Europeans described the Mayucas and Ays as cannibals.[27] Europeans perceived such people as a threat to the establishment of any sort of social order. Indeed, the presence of Indian "cannibals" lurking on the margins of nascent colonial societies could quickly transform curiosity into animus at times of tension, and tensions often escalated into bloodshed.

As the seventeenth century unfolded and eventually became the eighteenth, missionaries, explorers, colonial officials, and settlers continued to accumulate a growing repository of ethnographic information about Native American food and eating habits. For example, ethnographic observations about the consumption habits of the tribes that comprised the Creek confederacy had become commonplace by the eighteenth century.

In Creek country, the Tuscaloosa, Tallapoosa, Coosa, Cahaba, Talladega, Tallassee, and Alabama reportedly lived on a diet consisting of peanuts, squash, peppers, tomatoes, pumpkins, and corn.[28] Eighteenth-century ethnographic observations suggest to historians that the Creeks enjoyed a well-balanced diet. Every town in the Creek country was well supplied with eggs and poultry and was dotted with small garden plots that provided its residents with items such as sweet potatoes, corn, beans, and green leafy vegetables. Additionally, women and children foraged in the nearby brush for edible seeds and wild berries, while men provided additional sources of protein by hunting for game such as deer.[29]

Similar stories about the culinary culture of other Native southerners abound. For example, the diet of the Choctaw people resembled that of other large coalescent societies in the Native South during the eighteenth century. Choctaw women oversaw the planting, growing, and harvesting of corn, beans, pumpkins, and squash in communal gardens, while men added to the diet by hunting deer, bear, and a variety of small game. Fruits, nuts, and berries also supplemented the diet.[30]

Native southerners developed their own culinary cultures in addition to observing the habits of non-kin Native peoples. These observations sometimes included accusations of cannibalism when they believed that consumption behaviors differed from or were threatening to their own. For example, the Atakapa people, whose homelands were located in what is today southwestern Louisiana and the eastern coast of Texas, derived their name from the Choctaw *hatak* (man) plus *apa* (eater). There is no evidence that the Atakapa practiced cannibalism, but the name is suggestive of how Choctaws perceived the Atakapa as an external threat to the social order within Choctaw communities.[31]

Few external Native American groups terrorized the Native South quite as effectively as the Westo (also known as the Rickahocans or Chichimecos) during the late seventeenth century.[32] One historian estimates that from 1670 to 1715, between 24,000 and 51,000 Native southerners were captured and sold into slavery.[33] The Westo, a migratory Iroquoian people from the Northeast, played a major role in fueling the Indian slave trade throughout the eastern half of North America and the Caribbean.[34]

Westo power rested on their acquisition of European firearms and their mobility. In the English Carolina colony, the Westo formed strong economic alliances with Anglo traders and officials, while pitting other Native peoples, such as the Kussoes and Esaws, against the Westo and their English allies.[35] An economic and diplomatic relationship between the Westo and English that was based on captivity and slavery proved predictably unstable in a colonial context characterized by the regular movement of human beings and the fluid exchange of goods and ideas. Violence punctuated the Native South during the 1670s, ultimately leading to the extinguishment of the Westo by the early 1680s.

Although the Westo reign of terror in the Southeast was short lived, Native southerners were left with little doubt that these aggressors from the North posed a serious threat to their communities. Little wonder, then, that Native Americans in the southeast associated the Westo and other Indigenous slave-raiding parties with the practice most commonly associated with social disorder: cannibalism. Indigenous communities along the Florida coast, for example, allegedly exchanged stories about the threat posed by Westo raiding parties. Such stories spread rapidly throughout the Native South, culminating with claims that Westo warriors engaged in cannibalism.[36] English officials heard similar testimony from southeastern Native people; Native southerners allegedly characterized the Westo as "a ranging sort of people reputed to be man-eaters."[37] The Westo, in other words, were outsiders to the Native South. They hid in the shadows, had no permanent homeland in the southeast, and launched rapid-fire attacks on Native communities. The Westo therefore produced feelings of social anxiety and instability among local Indigenous communities. Hence, labeling these savage invaders as cannibals served to highlight the danger they posed to Indigenous communities in the southeast.

By the early eighteenth century, the Westo were gone, defeated militarily. But outside dangers still loomed in the Native South. The "northwards," as southeastern Indians referred to Native American warriors from the north, continued to raid towns and take captives throughout the southeast.[38] Although pressures from European settler communities continued to grow, Native southerners nurtured cultural and social traditions, many of which involved the consumption of a variety of foods and the perpetuation of culinary and ceremonial traditions.

These traditions established cultural rules. This meant that taboos were often invoked to prescribe human behavior. For example, Choctaw eating habits were guided by a few taboos. Choctaw perceptions about the types of flesh that were "natural" to eat informed various aspects of their social and cultural life. Choctaws considered flesh-eating birds such as crows and eagles as anomalies because "normal" birds ate vegetation. The Choctaws never consumed carnivorous birds.[39] Significantly, Choctaws also viewed cannibalism as taboo. In fact, they considered the flesh of the human body to be sacred. While Choctaws sometimes sacrificed their captives during religious ceremonies, they frowned on the consumption of human flesh.[40]

The care that Choctaws took in tending to the bodies of the recently deceased further highlights how they frowned upon cannibalistic behavior. When a Choctaw died, it was the sacred duty of the *hattak fullih nipi foni* (bone picker) to place the deceased on a scaffold. Once the body of the recently deceased had decomposed, the *hattak fullih nipi foni* used his or her fingernails to scrape and wash the bones of the dead. The deceased's kin would then come and regularly mourn over the bones of their departed loved one until those bones were dry and ready for placement in the bonehouse (*a-bo-ha-fo-ni*). The "feast of the dead" festival typically marked the conclusion of the mourning process.[41] The Choctaw people therefore saw the human body as sacred. The dead were not to be consumed; they were to be respected and prepared for the afterlife with great care and attention to detail. To Choctaws, this was the natural order of things. Eating human flesh was simply unthinkable to them.

What the Choctaws ate and did not eat, as was the case with other Native southerners such as the Creeks and Cherokees, reflected Indigenous spirituality in the southeast. Native people in the South lived in a world defined by a cosmology in which all living and nonliving matter was interconnected. Thus, what one chose to eat, when, and with whom, had profound social and cultural significance. In Louisiana, for example, preparing and consuming food were communal activities. Native women prepared food in "common pots," out of which men, women, and children would eat.[42]

The common pot was an important part of life in the Native south, as in other parts of eastern North America, during the seventeenth and eighteenth centuries. The tradition of eating from a common pot connected Native people to pre-contact traditions and to a sense of place. It also reminded people of the communal ties that bound kinship members together in a collective sense of belonging. Moreover, the common pot constituted a physical reminder of the centrality of women in matrilineal societies. Female knowledge helped cultivate the crops, prepare the food, and place the ingredients of a recipe in the common pot to cook a meal for the community to share.[43]

The tradition of the common pot proved so strong that the descendants of Native southerners forcibly removed to the Trans-Mississippi West in the 1830s recall the "iron pots" used to prepare meals for large numbers of people. For example, Matthew Maytubbie, a mixed-race

Choctaw, told a Works Progress Administration field worker in 1937 about the picnics that helped reweave the threads of community following removal, stating that "everybody would have a tin plate and wooden fork or spoon and we would go to the pot and help ourselves all the rest of the day."[44]

In the century before removal, southeastern Native Americans enjoyed communal feasts at different times on the seasonal calendar. During the Green Corn Ceremony among the Chickasaw, for example, dancing and feasting went on for three days in celebration of the first harvesting of corn.[45] Native southerners enjoyed feasts not only to give thanks for the earth's bounty but also to celebrate interpersonal relationships. In the 1770s, the trader James Adair, one of the better eighteenth-century ethnological observers in the Native South, wrote that each spring, "the Mississippi Floridians keep a great solemn feast of love, to renew their old friendships." Adair claimed this great celebration was known as *Hottuk Aimpa, Heettla, Tenaa,* "the people eat, dance, and walk as twined together." Although Adair believed that the ceremonial feasting and dancing he witnessed reflected the "lewdness and debauchery" of a "heathen" people, such ceremonies were in fact reminders to Native Americans in the South of their mutual responsibilities to kin and to the earth they shared with other animal and plant life.[46]

While southeastern Native Americans indulged in feasts for ceremonial purposes, they were sometimes puzzled by European feasting practices. For example, Choctaws struggled to grasp the meaning of the Euroamerican celebration known as Christmas. According to one observer

> One of the follies so incomprehensible to the ancient Choctaws was, and still is, that one day, near the close of each year, should be devoted by the "pale-faces" to eating and drinking, dancing and frolicking, carousing and fighting, called Christmas;–incomprehensible since so inconsistent with what the missionaries taught them what the Bible reasons for rejoicing were, and in what way they should be expressed to please God.[47]

In pre-Victorian America, Christmas celebrations tended to be rowdy and riotous affairs.[48] Little wonder, then, that Choctaws viewed such celebrations with a combination of skepticism and bemusement.

## Narratives of the Flesh

In the Native South, rituals of consumption typically had long-held cultural and spiritual meaning. Whether those traditions involved burning and smoking tobacco or consuming the "flesh" of game, Indigenous rituals of consumption and the importance of the common pot reinforced a deeply held sense of communal belonging in the two centuries after contact with European colonists.[49] In contrast, oral narratives that emphasized cannibalism revealed outsiders to be "other," threats to traditions and social stability.

Native Americans in the southeast and throughout eastern North America have a long history of using stories of cannibalism to differentiate themselves from other Indigenous communities. For example, the Lenape Indians referred to the Mohawk as "maneaters."[50] Alternatively, Native oral traditions deployed metaphorical allusions to cannibals (just as they referred to giants, water monsters, or serpents) to convey a sense of meaning about the unknown. The Powhatan, Cherokees, Creeks, Seminoles, and numerous other Native southerners told stories about the "water serpent" or "horned serpent" to Europeans, perhaps to dissuade the outsiders from traveling further into their homelands.[51] The Yuchi, who made their home in what we know today as Alabama, Georgia, and South Carolina, nurtured oral traditions of a monster that ate human flesh. For the Yuchi storytellers, the monster symbolized a constant threat to the social stability of their society. According to folklore, it is ultimately slain after warriors discover his weakness.[52]

Ogres, giants, and monsters engaging in cannibalistic behavior appear to have been common tropes in the oral traditions of Native southerners during the seventeenth and eighteenth centuries.[53] Native storytellers continued to nurture these oral traditions in the early nineteenth century. For example, late eighteenth- and early nineteenth-century Cherokee storytellers incorporated tales about cannibals into their oral narratives. The famous story of Kanati and Selu, the lucky hunter and the corn mother, refers to a foreign tribe known as the "Cookers." The "Cookers" were a sinister people, Kanati explains, because "they are cannibals, and if they get you they will put you in a pot and feast on you."[54]

Even though settlers and colonial officials sometimes referred to

Cherokees as "savages" when diplomatic relations deteriorated and war broke out during the eighteenth century, the Cherokees maintained strict prohibitions on cannibalism.[55] For the Cherokees, food consumption was part of trade and diplomatic negotiations with Europeans and other Native people.[56] The idea of consuming human flesh was both unthinkable and counterproductive to the cultivation of strategic "friendships" with the colonists, especially the English.

Having said that, Cherokee oral narratives did refer to cannibalism during the late eighteenth and early nineteenth centuries. In one instance, oral tradition warned Cherokees not to consume "the sinews of the thigh" of a woman.[57] Another tradition referred to a mythical cannibal as Cherokee warriors prepared for battle. One of the rituals these warriors allegedly performed was a prayer "to a being they call the Man eater, to come to their assistance and help them kill their enemies."[58]

Why would Cherokee warriors, a people with no history of engaging in cannibalism, pray to such a being? The surviving evidence is unclear, but it is not unreasonable to assume that the warriors hoped that by praying to such a being they could harness its physical strength and be victorious on the field of battle. In the latter third of the eighteenth century, references to human flesh in historical sources related to Cherokee hostilities with the Americans became fairly routine. General "Mad" Anthony Wayne, for example, used references to the destruction of human flesh to intimidate Native warriors. According to Wayne, Native warriors made similar threats in 1792 when the Western Confederacy Indians, which included Chickamauga Cherokee warriors, allegedly expressed a "hengre for white mans flesh."[59]

In 1793, rumors resurfaced about frontier violence between Chickamauga Cherokees and frontier settlers descending into cannibalism. Under the leadership of Doublehead, Chickamaugas captured and killed two frontiersmen. After the men were murdered, the Cherokees allegedly drank all their whiskey, scalped the men, and cut their bodies into pieces so they could cook and "eat chunks of the human flesh."[60] This story had all the hallmarks of a frontier legend. It fit settler stereotypes about savage Indians, but it also served a purpose for the Chickamauga Cherokees, who fought a war of resistance against American territorial expansion in the 1780s and 1790s.

Non-Indigenous ethnographers continued to record references to cannibalism in the Native South and to cannibals who were mythical gods that menaced Native southerners from an unspecified foreign location. Late eighteenth- and early nineteenth-century Chickasaw oral traditions, for instance, included cautionary tales that involved cannibals. Chickasaw storytellers spoke of a "race of people known as Cannibals who feasted on the bodies of their enemies, and who were also large." According to this Chickasaw oral tradition, this unnamed "race of people" used "the mastodon as their burden bearers and as their domestic work animals." Fortunately for the Chickasaws, this story had a happy ending. The cannibals "disappeared because they were a small number, and the Cannibals, together with the mammoths, were soon wiped out by a great epidemic."[61]

The Creek Indians also expressed an antipathy for cannibals and cannibalism into the late eighteenth century and beyond. According to James Adair, the Creeks were repulsed at the thought of ingesting human flesh. Adair insisted that there "is not the least trace among their ancient traditions, of their deserving the hateful name of cannibals." He added that taboos about the consumption of all forms of flesh meant "their taste is so opposite to that of the Anthrophagi, that they always over-dress their meat whether roasted or boiled." According to Adair, the Creeks went to great lengths to avoid eating raw flesh of any sort, even overcooking their meats to ensure they did not transgress such taboos.

Adair recorded his observations during a time of great violence and uncertainty across the Native South. This prompted him to add that during times of war, Indian warriors along the Florida cape were known to drink the blood of enemies out of their upturned skulls. Others allegedly consumed the hearts of their enemies to inspire courage. Such stories, however, borrowed heavily from racial stereotypes and the fantastical tall tales that were told along the frontiers of the American South. Moreover, such stories were out of step with the Creeks' revulsion for cannibalistic practices.[62]

## Conclusion

Cannibalism had no place in Native American culinary cultures of the Southeast. This reality, of course, did not stop settlers, missionaries, and political leaders from asserting that the practice was commonplace among the Indian population of the region. Such accusations persisted through the Revolutionary War period and the early decades of the American republic. When a Jesuit missionary sensationally reported, for instance, that he had seen a Native American mother feeding her children with the dismembered arm of an English prisoner during the Revolutionary War, the readers of that testimony might have felt justified in perceiving Native American people as the worst of savages.[63] These beliefs continued, as Native American oral histories reveal, into the twentieth century.

Using such falsehoods to pander to popular prejudices about Native American people at the dawn of the nineteenth century did not make such accusations true. This is not to suggest that cannibals did not exist in the Native South between the sixteenth and early nineteenth centuries—they did, in mythology and folklore. Whether we refer back to the "Man-eaters" who populated the Natchez story of "Lodge Boy and Thrown-Away" or examine the role of cannibals in the oral narratives of other cultural groups in the Native South, cannibalism existed in Native oral traditions to help elders prescribe social behavior, identify outsiders and threats to kin members, and reiterate acceptable habits of consumption.

CHAPTER 2

# First Reports of New World Cannibalism in the Italian Mercantile and Diplomatic Correspondence

ELENA DANIELE

A great amount of the information about the first stages of early modern European expansion in the Americas was written by and for Italians. Italian trading cities, with their high percentage of literate people and efficient networks for the transmission of political and commercial news, were initially the most receptive audience for reports about the Iberian overseas explorations.[1] The early information exchanged via the Italian network included highly stereotyped and contradictory representations of New World native populations. On one hand, the indigenous peoples of the Americas were portrayed as the innocent and peaceful dwellers of an Edenic paradise; on the other, they were described as fierce, indomitable cannibals. The longstanding controversy about the validity of primary sources for determining the history of the Columbian voyages and the ways of life of pre-contact indigenous cultures has spurred an ardent debate about the meaning and significance of the terms "cannibalism" and "anthropophagy" in such accounts. Our collection of essays is no exception, as different authors draw alternative conclusions about a common set of materials.

Three main lines of interpretation exist in this debate. Scholars read primary sources as fictions or discourses created (whether consciously or unconsciously) for various reasons that benefited Europeans in one form or another; accounts that drew upon a rich body of preexisting classical and medieval literature; or ethnographic accounts of a practice that actually took place in the Caribbean and was observed and recorded (although in the language and imagery available to fifteenth-century men) by those who had had contact with the alleged cannibals. Whether aggrandized or fictionalized, imbued with self-serving agendas or echoes of the well-established tradition of the marvelous East, the extant first- and second-hand accounts of the first two Columbian voyages were nonetheless originally intended as ethnographic accounts of the actual practice of cannibalism in the Caribbean Basin. In Nicolás Wey-Gómez's words: "What matters is that Columbus was convinced that he had walked in on a cannibals' lair in the Lesser Antilles."[2] And so were his contemporaries: by the return of Antonio Torres's fleet with Carib captives in 1494, New World cannibalism was an unquestioned fact for the Europeans of the time. But the reader will be surprised, perhaps, to find out that the first reaction to news of cannibalism was initially one of caution and disbelief, at least within the Italian mercantile and diplomatic milieu. In order to understand the origins of the notion that the Caribs engaged in cannibalistic practices and how this idea was received, how it was transmitted, and how it became consolidated, I will analyze the discourse on New World cannibalism as it emerged from the corpus of literary materials that were initially disseminated through the Italian network upon Columbus's return from his first and second voyages.

The first source for early representations of New World populations is Columbus's widely publicized 1493 letter announcing the positive outcome of his expedition. Although this letter made Columbus's name immediately known throughout Europe, scholars believe that the document is not an original by him. Initially penned by Columbus as a distillate of his diary, the original letter underwent substantial interventions by officials at court before its publication as the official announcement of the new Spanish possessions.[3] Mentions of fantastic elements contained in the diary were decontextualized and rearranged in the letter to appeal to a wide public that was familiar with a centuries-old tradition of travels to the East. According to the letter, dog-headed men, men with tails, and cannibals all lurked in the luxuriant vegetation of the newly found islands. But a reading of the diary shows that if Columbus did indeed mention such monstrosities in his log, he initially dismissed them as tales the "Indians" told about their warlike neighbors. It was only toward the end of his first voyage, after a first skirmish with belligerent natives (whom he deemed "non-Indian") that Columbus became convinced that some local tribes (the "Caribs") engaged in cannibalistic practices.

In contrast to the semi-fantastic content of the widely circulated letter, no mention was made of monsters or cannibals in the immediate transmission of information about Columbus's voyage via the Italian mercantile newsletters and in the 1493 papal bulls. But after the first participants in the second voyage came back in 1494 from the islands that Columbus had initially identified as inhabited by cannibals, multiple firsthand accounts of New World cannibalism became available in Europe, both by those who had traveled across the Atlantic and those who had interviewed the explorers upon their return. Humanists further propagated the sensationalistic image of a cannibalistic New World through their erudite embellishment of the original testimonies, imitating classical models. The information that circulated within the Italian mercantile and diplomatic milieu cautioned against a tendency toward the easy aggrandizement of news of cannibalism but nonetheless validated them.

## Columbus's Cannibals

Our journey must start with Columbus's 1493 letter, the very first document to describe the American continent, which served for centuries as the primogenial representation of Europe's first encounter with the New World. The natives' rudimentary weapons, nakedness, and positive reception of the first Europeans who landed on their shores garnered them a reputation for being a timid, harmless people, who would be easily converted to the Catholic faith. But toward its conclusion the letter also mentioned a race of warlike women, monstrous men with tails, and a ferocious population of man-eaters who inhabited unexplored islands—the Caribs, or cannibals. In part making sense of the unknown territories through his understanding of the world as he knew it, in part conditioned by the need to report positively on the outcome of his expedition and writing within a literary tradition with well-established conventions and tropes, Columbus interpreted new phenomena through the lens of a preexisting mental framework.[4] Myths such as those about Cipangus, Amazons, giants, mermaids, El Dorado, the Garden of Eden, and—of course—cannibals, feature prominently in this first account of discovery. By the time of Columbus's voyage, Italian humanists had long dreamed of a return to a former golden age of antiquity and to life in the state of nature. Late fifteenth-century intellectuals fantasized about a new golden age that had been foretold in classical texts, and they combined beliefs derived from the classical tradition with others related to Christianity. As the recipient and interpreter of such conceptions, Columbus applied them to his own experience:

> Most of the inhabitants were naked and unashamed, comely and gentle. There was no individual ownership of property, as all lived communally, sharing everything. There was no regard for rank, for religion, or for wealth, particularly gold, which was plentiful. The land was beautiful, fertile and bountiful with luscious fruits, spices, strange animals and exotic birds. . . . Columbus' description of the habitat of the New World, not wholly incorrect, but vague, general and selective of attractive features, conforms to the poetic landscape of Antiquity.[5]

How were myths and facts, literary legacy, and empirical observation brought together in the first account of the New World? Valerie Flint's analysis provides fascinating insight. If Columbus's observations were informed by the best of medieval authority, Flint says, that is not to say that he was unwilling or unable to contrast such authority and his own expectations with the reality he was facing. Still, medieval sources guided his eyes, and if they did not totally distort his descriptions, they at least determined the selection of items he chose to report about.[6] Medieval sources had a role in affecting both his perception and his writing, but, Flint asks, did the correspondences between those sources and his writing result from his unconscious transposition of his belief system into the written word? Or did he deliberately compound this resemblance so that readers who held those medieval sources in high esteem would accord the same esteem to his own writing?[7] More specifically, were his idolatrous man-eaters a tribute to the well-established literary tradition of the marvelous East (along with tailed men, bald men, and Amazons)? Or were his references to the existence of cannibals based on empirical observations of some sort? I now turn to Columbus's diary for insight on the matter.

The letter was written as a digest of the diary and thus condensed the original information it contained. Where this information came from, how it was obtained, and Columbus's reasoning as events unfolded cannot be inferred from the letter alone.[8] This is all disclosed in the diary. The original diary of Columbus's first voyage is lost, but it survives in Bartolomé de Las Casas's partial transcription and paraphrasing of Columbus's original text. In some passages, Las Casas copied Columbus's diary verbatim; in others, he provided a summary, thus referring to Columbus as "he" or "the Admiral." Since Columbus's very first encounter with the population that he referred to as the peaceful "Indians" (which took place as early as October 12, 1492), Columbus maintained the idea that the Indians had been attacked and enslaved by a different people:

> Some people I saw bore marks of weapons on their bodies, and I asked them with gestures what they were. They made me understand that occasionally people from neighboring islands came to capture them, and they defended themselves. I believed then and do now that people come here from the mainland to capture them and reduce them into slavery.[9]

As the days passed, Indians insisted that their oppressors would not only enslave but also eat them: "Far from there were men with a single eye and others with dogs' muzzles who ate men: as soon as they captured one they decapitated him, drank his blood, and cut off his genitals."[10] Remarks of this kind are consistent throughout the diary: whenever the Indians referred to the Caribs, they would repeat similar stories of their monstrous appearance and cannibalistic appetite. But what part of the tales Columbus included in his diary corresponded to his recording of the Indians' mythical lore about their enemies and what part instead matched his own imagination and sources about the East?

On November 26, Columbus made the association between maneaters and the ethnic name "*Caribs*" that would later crystallize in the synonym for man-eater, "*cannibal*":

> All the people he has discovered so far say that they have the greatest fear of those Canibas. . . . And he believes that the

> Canibas probably went and took these Indians from their own land and houses because they are so timorous and ignorant of arms. . . . They kept saying that the Canibas had but a single eye and the face of a dog. The Admiral felt that they were lying and thought that their captors must have been subjects of the Great Khan.[11]

Columbus did not uncritically accept the Indians' claims about the monstrous nature of their enemies as true. Rather, he introduced his supposition that "Canibas" meant "men of the Great Khan." On December 12, he concluded that "Caniba is none other than the people of the Great Khan, who must be very close by, and he must have ships and they must come and capture them, and since the captives do not return they are supposed to have been eaten."[12] Thinking that he had reached the islands off mainland Asia, Columbus associated the ethnic name "Caniba" with "Great Khan" and discarded the Indians' stories of cannibalism as belonging to the realm of myth, an expression of the fear the Indians felt toward their enemies. Based on the content of the announcement letter alone, one could argue that Columbus spoke of imaginary, monstrous man-eaters living on faraway, unexplored islands because his literary sources and own expectations influenced him and clouded his perception of the reality that was being displayed before his eyes. But while the letter does not provide sufficient context for the inclusion of elements of a fantastic kind, a reading of the diary shows that when Columbus did mention monstrosities, he also provided rational explications for them. In the diary, he repeatedly dismissed rumors of cannibalism. The entry on December 17 unequivocally states that "two men showed that they were missing some pieces of flesh from their bodies and gave them to understand that the cannibals had bitten them off. The Admiral did not believe it."[13]

But everything changed toward the end of his first voyage, when some of Columbus's men engaged in a skirmish with a non-Indian group of bowmen whose appearance and aggressive behavior matched the tales of Carib predation the Indians had recounted. One of the captured bowmen was brought before Columbus:

> That man, says the Admiral, was most ugly, much more so than the others seen up till then. His face was all blackened with charcoal . . . and he wore his hair very long, tied up in back in a net

> of parrot feathers. He was naked like the others. The Admiral thought he must be from the tribe of Caribs, who eat men.[14]

As a reading of his diary makes manifest, rather than rigidly adhering to some inherited belief or preconceived notion of the world, Columbus's interpretation of the Caribbean anthropological landscape evolved as events unfolded. Up until then, he had told himself that the Caribs, as "men of the Great Khan," could not possibly be so uncivilized as to eat people. An earlier entry is evidence of this stance: "The Admiral says he felt there was some truth to what they [the Indians] said, but if they [the Caribs] were well armed they would have to be reasonable people, and he was of the opinion that they had taken some prisoners, and when the prisoners had not returned home it was said that they had been eaten."[15] The men of the great civilization of the Great Khan, Columbus reasoned, would not engage in "unreasonable" ("uncivilized") behavior. Yet when finally faced with natives that he could only identify as Caribs, Columbus observed that they did not appear to be more "civilized" than the naked Indians. Once the equation between "Caribs" and "men of the Great Khan" proved wrong, Columbus concluded that the "lies" of the Indians were not lies after all. The entry of January 15 registered his conviction that "on the islands of Carib and Matinino is much copper, although Carib offers difficulties . . . inasmuch as those people eat human flesh."[16]

In brief, a reading of the diary shows that if Columbus was at times uncritically recording local fears of a mythical enemy in the form of Indian folklore, failing to distinguish between what the Indians said and what he believed was true, he did not readily believe in the literal existence of dog-headed men or other sorts of monstrosities. Rather, he was trying to make sense of his circumstances based on common sense and his own understanding of the world. And while his perception of the existence of two opposed populations (an innately good and an innately bad one, both defined in contraposition to civilized life) might have been heavily influenced by ancient ideas derived from his sources and his own expectations, it was also based on the observation that two different ethnic groups did indeed appear to antagonize each other in the islands and one group claimed that the other cannibalized them. The official version of Columbus's letter that spread a stereotyped image of naked inhabitants of a pristine land highly resonated with a preexisting mental framework that matched the public's expectations and validated Columbus's account. Yet from Columbus's perspective, nothing he had experienced seemed to contradict that framework. If one-eyed, dog-headed men and men with tails made their appearance in his writing, he dismissed them as the tales told by the Indians, but he unmistakably understood the islands to be inhabited by a warlike, cannibalistic population alongside a peaceful one. The second part of this chapter will address the other literary materials that became available in Europe as a result of Columbus's return from his first voyage, the context of their production and circulation, and what they can add to our understanding of how news of cannibalism was first received in Europe.

## Early Italian Mercantile and Diplomatic Correspondence on New World Cannibalism

In addition to verbatim copies of Columbus's announcement letter, news of the New World entered public discourse through a hasty series of abridged copies and transcriptions of the letter. Such copies spread rapidly through the European courts and the public at large in the form of correspondence by and to Italians. In contrast to the silence of the Spanish and Portuguese explorers (only one letter is known to have been written by a Spaniard on Columbus's first voyage), Italians generated a copious correspondence.[17] The reasons for this proliferation have been traced back to the diplomatic practice of the Italian states. By the late fifteenth century, the Italian states had developed a system of strategically positioned resident ambassadors whose aim was to maintain regular contact with their allies, gather accurate information about their enemies' intentions, and generally improve communication.[18] The figure of the diplomat had not yet emerged as standardized at the end of the fifteenth century: there was no concept of the diplomat as an individual with specialized technical training who was instructed to collect certain types of information. Diplomatic relations were thus conducted by a heterogeneous group of agents that consisted of merchants and traders, noblemen, state administrators, men of arms, clergymen, and more, who often performed several of these roles at once. Consequently, the content of the observations produced in diplomatic correspondence depended on individual perceptions and sensibilities.[19]

For the most part, Italian merchants and traders compiled the early correspondence exchanged in Europe about Columbus's first and second voyage. By the time of Columbus's expedition, the Italian trading tradition was centuries old. The nature of the profession required merchants to be up to date with the most recent information on markets and explorations. Economic agents located at the major European ports and trading cities were the first to be informed about the outcomes of the great overseas voyages. In the quick series of subsequent copies and transcriptions of Columbus's official announcement letter that first circulated within the Italian mercantile and diplomatic milieu, information was mostly reduced and details were sometimes added that are not found in the original letter, suggesting that authors had access to a variety of additional sources, such as word of mouth at the Spanish court, oral accounts by participants, and, in some cases, privileged access to Columbus's writings.[20] Although merchants' reports and diplomatic dispatches were not intended for general consumption, the information that eventually reached the wider public was largely derived from them.

These reports were indebted to the mercantile tradition: the style is straightforward and the content matter of fact. Precise and timely information was important in commerce. Reports that functioned as newsletters, which often circulated in multiple copies, were meant to inform partners and associates about relevant business issues. Information was usually put together quickly to inform a government or a business associate of some immediate circumstances and was not carefully organized, for the emphasis was on speed rather than style. We know, for instance, that the Genoese merchant Annibale de Zennaro, located in Barcelona (where the Spanish court was then seated), hastened to relay word of the voyage to his brother in Milan as soon as Columbus's letter had reached the court.[21] Based on details contained in the letter, news of the voyage was sent to Milan even before Columbus was able to appear before the Spanish monarchs in person. In his version, de Zennaro reduced the information contained in the letter and added details that echoed Columbus's log, thus showing that other information beyond the letter itself was available to the inner circle of the Spanish court.[22] Once the information had reached Milan, Giacomo Trotti, the Ferrarese representative to Ludovico Sforza, ruler of Milan, forwarded it to Ercole I of Ferrara.[23] Aside from Columbus's writings, this corpus of early Italian letters constitutes the most conspicuous source of documentation of both the first and second Columbian expeditions.

Merchants were concerned with quantifiable, objective data and their concrete application. The late medieval merchant's manual contained the kind of practical information (routes, distances, markets, products, prices, measures, and so on) that was necessary to conduct trade. This genre was open and flexible, for it could also include a wide range of subjects, such as ethnographic information about the social customs and political conditions of different populations, instructions for the merchant's behavior with the locals, social critiques, diary notes, and personal commentaries. But it could also include unverified (and encyclopedic) second-hand information and local lore. Yet attention to concrete facts and a concern with practical wisdom and common sense characterized the mercantile tradition.

The first circulated mercantile reports on the outcome of Columbus's expedition were not concerned with monstrosities. The immediate Italian reactions to news of the discovery largely omitted references to dog-headed men, one-eyed men, and the other fantastic races that permeated Columbus's announcement letter. Noticeably, these 1493 letters also made no mention of the cannibalistic Caribs. They focused on the Edenic qualities of the new territories and peoples: "A very large island towards the east, which had great rivers and frightening mountains and very fertile countryside and [was] inhabited by beautiful men and women, but they all go about naked, except that some have a leaf made of cotton over their genitals"; the economic potential of the new lands: "Some Spaniards have found certain islands, which were entirely unknown, abounding in gold, spices, and other good fruits"; and the civilizing and evangelical mission that was set for the second voyage: "every kind of thing necessary . . . is being sent there . . . to give measure and rules to these island-dwellers, who lead a life like beasts and in the same way as savages. . . . They will teach them the manner of living with religion and civility. . . . They will be taught in a short time, because they are docile, as has been reported."[24]

Sent from Rome, this last document echoed the themes of the papal bulls that had been issued in early May 1493. The Spanish pope Alexander VI, who had recently been elected with Fernando and Isabella's support, had sanctioned the monarchs' request for sovereignty over the lands Columbus had claimed for them. Following precedents set in the grants that had been conceded to the Portuguese Crown in bulls issued from 1452 to 1481, the pope endorsed the Spanish Crown's rights to the mainland and the islands Columbus had discovered and would discover in subsequent voyages. The pope linked the grant of sovereignty over the new territories with the duty of evangelizing the peoples that occupied them. Notably, the bulls emphasized the indigenous peoples' positive traits of peacefulness and their eagerness to receive the Gospel:

> In these islands very many peoples dwell who live peacefully and, it is asserted, go about naked and do not eat meat; and as far as your said envoys are able to suppose, the peoples dwelling in the said islands and lands believe that there is one creator god in the heavens, and they appear to be well prepared to embrace the Catholic faith and to be instructed in good morals; and it is hoped that if they were educated, the name of our Lord and Savior Jesus Christ would easily be brought into those lands and islands.[25]

I believe that the exclusion of monstrous races and other marvels from the bulls can be explained in terms of issues of literary genre, authorship, and readership of the texts. The papal bulls of May 1493 were legal contracts and contained practical instructions. Their concern was with the new human landscape and what should be concretely done about it, not with hypothetical monsters (the stuff of myth to which the law obviously did not apply). Man-eaters were likely excluded either because of their conceptual proximity to (and assimilation with) the other fantastic monsters of the literary tradition or because of the pope's interest in drawing attention to the good disposition and readiness of the naked men of the islands to embrace Christianity as a means of reinforcing the Catholic monarchs' propaganda.

We could extend such considerations of literary genre to the original semi-fictional narrative, the 1493 letter. It contained the statement that Columbus had "so far found no human monstrosities, as many expected." But who was expecting such monstrosities? Was it Columbus, the experienced navigator, and his crew? Or was it the wider European public for whom the letter was conceived? The statement seems to correspond more to the expectations of the public than to reflect Columbus's real concerns and focus of attention, as shown in the diary. The letter deliberately mixed fictional and factual elements. Drawn from the diary but decontextualized and rearranged, the fictional elements in the letter created a narrative in which a broad European public was likely able to recognize literary features that were coherent with the long-standing tradition of travel to the East. In this sense the letter can be inserted in the tradition of extremely popular texts about the East that were bestsellers in Columbus's time.[26] And when we consider its widespread diffusion and the high number of reprints that were made of it, it appears clear that the letter had the literary and editorial characteristics of a bestseller of its time. News of geographic explorations offered late fifteenth-century audiences the opportunity to expand their knowledge of the known world, but the sensationalistic appeal of exotic features was also exploited for entertainment purposes. In the last part of this study, I will show how new information and literary appeal were tied together in a delicate balance in the texts that relate Columbus's second voyage.

## New World Cannibalism in the Accounts of the Second Voyage and Related Documents

On his second voyage, Columbus set sail directly toward the islands where the population of the Carib/Cannibals was supposed to live, according to the information gathered during his first journey. As soon as the first ships of the second journey returned to Spain halfway through the expedition, a wealth of additional details about New World cannibalism became available to the European public. Participants in the second expedition claimed that they had visited those islands and found evidence of cannibalism. Moreover, they had captured some Caribs and brought them back to Europe for display. I will consider here these original accounts by eyewitnesses of the second Columbian voyage and other reports by contemporary observers.

In February 1494, Columbus sent Captain Antonio Torres back to

Spain with news, goods, and natives. Torres carried a report written by Columbus to the sovereigns, a letter addressed to the municipality of Seville by the Andalusian physician Diego Alvarez Chanca, and a letter by a man named Guillermo Coma.[27] This last letter has not been preserved in its original Spanish version, but it exists in the Latin translation that the Sicilian humanist Nicolò Scillacio made of it.[28] The last extant firsthand account of the second journey is a letter by Michele da Cuneo, a merchant from a noble family from Savona.[29] While the first letters were written shortly after the 1494 events they recount, da Cuneo's account was written upon his return to Italy one year later. Yet its narration of the events of the second voyage coincides with the others for the most part. With the exception of Scillacio's translation of Coma's account, all of these documents were written by authors who were directly involved in the events they narrated. Because Columbus's diary of the second voyage is lost, these letters are particularly relevant as sources of information on this expedition.

All of the documents are consistent in validating the established dichotomy between the peaceful Indians (the inhabitants of the island of Hispaniola), and the Caribs or cannibals (located on the smaller islands that are today called the Lesser Antilles). The few discrepancies that exist among the texts do not affect the unanimous consensus among eyewitnesses that the Caribs practiced cannibalism. Da Cuneo reported that while exploring one of the Carib islands, a party of Europeans rescued some young Indian captives who had been abducted from the other islands. Among them were some young boys whom the cannibals had castrated:

> On that island we seized twelve beautiful and very fat females, aged between fifteen and sixteen, with two boys of the same age whose genital members had been cut away clean to the belly. We figured that they had done it to keep them from mixing with their women or perhaps to fatten them up and eat them later. These boys and girls had been captured by the Cannibals.[30]

Chanca registered that later, the captain of a party of about thirty men who had ventured to inspect the villages that had been abandoned by the time the Europeans arrived allegedly found "a good deal of spun cotton, yarn and edible provisions and of everything he took samples. In particular, he took away three or four human arm and leg bones.

When we saw this, we suspected these islands were inhabited by the Caribs, human-flesh-eating people."[31] According to Chanca, human remains were repeatedly observed in multiple dwellings of the natives: "Several times we went ashore, exploring all dwellings and villages that lay along the coast where we found quite a few human bones and skulls hanging inside the houses and used as containers to hold things."[32] Additional details were gained through the captive Indian women, whom the Europeans had set free from Carib villages:

> They [the cannibals] assault the other islands and take with them the women they are able to seize, especially young and beautiful girls whom they keep as servants as well as lovers, and they take so many of them that in the fifty dwellings they had fled from, more than twenty imprisoned girls followed us. The same women also reported the Caribs act with unbelievable but true cruelty, eating the offspring generated with the imprisoned women while raising only those conceived by women of their own kind. The men they are able to capture alive are brought into their huts for slaughtering and immediate consumption. They claim human flesh is so exquisite that a similar delicacy does not exist in the world, and this is clearly indicated by the fact that, of the bones we found in their dwellings, all that could be gnawed on had been gnawed on, and all that was left was what could not be eaten, because it was inedible. There, in one of the huts, a human neck was found boiling in a pot.[33]

Da Cuneo's account added: "The Cannibals, when they capture some Indians, eat them like we eat young goats, and they say that the flesh of a boy is much better than that of a female. They have an insatiable appetite for that human flesh."[34]

These quite sensationalistic remarks on Carib cannibalism—in part suspiciously reminiscent of passages from previous travel literature—have been systematically questioned in a lengthy scholarly debate. No European observer witnessed actual acts of cannibalism in the New World, skeptics argue; cannibalism was merely inferred from the Indians' testimony and substantiated by the observation of castrated captives, the fact that the rescued Indians willingly followed the Europeans on the ships to escape Carib captivity, and the finding of human remains in the villages. One frequent reservation is the argument that the explorers' testimony, "far from being, as sometimes claimed, a 'matter-of-fact' description, is a highly mediated piece of prose deeply embedded in the assumptions which governed Columbus's second voyage."[35] According to this view, even before embarking on the expedition, Chanca would have derived his expectations that the Caribs were cannibals from Columbus's propounded "official version," which he would have then espoused through his use of the first-person plural.[36] Chanca was not a member of the landing party and only reported what was told to him second-hand. Consequently, "in no way can he be seen as an independent or fresh witness who 'just' reports what he sees."[37]

Similar to frequent assumptions that Columbus had a prejudiced mindset, we find that at the heart of the dismissal of these documents' validity as reliable ethnographic accounts of an actual practice lies the idea that early modern men's perceptions were highly influenced by a predefined framework that was directly transposed onto the New World from the Old. Chanca's letter can certainly be read as a mediated piece of prose (just as Columbus's and da Cuneo's writings can), especially when it comes to the colorful embroidering of the most gruesome details of Carib cannibalism. Yet the sensationalism in these accounts is counterbalanced with passages that are unequivocally drawn from direct observation and experience. In that respect, these reports are fresh and original. In the last part of this chapter, I will further address the issue of the reliability of these accounts.

Michele da Cuneo was born in 1448 in Savona to one of the city's wealthiest and most prominent families. Michele's grandfather had sailed the Mediterranean and had served as a diplomat in Milan and Genova. Following in his footsteps, Michele's father and uncles were traders and sailors who also held public office in Savona. Corrado da Cuneo, Michele's father, became a member of the city's Consiglio degli Anziani in 1471. From 1446 to 1482, Corrado conducted trade in Chios, the Maghreb, Spain, London, and Flanders. He also owned land, buildings, and shops in Savona and its surroundings, and in 1474 he sold a small property to Columbus's father, Domenico, who had moved from Genova with his family in 1470.[38] Michele da Cuneo and Christopher Columbus came from the same mercantile milieu, and Columbus took him as a friend and a business associate on the voyage to survey the new lands. Da Cuneo did not disappoint: the gaze he cast upon the new lands was that of a skilled merchant, a man trained in the careful and detailed observation and assessment of anything that could be profitably sold in the markets of the known world. His descriptions have been called "the first methodical systematization of the whole nature of the Indies, beginning with the plants and going on through the animals to conclude with the men."[39] Da Cuneo's meticulous classification of New World species and goods (their shape, quality, taste, use, and marketability) marks the distance of his world view from that of his traveling companion, the Andalusian doctor Chanca, who had not received the same training in commercial pursuits.

If on the one hand, Columbus and da Cuneo shared common roots in the late medieval mercantile tradition, on the other their readership heavily determined the content of their communications. Columbus was obviously limited in his writing, as his reports were official documents to the Spanish Crown, while da Cuneo was much freer to express his true thoughts and sentiments. Because his letter was addressed as a private communication to a friend and business associate in his Italian hometown, it included unfiltered information such as his disappointment about the scarcity of gold on the islands, the disagreement between Columbus and a cosmographer over whether Cuba was to be considered an island or a continent, and even the candid account of his own rape of an Indigenous woman. Given the scope and depth of observation of da Cuneo's writing, a set of questions could be productively raised regarding his assertions about the cannibalistic habits of the Caribs. As a man who had traveled extensively, who was used to conducting trade with peoples of different languages and cultures, and who had the ability to thoroughly describe what he saw because his attention was focused on objective assessments of landscapes and goods, it is hard to imagine reasons why da Cuneo would report on the cannibalism of the indigenous natives other than that he was genuinely convinced that the practice was taking place on the islands. His letter contained no tales of the expected marvels and monstrosities that had circulated in Europe after Columbus's return. Even the mythical island of women without men, which Columbus had judged would not be far from the islands of the Caribs, vanished in da Cuneo's account. Why would Amazons fail to survive and cannibals thrive in da Cuneo's landscape of Columbus's second voyage, if it were not for the fact that he considered the latter to have a bearing in empirical reality?

This is not to say that da Cuneo's and other contemporary accounts of New World cannibalism lacked the characteristics of highly mediated prose. As the well-known skeptic of cannibalism, William Arens, put it, it would be unreasonable to imply out of hand that all observers misrepresented their observations; "but they might have resorted to a common shortcoming of authors both past and present called plagiarism."[40] In other words, a learned man like da Cuneo might have drawn his most graphic details from preexisting literary representations to supplement his account, even if other sections of his brief treatise on the Indies reflected his own firsthand experience and observation. Even if his main concern was with commercial pursuits, he was nevertheless a well-educated man and must have had access to the kind of literature we know Columbus had read before sailing. Although cannibalism loomed large in the early modern European imagination, the embellishment, aggrandizing, and plagiarism of tales of cannibalism in travel accounts do not necessarily undermine the validity of those accounts as sources of historical evidence. The fact that representations of cannibalism could be deliberately plagiarized and augmented using models derived from existing sources does not invalidate the possibility that reports of cannibalism could also be based in empirical reality.

The translation that Nicolò Scillacio made of Guillermo Coma's report is admittedly one such operation of literary embroidery upon firsthand sources. By his own admission, Scillacio engaged in the embellishment of his original source through self-conscious imitation of classical models:

> I very recently received an account by letter from Guillermo Coma, a very noble Spaniard, written in his native language, and . . . I translated it into Latin in the truthful style of Lucian and perhaps, in a style more amusing than Siculus's. . . . Afterwards . . . I will very carefully add to the books of the ancient authors what has been handed down to us by our predecessors concerning the savagery, customs, and laws of the various peoples and about their ways of life.[41]

The specific features of Italian humanism emerge through Scillacio's reworking of Coma's text: his Latin letter, compiled in Pavia after December 13, 1494, for his patron Ludovico il Moro, Duke of Milan, was a typical product of courtly humanism.[42] The Sicilian Scillacio was doctor of arts and medicine and a professor of philosophy at Pavia. His work originated in the social and intellectual milieu of the early modern lecture hall, whose language "relied heavily upon a corpus of authorities (*auctoritates*) or tropes (*loci communes*) and on the arguments to which these in turn referred."[43] Scillacio never traveled to the New World, but he was in Barcelona shortly before compiling his letter (which was published in Pavia in 1495 or 1496). He had likely obtained his firsthand source through the same medical circle that Chanca belonged to.[44] Scillacio's manipulations of Coma's account illustrate the specific contribution of Italian humanists to the creation and dissemination of an idealized image of the cannibal. Scillacio appears to have deliberately glamorized cannibalism and other exotic elements for their literary appeal.[45] He also openly engaged in a conscious effort to put ancient and recently acquired knowledge in dialogue. The figure of the cannibal was colored by the superimposition of classical terminology over the original eyewitnesses reports: "The people there are ferocious and unconquered, and live on human flesh, and so I may rightly call them anthropophagi."[46] He also reinterpreted through classical myth the Indians' claims that the cannibals ate their own sons: "If any of these [captive] women happen to give birth, they eat the child as they do the other captured children; this is a truer version of the legend of Saturn, who the poets claim gorged himself on his own children."[47]

Another Italian humanist, Peter Martyr D'Anghiera, augmented reports of cannibalism through his elegant and erudite Latin remodeling of firsthand accounts after the classics. D'Anghiera, a prolific and influential writer, was an attentive observer of the American enterprise, which he recorded from his advantageous location at the Spanish court and interpreted through the lens of his education as a Renaissance scholar. His *Decades de Orbe Novo,* a systematization of information about the new overseas lands and the Spanish exploration of them, was widely circulated throughout Europe in both translations and adaptations and was thus extremely influential as one of the most important sources of information about the American lands. The humanistic tradition led him to identify the condition of simplicity of the peoples Columbus encountered with the golden age of antiquity. The exotic appeal of cannibalism is prominent in his writings. In his letter of December 5, 1494, to his friend Pomponio Leto in Rome, Peter Martyr D'Anghiera, like Scillacio, drew parallels between the newly found cannibals and the man-eaters of ancient tradition:

> Be careful not to doubt they were Laestrygonians or Cyclops who fed on human flesh, and take care not to let your hair bristle in horror! When from the Fortunate Islands (which some want to call the *Canaries*) one moves toward *Hispaniola* . . . you run across many islands of savage men, whom they call *Cannibals* or *Caribs*.[48]

The enthusiasm with which the erudite embroidered their firsthand sources was paralleled by a display of concern with the careful selection of reliable information in the correspondence of merchants and diplomats. The Tuscan Simone dal Verde was a purveyor of velvet and brocade to the Spanish court at Valladolid when Torres's ships returned from the Antilles. His letter of May 10, 1494, to a business agent in Florence exhibited skepticism about the truthfulness of news from the New World, which he felt compelled to validate:

> I have spoken with three persons who returned with those twelve caravels; one of them was a captain of those caravels, another the pilot, and another was master of one of the caravels that went there. I will tell you what I learned from them, not without fear of writing uncertain things. So as not to err or place myself at risk of telling lies, I will tell that part of what I heard which seems likely to me. . . . They found in those houses two young girls and two young boys who had been taken from the other islands. The genital member of the males was cut away close to the pubis: they say that they fatten them for eating. Since this is a horrible thing to think about, let alone assert that it actually happens, I have made every effort to obtain reliable information, and I find it without any doubt to be true.[49]

Dal Verde reported his efforts to verify rumors of cannibalism through his direct interrogation of the people involved in the enterprise and one of the cannibals himself, who was brought to Europe as a captive:

> The captain of those caravels that returned certified to me that very many bones of the dead were found in their houses and in one house human flesh was roasting and a man's head was on the coals; and those things were brought to the admiral so that he could see them. I do not know if this is true, given the facility that those men have for telling lies. What I do believe, based on what everyone says, is that they eat human flesh; and the inhabitants of the other islands say the same thing. . . . I have spoken with one of the men they brought back, who understands a little of our language, and learned from him that it was true: it appears that over here he is ashamed of it and shows signs of regret.[50]

With the common sense typical of the businessman, dal Verde questioned the truthfulness of the reports that were brought back from the New World and even openly exposed the ease with which tales about it could be aggrandized by those who had been there. His letter adduced the same evidence for cannibalism as the other sources of the second voyage, but in a concise, skeptical tone devoid of sensationalistic details. Dal Verde was well aware of the dangers of exaggeration in travel stories. But it seems to me that despite his initial skepticism, his letter clearly attests to the fact that his conclusion on the matter was that Carib natives did actually engage in cannibalism.

In the heterogeneous corpus of literary materials that was quickly spread through the Italian diplomatic and mercantile network as an immediate reaction to the news of Columbus's return from his first voyage, the naked peoples of the newly found islands were initially characterized by their good disposition. Mostly concerned with the novelty of the new territories, the quality of the land and the goods, and the profit that could accrue from trade, these first documents largely omitted the references to monstrosities or cannibals that were popularized by Columbus's widely circulated announcement letter. The early information on the Americas was transmitted via the Italian mercantile and diplomatic correspondence with an immediacy unparalleled by other literary genres. Instead of drawing on the authority of the ancient books on the East or catering to a wide reading public that was expecting tales of marvels, these writers directed their letters toward traders and state administrators concerned with facts and practical details. This body of literary materials was generated using firsthand information that was passed by word of mouth, often through directly interrogating participants in the expedition. The telegraphic format of the mercantile circular letter, the rapidity with which missives were sent out, and the utilitarian gaze cast upon the new lands leaned toward content that was factual and essential. It seems likely to me that these letter writers intentionally discarded fantastic elements or unverified data because they did not suit the interests and needs of a public that was eager for practical and reliable information.

Following Columbus's second voyage, as more islands were explored, more information trickled back from the Caribbean. In contrast to the vague ideas about cannibals that were initially disseminated through Columbus's letter (ideas that were highly reminiscent of preexistent literary tropes), accounts by participants in the second voyage related a whole new set of details about cannibalism. Italian humanists immediately emphasized this information with sensationalistic tones in their embellished reworkings of the firsthand sources. An augmentative process often marked both the recounting of the experience in the original accounts and the passage of information from one context to another, and prurient details were easily sensationalized to create more entertaining and vivid narratives. Yet, although contemporary observers were aware of the phenomenon, they did not believe that it invalidated accounts of cannibalism. At the turn of the sixteenth century, adventurers were willing to undergo great risks for any scrap of gold. They thoroughly scrutinized new landscapes to extract value from anything they could offer, be it in mineral, vegetable, animal, or human form. It is no surprise that adventurers and explorers and those who revised the texts they produced also exploited new lands for their exotic appeal and the imaginary that they activated in European audiences. Judging from the editorial success of the numerous editions of Columbus's announcement letter, such tales were highly marketable. To discard the cannibal trope as a myth with no foundation in reality because the literary sources that conveyed such information are too ornate to be believable (as Peter Hulme and other scholars have suggested) seems reductive.[51] The seemingly unreliable interpolations from previous texts only attest to the fact that "humanist culture was not that of a self-enclosed community of scholars, but rather, through literacy and other channels, affected various levels of society, connecting the urban classes of patricians, merchants, lawyers and doctors to the court and its domesticated aristocracy."[52] The first Italian accounts in the mercantile tradition were imbued with humanist culture but were mainly concerned with the concrete assessment of facts and new commercial landscapes, not with embellishment in sophisticated prose. These sources recount the history of the early contact with the Americas with a freshness unencumbered by editorial considerations or by the political interests of colonialists.

CHAPTER 3

# Sex and Cannibalism

## The Politics of Carnal Relations between Europeans and American "Anthropophagites" in the Caribbean and Mexico

KELLY L. WATSON

Christopher Columbus was, by most accounts, a man of steadfast principles and unwavering confidence in his vision. Long before setting foot in the Americas, Columbus argued vociferously with some of Europe's leading experts in geography and cartography about the ratio of land to water in the cosmos and the potential for humans to thrive in the torrid zone. Each time Columbus requested funds for his voyage, he encountered strident dissent from powerful men who clung to an outdated perception that the earth was almost entirely made of water except for one continent that was separated into three sections: Europe, Asia, and Africa. Columbus's detractors argued that if he sailed west and south, he would not find land, and that even if by some miracle he did find land, it would never be truly habitable. Thus, they lobbied the Catholic monarchs to turn down his requests for funding for a voyage of proof. However, Columbus had powerful friends who shared his understanding of the potential for land and human settlement to the west and south of Europe and together they were eventually able to convince Ferdinand and Isabella to allow the voyage, but only after the Reconquista was complete. In addition, Columbus had to promise that almost all funds would be provided by private sources and that the Crown would get one-fifth of all profits from the venture.[1]

Throughout his life, Columbus demonstrated the solidity of his convictions even in the face of great opposition.[2] However, the strength of his convictions also made it difficult for him to recognize the empirical reality of what he saw on his voyages. This was true not only in his belief that the Americas were actually a part of greater Asia but also in his perceptions of the people who resided there. Before setting sail, Columbus knew what kinds of people he might find, particularly in the tropical regions. He was familiar with popular medieval and classical literature that described the flora, fauna, and geography of the lands on what was thought to be the fringes of the earth and he often looked to such texts to determine what he should expect to find. For example, based on the precedent the fanciful tales of medieval travelers had established, Columbus expected to find mermaids in the Indies. He wrote in his journal that he did indeed find mermaids, although they were not as beautiful as he expected (most likely because the "mermaids" were actually manatees).[3]

In a letter to the Spanish sovereigns during his third voyage to the Americas, Columbus reaffirmed his confidence in his cartographic calculations and said that his voyages would be remembered by future generations because they would offer corrections to thousands of years of misunderstandings about the distribution of lands and people on the surface of the earth. Columbus also suggested some adjustments to previous understandings of the shape of the earth and the location of Eden, or terrestrial paradise, which most previous scholars had placed somewhere in the eastern northern hemisphere.[4] He argued that contrary to popular belief, the earth was irregularly shaped and that the western hemisphere had a protrusion shaped like a woman's breast. Columbus believed that Eden would be found at the high point of this protrusion, where the nipple would be.

> But this western half of the world, I maintain, is like the half of a very round pear, having a raised projection for the stalk, as I have already described, or like a woman's nipple on a round ball. Ptolemy and the others who have written upon the globe, had no information respecting this part of the world, which was then unexplored; they only established their arguments with respect to their own hemisphere, which, as I have already said, is half of a perfect sphere.[5]

While we know that Columbus was not quite correct in his understanding of the shape of the earth, his description of the world as a sexualized woman's body part is quite telling. Columbus was certainly not alone in describing land as feminine. As this was a fairly common way to speak of landscapes, such descriptions help us think through how Columbus and others understood their accomplishments.[6] European visitors to these "new" lands had ideas about gender and sex that, more often than not, they imposed upon the local context instead of attempting to understand new peoples and cultures on their own terms. Thus, men like Columbus already knew, at least in general terms, the wonders that would await them in the Americas. They knew that the sexual practices of the inhabitants would not match up with European values and they also knew that in the "wildest" and "least cultivated" regions of the world they would find cannibals.

This chapter examines the connections between the discourses of cannibalism and sex in the Caribbean and in Mexico from the late 1400s through the mid-1500s. Cannibalism and sex intersected in the discourse of these regions in two main ways.[7] First, European men who traveled to the Americas, especially at the end of the fifteenth and the beginning of the sixteenth centuries, believed that certain groups of American Indians were cannibalistic and others were not. They used this determination of cannibal status as a way of judging who was and was not an acceptable intimate partner.

The second way these discourses intersected was through European conquerors' use of cannibalism as a heuristic for a variety of unrelated practices. In other words, early visitors to the Americas assumed a great many things about peoples they believed to be cannibalistic. As acts of cannibalism were consistently linked with discourses of savagery and civilization in early modern writings, being accused of cannibalism was far more complex than simply being perceived as someone who consumed human flesh.[8] Cannibalism connoted savagery, and savagery was never limited to just one practice. So those accused of cannibalism were commonly accused of violating a variety of European cultural taboos. Savages ate the wrong foods, often at the wrong times and in the wrong amounts.[9] Their sexual practices were perceived as equally flawed. Savages did not understand modesty, did not value chastity, or did not give men enough sexual power.

It can be easy to fall into one of two camps when discussing European descriptions of supposed acts of Indigenous American cannibalism. The first camp insists that these accounts are useful only for learning about European preconceptions. Thus, such sources demonstrate the persistence of classical and medieval conceptions of cannibals but reveal nothing about actual Native American practices. The second camp argues that while European descriptions of Indigenous American cannibalism obviously bear the hallmarks of stereotypical thinking and imperialist motivations, reading carefully between the lines can reveal important details about Native lives and practices. Thus, while European sources that describe cannibalism in the Americas are not completely accurate, they nonetheless contain important truths if one looks carefully enough.

There is a wide spectrum between these two positions, and this essay examines the murky middle between them. Modern ideas of truth and falsehood cannot simply be retroactively applied to early modern writers. Men like Christopher Columbus or Amerigo Vespucci were not lying when they wrote about wondrous dog-headed people in the Americas, but they were not telling the truth either. Another distinction is that scientific observational techniques were in their infancy in the sixteenth century and neither of these men were trained observers of other cultures. Early modern depictions of Indian life do perhaps reveal more about the authors than the subjects, but archaeological and anthropological evidence has shown that cannibal practices were present in some Native communities (as they were in Europe). Nothing has quite shown that Native Americans were the rapacious cannibals European extremists described, but that doesn't indicate an absence of anthropophagy. We cannot fully discount European writings, but we cannot use them as reliable evidence of Native practices either. If this feels unsatisfying, that discomfort is not lost on me. It is uncomfortable to write and read in the murky middle.

## Sex with Cannibals

In the first few decades of the European presence in the Caribbean and Mexico, European men engaged in sexual relations, both forced and consensual, with Native women. Despite their consistent demonization of Indigenous man-eaters, eyewitness accounts reveal that sex between reportedly cannibalistic women and European men occurred. In some instances, the fact that a particular woman was believed to be a cannibal was the very thing that made her a potential sexual partner. In other instances, European men saw sex with anthropophagic women as a threat to European civilization. The distinguishing factors related to the status of the woman and the goal of the sexual encounter. Long-term relationships and/or politically advantageous partnerships with cannibalistic women were not encouraged, while sporadic, casual encounters between "cannibal" women and European men were not perceived as a threat to Europe's civilizing agenda.

One of the clearest examples of the role of cannibalism in the determination of sexual partners comes from the account of Michele da Cuneo, who accompanied Columbus on his second voyage to the Americas. Cuneo was an Italian aristocrat and likely a childhood friend of Columbus who volunteered for the voyage. After he returned to Europe, in October 1495, he wrote a letter to his friend Gerolamo Annari.[10] He devoted much of this letter to describing the geography, flora, and fauna of the Caribbean, but he also penned a significant record of the customs of Caribbean peoples. By 1495, the tales of Columbus's first voyage were well known in intellectual circles in Europe, and Cuneo drew from both these accounts and his own observations for his descriptions of Indians. He reinforced the notion in earlier accounts that there were two main groups of people in what we now call the Caribbean: a gentle, tractable people and a fearsome group of cannibalistic warriors. In the earliest records of encounters between Europeans and Caribbean Natives, there was a great deal of confusion over the distinction between cannibals and noncannibals as these categories were often superimposed upon the tribal designations of Carib and Arawak, respectively.[11] In fact, the modern word "cannibal" is derived from the word "Carib." Thus, there was a great deal of slippage between the use of "carib" and "cannibal" in early accounts; almost always the two were used as synonyms. The Caribs were cannibals, and cannibals were Caribs. When Cuneo described a battle between Columbus's fleet and a canoe of Indians that he labeled as "Camballa" in Italian, this designation carried a great deal of symbolic weight.

In Cuneo's description of this encounter between Columbus's crew and a group of Caribs in canoes, the battle did not end well for the Indians, as all were either captured or killed. Cuneo related that the people in the canoes fought fiercely, which, along with the presence of castrated captives (whom I will discuss later), led him to believe that they were cannibals/Caribs rather than supposedly pacifistic Arawaks.[12] Later in this letter, Cuneo outlined the similarities and differences that he perceived between the two groups: "The Cannibals and the Indians . . . all have one language and live in the same manner and seem in appearance to be of a single nation, except for those Cannibals who are more fierce and clever than the Indians. The Cannibals, when they capture some Indians, eat them like we eat young goats. . . . They have an insatiable appetite for that human flesh. . . ."[13]

When the aforementioned battle ended, the Spanish crew took the remaining Indians captive so they could sell them into slavery. Columbus gave one of these captured slaves to Cuneo as a gift. His description of the fate of this unfortunate young woman after she came into his possession vividly illustrates the intersection between sex and cannibalism.

> While I was in the boat I laid my hands on a gorgeous Cannibal woman whom the lord admiral granted me; when I had her in my quarters, naked, as is their custom, I felt a craving to sport with her. When I tried to satisfy my craving, she, wanting none of it, gave me such a treatment with her nails that at that point I wished I had never started. At this, to tell you how it all ended, I got hold of a rope and thrashed her so thoroughly that she raised unheard-of cries that you would never believe. Finally we were of such accord that, in the act, I can tell you, she seemed to have been trained in a school of harlots.[14]

Given what we know about European men's beliefs about the inhumanity of cannibals, it is likely that he believed that his rape of this woman was justifiable. For our purposes here, it matters very little if she was actually a Carib Indian, much less whether or not she had ever eaten another human; the fact that Cuneo assumed her to be a cannibal was enough to strip her of her human dignity. The literal possession of the Carib woman's body echoed the process of imperialism writ large; European conquerors portrayed both the land and the people as unconsciously desirous of subjugation. This sad tale is the only historical record of this woman's existence.

In other parts of his letter, Cuneo carefully recorded his observations about the beauty, breasts, stomachs, and procreative practices of Native women.[15] He also gave a detailed account of their supposed orgiastic religious practices and their sodomitic tendencies.[16] Considering this alongside Cuneo's suggestion that his Carib victim was "trained in a school of harlots," we are left with a description of the Caribs as little more than hypersexualized animals. However, by indicating that she *trained,* Cuneo seems to be subtly implying that while this young woman was perhaps more instinctively knowledgeable about sexuality than European women, she had learned her skills through practice. A mere animal would not need training to be a skilled lover. For Cuneo, because she possessed knowledge that was more than instinct, her ability to refuse his advances was curtailed, since "fallen" women had limited agency in such matters. Her supposed sexual prowess was further confirmation for Cuneo that she was not a pure, civilized woman deserving of his care or consideration. He saw her as tainted by her association with cannibalism and by her ability to engage in pleasurable sexual congress.[17] She and other Carib women appeared in early writings as beings whose bodies triumphed over their reason.

Other eyewitness accounts linked sexuality and savagery, particularly the writings of Amerigo Vespucci. While the veracity of Vespucci's accounts is questionable, his popularity among the learned readership of Europe is not.[18] He reportedly traveled to the Americas on four separate occasions in the period 1497 to 1504, twice for Spain and twice for Portugal. He described the sexuality of Native peoples of the Caribbean and mainland South America in far more detail than other eyewitnesses. Vespucci wrote that Carib women were inordinately lustful but "not as revolting as one might think."[19] Their lustfulness was not directed only at men of their own tribe, however; according to Vespucci, Carib women were also "driven by their excessive lust to corrupt and prostitute their modesty" in order that they might "copulate with Christians."[20] Unlike Cuneo, Vespucci avoided explicitly mentioning any sex acts between European men and Indian women, even though he obliquely referred to such acts as quotidian.

He also indicated several different times that circum-Caribbean American Indians were overly generous, both with their possessions and their bodies. He revealed that he was disturbed by the Indians' tradition of offering their virginal daughters as diplomatic presents to the European visitors.[21] Vespucci also contradicted almost all previous accounts by indicating that the Caribs consumed both men and women "with such ferocity that merely to speak of it seems a brute thing."[22]

Transnational awareness of the practice of cannibalism came with a steep cost both for individual Indians and for tribes as a whole. In 1503, the Spanish Crown directly addressed the supposed problem of cannibalism in the Americas through a *real cédula* sometimes known as the cannibal law.[23] This decree established the spiritual value of Indians and demanded that they be given the chance for salvation, but it also recognized that some peoples might be beyond redemption. Because Indians deserved the chance to be saved, the law disallowed wanton enslavement. However, it also set forth a protocol for dealing with cannibalistic Indians who vociferously resisted conversion:

> Therefore, by means of the present [letter] I give permission and the authority to any and every person under my command who should go to the islands and Tierra Firma of the said Ocean Sea that up to the present have been discovered or that will be discovered, that if the said cannibals should resist and not wish to receive and welcome into their lands the captains and peoples who by my command go and make the said voyages and if [the cannibals] do not wish to listen to them in order to be indoctrinated in the things of our Holy Catholic faith and enter my service and become subject to me, [then the persons under my command] may and can capture [the cannibals] in order to take them to whichever lands and islands . . . they wish, paying us the share of them that belongs to us in order that [the cannibals] might be sold and a profit be made without [the seller] incurring any penalty whatsoever, and this is so that, being brought to these parts and being in service of Christians, [the cannibals] can be more easily converted and attracted to our Holy Catholic Faith.[24]

This law was followed by several other laws related to cannibalism and enslavement over the next few decades and in 1518 a council was created to formalize the list of regions inhabited by anthropophagites.[25]

But these laws did not specifically address gender until 1569. Prior to this, women were implicitly excluded from enslavement regardless of their tribe's supposed cannibalistic practices. Thus, in the early sixteenth century, men were legally and spiritually culpable for cannibalism (despite many descriptions of Indian women's active participation in acts of cannibalism).

When the Spaniards shifted the major focus of their exploration and conquest to the mainland in the first decades of the sixteenth century, what did not change was observers' desires to separate Indigenous groups into good or bad, civilized or savage—their desire to describe, exploit, and fantasize about the shocking things Indians did with their bodies, or their continued commentaries on cannibalism. Spanish writers were no longer able to assert a clear difference between savage, uncivilized cannibals and peaceful, innocent Indians. Instead they faced a new set of circumstances where peoples that had seemingly much more complex governments, cities, and religious traditions also sometimes indulged in cannibalism and human sacrifice. The Maya and Nahua peoples the Spaniards encountered defied the simplistic descriptors writers had used when discussing the Caribs and the Arawaks. Spanish writers still appeared to be conflicted about their attraction to Native women and the cultural traditions of the objects of their desires. This conflict appears quite clearly in firsthand descriptions of Cortés's conquest of Mexico.

In order to cement their new alliance with the Spaniards, Yucatecan Maya groups engaged in traditional forms of diplomatic exchange. Typically, groups exchanged gifts meant to demonstrate their commitment and sincerity. The commodities the Maya exchanged to seal relationships and create kinship ties between groups included people, particularly women. Thus, for the Maya, sexual relations between their people and the Spaniards would deepen the connection between groups. Any children born of these unions would perform an important role as cultural mediators. Local caciques gave their daughters or other important relatives to Spanish men as a gesture of trust and submission.[26] They also gave enslaved women as gifts to a member of an alliance or occasionally as tokens for sacrifice. The woman Cortés and his men collected on their journey across Mexico may not have been official negotiators of the alliance between Spain and various Maya groups as the Spaniards would have perceived it, but their role in a form of sexual diplomacy should not be understated. These women forged links between the newcomers and the enemies of the Aztecs through their bodies.

The conquistadors did not have a clear protocol about what to do with the women they were given. In diplomatic exchanges, Spaniards regularly expected high-ranking Native women to convert to Christianity before they could fulfil their role as cultural mediators. Although Cortés regularly distributed noble women among his most trusted compatriots, before he would sanction sex between his men and Indigenous women, he wanted to be sure that the women were acceptable sexual partners for important, respectable Spanish men. While Cuneo had no moral qualms about raping a Carib woman, he would not have seen her as an acceptable long-term partner or mistress. We have very little information about the scores of lower-class women Yucatecan Maya groups gave Spaniards as part of cultural diplomacy. But we know that Cortés and other Spaniards expected the noble women Natives gave them to convert to Christianity, give up their "savage" practices, form lasting ties with them, and bear them children who would lead the next generation of the conquest.[27]

In one significant instance when local caciques gave Cortes women as gifts, instead of simply accepting the women as objects for labor or sex, he required them to give up their traditional beliefs and practices before they could act as ambassadors.[28] Bernal Díaz del Castillo described the incident in his account of the conquest, indicating that Cortés believed "that these damsels must become Christians before we could receive them." The women belonged to groups that practiced cannibalism, as Castillo recorded:

> Every day we saw sacrificed before us three, four, or five Indians whose hearts were offered to the idols and their blood plastered on the walls, and the feet, arms, and legs of the victims were cut off and eaten, just as in our country we eat beef bought from the butchers. I even believe that they sell it by retail in the *tianguez* as they call their markets.[29]

The women were thus presented both as objects of exchange and as potential victims of cannibalism and sacrifice. It follows that Cortés and other Spaniards assumed that the women were savage and anthropophagic but also redeemable. The women from this example were baptized quickly and then distributed among Cortés's trusted leaders.[30] Given the speed with which these conversions took place, it seems fairly unlikely that the women were sincere in their desire for baptism. Indeed, baptism appears more like a convenient ritual meant to turn these women into Catholics who would then be potential intimate partners. While many Spaniards were untroubled by the thought of having sex with Indigenous women, they saw taking heathen women as wives or mistresses as unacceptable. In other words, meaningless sex (which, of course, was probably far less meaningless for the women, who were often forced) was acceptable with women who did not meet the standards of Spanish civilization, but it would have been inappropriate to develop deep attachments to anthropophagic women.

Cortés occasionally seemed conflicted about the fate of the women he was given. He hoped these women could serve important roles as translators and cultural ambassadors and as potential emissaries for Catholicism. When he asked a friar who was part of the small Spanish contingent in Mexico whether he should accept non-Christian women as gifts and potential brides, the friar told him that bringing these women into the fold could provide the Spaniards with viable "material to work upon." But he also said that it was reasonable for Cortés to say that he would not accept women who had not disavowed their most savage practices, like sacrifice and cannibalism.[31]

Bernal Díaz also struggled with conflicting desires. He found himself both impressed and horrified by the Aztecs' treatment of women and by their sexual practices. Díaz was amazed by the size of Motecuhzoma's harem but repulsed by his unsavory desires, which reportedly included sex with young men, whom he occasionally consumed. (Despite his knowledge of such practices, Cortés entrusted a young Spanish page to Motecuhzoma's care.) Díaz was willing to ask Motecuhzoma to give him a "very pretty Indian woman."[32] Thus, while Díaz might have been uncomfortable with the appetites of the Aztecs, this did not prevent him from desiring the bodies of anthropophagic Aztec women.

## The "Savage" Sexual Practices of Cannibals

Being accused of cannibalism almost always meant being accused of breaking other taboos of European civilization. Man-eating has been discursively linked to barbarity in the literature of Western Europe and the Mediterranean for thousands of years. It was also something that reportedly occurred most often on the fringes of civilization, in the regions most removed from metropoles.[33] Being called a savage has long had consequences beyond personal slander, as accusations of savagery and cannibalism were used as justifications for conquest, enslavement, and other forms of violence. Just as cannibalism was an indicator of savagery, sexual practices were part of how Europeans understood barbarity. Or, to put it another way, the written record suggests that Europeans believed that groups of people they believed to be cannibals also engaged in a variety of inappropriate sexual and gendered practices. The obverse was also true: groups that they believed engaged in sexual and gendered practices that Europeans deemed inappropriate were also more likely to be accused of acts of man-eating.

The writings produced from Columbus's voyages show that the discourse of cannibalism was inextricably intertwined with the discourse of other "savage" practices. The only surviving pieces of Columbus's journal are found in the writings of his son Ferdinand and the writings of Bartolomé de las Casas; the latter presented the greater portion. It is clear that both Ferdinand Columbus and Las Casas had copies of the original journal because they both quote it at length; they provide summaries of other parts. For the sake of clarity, this essay will refer to Columbus as the author of this journal, even though its authorship is far more complex.

The first description of an act of cannibalism in the Americas comes from an entry in Columbus's journal just three weeks after first landfall in the Caribbean and clearly links sexual practices and anthropophagy.[34] In this entry, Columbus indicates that a group of (presumably) Arawak Indians he met informed him of a terrible threat on a nearby island, where "there were one-eyed men, and others, with snouts of dogs, who ate men, and that as soon as one was taken they cut his throat and drank his blood and cut off his genitals."[35] Given his familiarity with the writings of Marco Polo and John Mandeville that featured anthropophagic cynocephali, Columbus did not seem terribly surprised to hear about dog-headed men.[36] A modern skeptical reader might have a few questions about Columbus's observations:

How did Columbus learn all of this information from the Arawaks when no one on the voyage spoke their language? Can creatures with the heads of dogs and the bodies of humans really be considered *human*? And if they are not human, can their consumption of humans really be considered cannibalism? But for our purposes here, what is most interesting about this observation is the link between cannibalism and sex. The removal of the captives' genitals by the male members of the cynocephalic tribe has clear sexual overtones. Castrating captives is obviously intended to emasculate the victims, but it also serves to prevent any procreation between captives and conquerors and thus ensures that no kinship relationships could be forged. It also leaves the reader wondering what exactly these dog-headed cannibals did with the genitals that they removed. Did they consume them with other body parts, as Columbus said they did? If so, this act of cannibalism might also be perceived as not only a symbolic emasculation of the consumed by the consumer but also as an act that mimicked sodomy through the ingestion/insertion of genitals into the body of the consumer.[37] Thus, from Columbus's perspective, the cannibalistic appetites of these dog-headed men might easily be seen as a threat to European masculinity through their taboo violations of men's bodies.

Columbus also reported on his first voyage that he heard about cannibals on neighboring islands whose mating habits seemed at odds with European notions of propriety.[38] He described this society of supposed cannibals as entirely male and reported that they seasonally mated with the all-female population of the nearby island of Matinino. The descriptions of the women of Matinino closely resemble the Amazons of classical legend.[39] Female children born of the copulations between the male cannibals and the women of Matinino were left to be raised by their mothers, while male children born of these unions were raised by their cannibal fathers.[40] In this example, we again see a link between cannibalism and nontraditional sexual practices. While the women of Matinino were not directly accused of cannibalism, it seems reasonable to conclude that by procreating with anthropophagic men and by relinquishing their sons to be raised as cannibals, they at least condoned the eating of human flesh. Furthermore, from Columbus's perspective, having anthropophagic fathers would have only increased the women's reputation as savages.

He described both groups as savage and animalistic, for seasonal mating is only practiced by "lesser" animals, never by humans. Similarly, the inability to recognize and appreciate appropriate foodstuffs was a habit associated with animals. The nontraditional kinship networks and strange same-sex living arrangements would also have seemed quite shocking by genteel European standards. Thus, Columbus's descriptions of these Caribbean Indians reinforced the notion that one savage practice often led to another and that because cannibalism and sex are both embodied acts, they are closely linked.

As European exploration and conquest continued in the Caribbean and tales of these exploits traveled, the connection between accusations of acts of cannibalism and the perception that European sexual norms were being violated became even more explicit. Many secondhand accounts, for example, related that New World cannibals immediately castrated young male captives and took them, along with any female captives, back to their communities. The young castrated men were fattened and kept for food, while the women were used as slaves and breeding stock.[41] The castration of the young men paralleled the sexual abuse of captured women. Reports of the Caribs not eating women but instead keeping them as slaves also became a common feature of many early accounts of European conquest of the Caribbean.[42] Male European writers presented Carib society as the mirror image of what they conceived of as civilization. Using women as slaves to perform physical labor while "wasting" the labor of men by eating them was fundamentally illogical to western Europeans in the late fifteenth and early sixteenth centuries, who always valued men's labor and male bodies more highly than women's. In fact, according to Diego Alvarez Chanca, a crew member on Columbus's second voyage, the Caribs believed that "the flesh of boys and women is not good to eat."[43] Chanca indicated that the Caribs captured women so they could exploit their bodies through labor and sex. According to Chanca, the tribe consumed any children that resulted from these unions.[44] Not only were the Caribs violating European sexual norms by sanctioning extramarital intercourse but the products of these unions were created to increase the community's food supply instead of increasing the population.

Amerigo Vespucci also linked gendered and sexual practices with cannibalism in his writings. He devoted significantly more space to describing the sexual habits of Indians than Columbus and his compatriots did. For example, Vespucci reported that "they have another custom that is appalling and passes belief."

> Their women, being very lustful, make their husbands' members swell to such thickness that they look ugly and misshapen; this they accomplish with a certain device they have and by bites from certain poisonous animals. Because of this, many men lose their members, which rot through neglect, and they are left eunuchs.[45]

While other writers, as we saw earlier, argued that the eunuchs who were present among the Caribs were castrated Arawak captives being prepared for consumption, Vespucci's explanation is strikingly different. In Vespucci's version, the eunuchs were Carib men whose masculinity had been diminished by the women of their own tribe. It is unclear whether Vespucci was indicating that men lost their penises from their own neglect, for example by failing to take care of basic hygiene, or if he was implying that men lost their members from women's extreme sexual habits. The latter seems most likely, as Vespucci appears to be hinting at two seemingly contradictory dangers of women's inordinate lust. First, their out-of-control desires led them to deform their male partners' genitals. And second, for some reason this overwhelming desire also led to misuse and literal emasculation. Thus, in his writings, the Caribs violated many of the most treasured tenets of European civilization.[46] They ate human flesh, the women were sexually aggressive and lewd, and the men were weak and emasculated. In other words, the Caribs' understanding of the functions and purposes of the human body were absolutely at odds with Christian Western European conceptions.

Vespucci's writings demonstrate that he was simultaneously repulsed by and attracted to Indians and their practices. He devoted significant space in his works to the embodied practices of Indigenous Americans, but he consistently deferred to European norms of decorum by not sharing too much (possibly incriminating) detail. For example, he wrote: "They are not very jealous, and are inordinately lustful, the women much more than the men, though decency bids us pass over the wiles they employ to satisfy their inordinate lust."[47] He was less cautious about describing acts of cannibalism, however.

Vespucci described Caribbean Natives as having very different gendered and sexual mores than Western Europeans. Not only were women more sexually aggressive, but they also had significantly more social power, and that power was not derived from purity or domesticity. These contrasting understandings of gender are clearly demonstrated in one of the more famous accounts of cannibalism in Vespucci's writings. The crew spotted a group of Indians on the shore and spent several days trying to entice them out of the woods where they had fled. Eventually, once a number of Native women had gathered on the shore, the crew decided to send a single young man to treat with them.

> He went among the women, and they all began to touch and feel him, wondering at him exceedingly. Things being so, we saw a woman come down from the hill, carrying a great stick in her hand. When she came to where our Christian stood, she raised it, and gave him such a blow that he was felled to the ground. The other women immediately took him by the feet, and dragged him towards the hill. The men rushed down to the beach, and shot at us with their bows and arrows. Our people in great fear, hauled the boats towards the anchors, which were on shore; but, owing to the quantities of arrows that came into the boats, no one thought of taking up their arms. At last four rounds from the bombard were fired at them, and they no sooner heard the report than they all ran away towards hill, where the women were still tearing the Christian to pieces. At a great fire they had made they roasted him before our eyes, showing us many pieces, and then eating them. The men made signs how they had killed the other two Christians and eaten them. What shocked us much was seeing with our eyes the cruelty with which they treated the dead, which was an intolerable insult to all of us.[48]

Vespucci continued, describing the anger and shame he and most of the crew experienced while witnessing this event. The captain of the ship (despite the credit he is often given, Vespucci was not the captain) refused to allow the crew to retaliate and Vespucci felt emasculated by the whole experience.[49] His crew clearly underestimated the Native women and assumed that they were not as threatening as Native men. They also assumed incorrectly that these women would not perceive a single young European man as a threat. The horror Vespucci experienced came not just from witnessing a wanton act of cannibalism but also from the fact that women were the perpetrators.

In the context of the conquest of Mexico, conquistadors also expressed fear of the sexual proclivities of Maya and Aztec men. A common theme in the original and secondhand accounts of the conquest of Mexico is the combining of accusations of cannibalism and taboo sex acts, particularly sodomy.[50] For example, Alonso Zuazo remarked that Indians possessed "the 'trifecta of sin' as the Italians say: they do not believe in god, they are almost all sodomites, [and] they eat human flesh."[51] In his letters to the Crown, Cortés pointed out the supposed ubiquity of cannibalism among the Indians of Mexico: "They are all cannibals, of which I send Your Majesty no evidence because it is so infamous."[52] Francisco López de Gómara indicated that abolishing cannibalism was a primary obligation and a catalyst for Cortés's conquest of Mexico.[53] In addition to eliminating man-eating, Cortés needed to develop allegiances with mainland Indians to achieve his goals. Developing kinship ties through sex, marriage, and procreation was a tried-and-true method of gaining allies.

It is clear in the firsthand accounts that the Spaniards believed that man-eating was widespread in the Americas and that they assumed that cannibalism always existed alongside other "savage" practices. Indians practiced sodomy and human sacrifice, they did not value virginity, and they treated women either too well or too poorly.[54] Observers consistently connected uncivilized habits to cannibalism. For example, the Anonymous Conqueror, who is also referred to as a companion of Cortés, wrote that "all of this province of New Spain and of those other provinces eat human flesh, which they have in greater esteem than any other food, so much so that many times they go to war and place themselves in peril only to kill someone to eat. They are commonly sodomites as I have said and drink without moderation."[55] He made no real distinction between different Indian groups and assumed that they were all cannibals, sodomites, and drunkards.

The Aztecs and Maya were frequently accused of being sodomites, and these practices were particularly troubling to Cortés and his men. The Spaniards drew some distinction between the passive and active participants in male homosexual acts. The penetrated partner was viewed as similar to a woman and thus as something less than a man. This was not the only concern that conquistadors had about Indian homosexual practices, however. If men were having sex with other men, then Indian women must have been failing in their responsibilities: if men did not desire women, then women were failing to be desirable. Spanish writers often argued that if women were afforded what they considered to be too much power in a community, they were automatically less desirable. Sexual relations were almost always understood as acts of dominance and submission. Dominant women would lead to submissive men, and this would possibly drive men into the arms of one another.[56]

One well-known chronicler of the events in Mexico was Bartolomé de las Casas. Unlike many of his contemporaries, Las Casas tended to be more sympathetic to Indian beliefs and practices. He consistently criticized what Spaniards did in their efforts to conquer and forcibly convert Indians. He also refuted many earlier arguments about the supposed barbarity of Native peoples. Las Casas believed that while Indians might be less civilized than Europeans, they were not ignorant or irredeemable.[57] While he also understood that many kinds of sexual immorality went hand in hand with barbarism, he believed that this connection was also evident in European societies.[58] For Las Casas, the presence of sexual immorality was worse than the practices of human sacrifice and cannibalism. Thus, while he recognized that cannibalism and sexual deviance often coincided in what Europeans interpreted as savage societies, he did not see these as equal crimes.[59] Furthermore he hinted at an evolving understanding of the intersections of cannibalism and sexuality by recognizing that even if aberrant behaviors like man-eating or sodomy were often present together in Native societies, they could be disentangled.

## Conclusion

As the Spanish conquest continued and as new imperial powers sought to secure footholds in North America, the connection between sex and cannibalism became somewhat less pronounced. By the seventeenth century, fewer significant descriptions linked cannibalism and sexual availability. French, Spanish, and English accounts did continue to lump cannibalism and sex together under the umbrella of savagery. And although the presence of sexually deviant behavior and man-eating continued to be justifications for the ill treatment of Indians, they were no longer primary catalysts for conquest.

For example, in southern Canada during the spring of 1678, Catherine (or Kateri) Tekakwitha, possibly the most famous Catholic convert in North America, met another Iroquois woman named Marie-Thérèse Tegaiaguenta, who became one of her closest companions. Marie-Thérèse and Catherine were kindred spirits; they were two young Iroquois women who found themselves both incredibly committed to their new faith and torn between the traditions of their people and a desire to devote their lives to the pursuit of spiritual perfection. Together they practiced mutual flagellation and other acts of extreme bodily mortification. But history remembers Catherine, the so-called Mohawk Saint, while Marie-Thérèse is relegated to a footnote.

In his biography of her life, Catherine's confessor, Father Pierre Cholenec, tells a story about Marie-Thérèse's past that hints at why these two women are remembered so differently. Sometime before she came to the mission at Kahnawake but after she converted to Catholicism, Marie-Thérèse went on a hunting expedition with her husband, her nephew, and eight or nine other Iroquois men and women. The party soon found themselves in dire straits; they had run out of food and would soon starve to death. Like so many before them, the hunting party's thoughts turned to the flesh of their fellow travelers. While debating their course of action, one member of the party asked Marie-Thérèse about the Catholic perspective on starvation cannibalism. Cholenec reports that "she did not dare reply as she did not know enough about this important question and she was afraid of contributing to a homicide."

> More to the point, she quite naturally felt that her own life depended on the answer, for she believed that, after they had eaten the woman and her children [the widow of a Seneca man who had already died], as they did in fact do, she herself would then be killed. As her eyes opened to the danger to her body, [Marie-Thérèse] also began to realize that the deplorable state of

> her soul was infinitely more pitiable than that of her body. She felt great horror for the disorder of her past life and the fault she had committed in going on the hunting trip without first going to confession. Asking God's pardon with all her heart, she promised that if He delivered her from this danger and returned her safety to the village, she would not only confess immediately, but reform her life and do penance. God wished to use this woman to make Catherine known, and so he answered her prayer and after incredible pains and exertions, five [of them] returned to [the settlement] toward the middle of winter. Among them were this woman and her little nephew.[60]

Interestingly, in this account, Cholenec hints that Marie-Thérèse did not actually consume human flesh, but since she survived the ordeal, it would be fairly surprising if she did not. Her version of events, as filtered through a Jesuit pen, seems quite similar to tales of English captives among Iroquoian and Algonquian peoples. Many of these captivity narratives tell of men and women who are reduced to the contemplation of cannibalism but are redeemed from having to commit such a terrible act through the providence of the almighty.[61]

Despite her fervent commitment to God, Marie-Thérèse Tegaiaguenta never achieved the notoriety of Catherine, who was officially canonized in 1980. Unlike Catherine, Marie-Thérèse was not a perpetual virgin; she was a widow. Catherine's most recent biographer, historian Alan Greer, argues that in the hagiographical literature the story of Marie-Thérèse and her sinful past are used as a contrast to Catherine's most saintly virtues.[62] Thus, no matter how good a Catholic woman Marie-Thérèse might have been, her sexual and anthropophagic past keep her from moving from simply pious to saintly. Indeed, it can be argued that more than any of the reported miracles that she performed or were performed in her name, the thing that made Catherine Tekakwitha so widely revered is that her French Jesuit supporters believed that she had somehow risen above the savagery they thought was an inherent characteristic of all Indians. Her most famous supporter, Cholenec, entitled his hagiography the *Life of Catherine Tegakowita: The First Iroquois Virgin*.[63] Obviously Catherine was not the first Iroquois virgin, but Cholenec and others argued that she was the first Iroquois to dedicate her purity and chastity to God and to fully shed her "savage, cannibalistic" ways. In other words, Marie-Thérèse forever bears the taint of European views about sex, cannibalism, and savagery among Native Americans while Catherine Tekakwitha rose above her "nature" and became a saint.

Viewed alongside the earlier examples from the Caribbean and Mexico, the story of Marie-Thérèse helps us see how a connection between sex and cannibalism persisted into the last quarter of the seventeenth century in New France, albeit in a substantially different form. While early European visitors to the Caribbean struggled to make sense of their desire for sex with Native women and their disgust at their cultural practices, they were able to figure out ways to justify sexual intercourse. Michele da Cuneo forced sex upon an unwilling woman after suspecting that she was a member of the cannibalistic Carib tribe. The vast gulf that existed between Cuneo's understanding of civilization and the practices of the Caribs allowed him to see her as something less than himself: a being from whom consent was neither necessary nor possible. Cortés, in contrast, had conflicted feelings about the gifts of Native women he received. While he wanted to cement his bond with the Yucatecan Maya through sexual diplomacy, such bonds could not easily be formed through sexual relations that occurred outside the realm of accepted Spanish sexual standards. Thus, the women he received were simultaneously objects of desire, tools of conquest, and the recipients of Cortés's cultural imperialist agenda. They had to first become Christians before they could be made into useful cultural ambassadors and progenitors of the next generation of conquistadors.

The discourse of cannibalism in early North America also reveals that the supposed savagery and barbarism of Native peoples was multifaceted. In other words, to be savage meant that a group demonstrated an array of what Europeans saw as uncivilized behaviors that included nakedness, heathenism, promiscuity, a lack of centralized government, intense jealousy or avarice, rampant thievery, and cannibalism. In the earliest accounts of European men in the Americas, we can clearly see that inappropriate sexual behaviors and anthropophagy were two "savage" characteristics that often overlapped. Native peoples who were accused of one of these violations of the norms of European civilization were quite often accused of the other.

Because both deviant sex and the consumption of human flesh were practices that Europeans believed demonstrated a lack of proper respect for the human body, accusations of sexual deviance and cannibalism alongside one another served to reinforce Western European, particularly Catholic, perspectives that bodies were dangerous sites. Too much emphasis on the body led to dangers for the soul. Thus, eliminating the practices of cannibalism and inappropriate sexual acts among the Indigenous peoples of the Americas was central to the agenda of European imperialism.

CHAPTER 4

# Spaniards, Cannibals, and the Eucharist in the New World

REBECCA EARLE

> *What temperance or docility can you expect from men who devote themselves to every sort of excess and shameful weakness, and who eat human flesh?*[1]

A recurrent feature of Spanish colonial discourse in the early modern era is the lament that Amerindians from Florida to Patagonia suffered from two grave defects: they were hopeless drunks and they were prone to cannibalism. Examples of such allegations are legion. Drunkenness, insisted one seventeenth-century writer, "is such a common vice among Indians, that you scarcely find a single one who having some wine or *chicha* [maize beer], which is what they usually drink, does not get drunk."[2] "Wine," wrote the sixteenth-century chronicler Gonzalo Fernández de Oviedo, is "the thing they esteem most."[3] The Spanish Council of the Indies summed the situation up at the end of the sixteenth century: "All Indians are inclined to vice and drunkenness and to being idle, never applying themselves voluntarily to any sort of work whatsoever."[4] Colonial complaints about drunkenness were unrelenting throughout the colonial era and they also came to form a standard element of postcolonial creole discourse.[5] Such comments make clear that settlers considered drunkenness to be a characteristic indigenous vice.

In addition, from Columbus's arrival in the Caribbean in 1492, European colonists and explorers consistently associated cannibalism with the New World. As scholars have shown, Columbus at first could not decide whether the peoples he encountered in the West Indies were civilized subjects of the Great Khan or were instead man-eating cynocephali, but a consensus quickly formed that the newly discovered lands were a zone of anthropophagi. The association between cannibalism and the Caribbean was particularly strong; Amerigo Vespucci reported matter-of-factly in 1503 that the island peoples of the Caribbean "slaughter those who are captured, and the victors eat the vanquished; for human flesh is an ordinary article of food among them" and for centuries "Carib" was practically synonymous with the word "cannibal."[6] Nonetheless Europeans believed that cannibalism extended across the hemisphere. Chroniclers of all regions reported carefully on whether particular groups did or did not eat human flesh and the fear of being eaten permeates many conquest narratives. The expectation of meeting cannibals was such that when their captors prodded a party of Spaniards who had been captured in Patagonia, the Spaniards immediately assumed "that they wanted to eat them, and wished to inform themselves about the taste of their flesh and what they were like inside."[7] The association between the Indies and cannibalism was immortalized in popular prints, in theatrical works such as *The Tempest,* and in the very word "cannibal."[8] (See Image 1.) "From the discovery," writes Carlos Jáuregui in his authoritative cultural history of the New World cannibal, "Europeans found anthropophagites everywhere, creating a sort of semantic affinity between cannibalism and America."[9] It is clear that for many colonists and colonial writers, drunkenness and cannibalism, like sodomy, stupidity, and general incivility, were part of a spectrum of distinctive behaviors associated with Amerindians that showed them to be quite different from and almost certainly inferior to their colonizers.

Many of the interpretative routes we can follow to explain this web of associations are by now clearly marked. It is evident, to begin with, that the claim that Indians were cannibals formed part of a larger European dismissal of Amerindians as unfit for self-government, a view that drew upon long-standing European traditions of locating aberrant behavior in distant or mythical locations. The pioneering research of scholars such as William Arens and Peter Hulme has shown that the discovery of cannibals in the New World cannot be separated from the process of colonization that brought Europeans

*Image 1.* "Early German Woodcut of a New World Scene," 1505. Spencer Collection, The New York Public Library. *Courtesy of the New York Public Library.*

to the Indies in the first place.[10] Cannibals, in a sense, were a necessary part of colonial space. As Gareth Griffiths put it, "For whites engaged in the activity of 'conquest' the dominant sign of the Indian is that of the cannibal."[11] Many other scholars have linked charges of both cannibalism and drunkenness to wider dismissals of indigenous society and to justifications of colonial violence.[12] Such research also informs a related body of scholarship that considers whether European colonial discourse, whatever its motivation, accurately captured any aspect of indigenous culture. Perhaps, as some scholars suggest, Spanish sightings of cannibals or drunks are no different from Columbus's implausible claims that he engaged in meaningful communication with the "Indians" he encountered, which have been so effectively dissected by Stephen Greenblatt. New World cannibalism was from this perspective a colonial mirage, not a meaningful indigenous practice.[13] Other scholars maintain that we can glimpse aspects of the indigenous experience through the colonial wrappings. Neil Whitehead, for example, used the German sailor Hans Staden's 1557 account of his captivity among the Tupinamba to illuminate the meaning of Tupinamba cannibalism.[14] Likewise, scholars for decades have examined the repeated Spanish claim that Amerindians were unable to resist the lure of alcohol and have debated whether this reflects a European failure to understand the very different Amerindian ideas of moderation and the purpose of alcohol or whether it instead reveals the reality of a demoralized indigenous society rent asunder by colonialism.[15] A rich scholarship, in short, situates accusations of drunkenness and cannibalism within a broader analysis of Spanish justifications for colonization and highlights the dilemmas scholars must confront as they try to disentangle Spanish rhetoric from indigenous experience.

There is, however, another context into which we can place early modern discussions of drunkenness and cannibalism: the Christian sacrament of communion. Communion, after all, entailed the (mediated) consumption of wine and the (mystical) ingestion of divine flesh made human. The centrality of the Eucharist to Reformation debates about Christian doctrine is reflected in the colonial Church's sustained focus on this sacrament. It is clear that the Mass was not just one of many Iberian practices that colonial actors aimed to transfer to Spain's new possessions; it was a fundamental element of early modern Catholic identity and belief. Many scholars have explored the varied efforts missionaries made to translate this sacrament to the Indies. These efforts were never separate from the hierarchies that structured life in the colonial world. Discussion of whether indigenous people could comprehend the mysteries of transubstantiation informed (and was informed by) Amerindians' alleged irrationality and inability to govern themselves. Celebrations of Corpus Christi, the festival honoring the Mass, marked out Amerindians as incomplete converts even as they provided spaces for indigenous participants to insist on their status as members of the communion of saints. This research has also stressed the intrinsic connections between the Eucharist and other forms of literal or metaphorical consumption, including cannibalism. Corpus Christi, notes Carolyn Dean, was "*semiophagous*: it was a feast that dined on signs of difference, gaining sustenance for its triumph from the Andean subaltern. From the moment of its instigation the ravenous festival fed on the colonized."[16] To understand the meaning of indigenous drunkenness and cannibalism within Spanish colonial discourse we therefore need to consider their relation not only to broad rhetorics of colonial power but also to the very specific early modern debates about this most sacred of Catholic sacraments. By charting the shifting relationship between bread and wine and flesh and blood we gain a richer understanding of the Spanish colonial imagination and what it meant when settlers accused Amerindians of being drunkards or cannibals. Building on a rich and imaginative body of work, this chapter argues that cannibalism highlights a central feature of all colonial regimes—what Kate Teltscher has described as "a fundamental sense of insecurity which can rarely be allowed direct expression, but which keeps surfacing to be repeatedly allayed."[17]

The chapter first explains the central role that wheat bread and wine occupied within Spanish religious and dietary regimes and how these substances marked out the distance that separated Spaniards from Amerindians. For Spanish Catholics, bread and wine represented both the essence of their Catholic identity and the sine qua non of bodily health. The consumption of earthly bread and wine ensured corporeal health, while the heavenly bread and wine of the Mass ensured that of the soul. Amerindians were supposedly incapable of consuming these healthy, necessary substances in an appropriate fashion. Indeed, many priests refused to administer communion to Amerindians on the ground that their continual drunkenness rendered them ineligible. Far from providing spiritual succor, in the hands of Amerindians, alcohol brought about their exclusion from the Catholic polity. Beyond this, many writers alleged that the terrible mortality that decimated indigenous communities across the hemisphere after the advent of colonialism was due in part to the failure of Amerindians to drink in moderation. Europeans believed that the same wine that ensured health in the Spanish body was lethal to the indigenous body. Worse, while Catholics worshipfully received the body of Jesus Christ made flesh in a communion wafer, Amerindians indulged in the terrible sin of earthly cannibalism. The distance that separated Amerindians from Spaniards could thus be measured in the difference between a drunken cannibal and a sober Catholic. These differences, however, were fragile, and the distance was perhaps not as great as colonists might have desired. The chapter's concluding section considers the colonial anxieties that dogged such attempts at differentiation.

## Sober Catholics and Drunken Idolaters

*Wherever this wine is made there is hidden idolatry.*[18]

We need to begin with the Spanish diet, for food, just as much as religion, lies at the heart of early modern discussions of drunkenness and cannibalism. Even though a variety of foods were consumed in early modern Iberia, there was consensus on the preferred diet. A perfect meal would contain wheat bread and red wine, some fresh lamb or other familiar meat seasoned with olive oil and vinegar, and perhaps a bit of salad, some olives, or a fig.[19] These were the things that settlers missed in the New World; all the pineapples and chocolate in the world could never compensate for their absence. Colonists across the Indies waxed lyrical on the foodstuffs that made up the ideal Iberian meal. From Mexico, the Spanish doctor Francisco Hernández wrote that wheat was a "gift from Mother Nature as precious as health itself."[20] The grapevine was the "most beneficial and necessary plant that the Spanish brought and planted in this New World," wrote Jesuit Bernabé Cobo.[21] Meat was absolutely vital. "Spanish people . . . cannot survive without the sustenance of meat," insisted one viceroy.[22] These foods were redolent of health, of civilization, and of Christianity.

That they were healthy was beyond doubt. Wheat bread and grape wine, in particular, were regarded as exceptionally nourishing and digestible.[23] Early modern Spanish texts are full of encomia to wine, which was praised for its healthful, medicinal effects, provided it was drunk in moderation. Immoderate consumption came in for universal criticism—the examples of Noah and Lot were frequently cited—but most writers agreed that Spaniards were less prone to the vice of drunkenness than other Europeans, and even those who were most outspoken in their condemnation of drunkenness generally refrained from recommending total abstinence.[24] Spaniards boasted of their moderation, which they regarded as proverbial.[25] Far from being a menace to health, wine was practically a medical necessity. "To deprive an old man or a youth of a little wine," observed one colonial writer, "is to send him straight to the grave."[26]

More importantly, wheat flour, like grape wine, was a symbol of Christianity itself. These were the substances that through the mystery of the Mass were transformed into the very body and blood of Jesus Christ. Indeed, they were the only substances capable of undergoing this transformation. From the Middle Ages, Church doctrine required that communion be celebrated using only wheat bread and grape wine.[27] These substances were essential to the execution of the most important of Catholic mysteries. Indeed, they were in some ways fungible, since, as the Council of Trent determined, Christ was fully present in both components of the Mass.[28] Bread and wine represented for Spaniards both the idealized, healthful diet, and the essence of Christianity in their potential to become the very body and blood of Christ.

Amerindians, in contrast, appeared to Spaniards to possess an entirely dysfunctional relationship to these basic foods. Everything was the reverse of what it should be. "Everyone in this province of New Spain, and even in the neighboring provinces, eats human flesh and esteems it above all other foods," complained one sixteenth-century writer, adding that "they are commonly sodomites, as I have said, and drink excessively."[29] Spaniards argued that wine was positively lethal for Amerindians. Many writers argued that even a small amount was dangerous to the indigenous body. Giving alcohol to Indians "has the effect of killing them off," insisted a Mexican viceroy.[30] Everyone knows that "this drink destroys their health and kills them," observed another.[31] In the view of many writers, overconsumption of alcohol was behind the terrible mortality that afflicted the indigenous population from the advent of colonialism.[32] Alcohol was medicinal for Spaniards; it was a poison for Indians. This conviction undermined the widely expressed hope that Amerindians would adopt a European diet in ways that point to the fundamental insecurities that shaped early modern colonialisms, a subject to which I will return.[33]

Moreover, while the Christian Mass involved sober and moderate consumption of wine, colonialists condemned indigenous religious festivals as little more than drunken orgies. The sixteenth-century chronicler Juan Rodríguez Freyle, for instance, alleged that such events were nothing more than "great drinking sprees."[34] In the view of the Jesuit priest José de Acosta, getting drunk was "their principal cult and religion."[35] For Europeans, Amerindian drinking led inevitably to drunkenness and idolatry, practices that Europeans believed indigenous people were prone to in the first place. Colonial prohibitions on the sale of alcohol to Amerindians often stipulated that not only was alcohol dangerous to indigenous health, but it also opened the door to idolatry. In the words of another Jesuit, drunkenness was "the ancient root of idolatry."[36] For these reasons settlers should under no circumstances sell wine (let alone spirits) to Indians "because of the serious harm that ensues to both their bodies and souls."[37] For Amerindians, drinking was fundamentally incompatible with Christianity and corporeal well-being, while for Spaniards it was a source of spiritual and physical health.

This unhealthy relationship to alcohol led a number of colonial writers to conclude that Amerindians should be excluded from taking communion altogether. Catholic doctrine prohibited administering the sacrament to individuals who attempted to receive communion while drunk, and it seems that many priests believed that Amerindians were so often drunk that they should be excluded as a matter of course.[38] Instead of treating the sacrament with respect, Indians just used it as an occasion to get drunk. "Often on the very day that you take communion you get drunk just as you used to do before you became Christians," one confessional manual complained.[39] Those who opposed this exclusionary practice insisted that as communion was necessary for salvation, denying it to Amerindians was tantamount to denying them salvation. In this view, the Amerindians' inability to consume alcohol appropriately resulted in their exclusion from the Christian community.[40] For instance, the Council of Lima, which met in the mid-sixteenth century to implement the resolutions of the Council of Trent, found it difficult to reach a decision about the capacity of indigenous people to engage in this most sacred ritual. The First Council of Lima, which met from 1552, restricted participation in communion to those indigenous people (and a few others) the bishops had approved. The Second Council of Lima determined that Amerindians should not receive the sacrament until they had a firmer grasp of the faith and had abandoned their bad habits, which included drunkenness. Communion was a "delicacy" not suited to them, in the view of the Council.[41] In the 1580s, the Third Council of Lima reversed this position and urged priests to encourage Amerindians to take communion. Overall, the colonial Church was uncertain about whether Amerindians should be permitted to take communion, frequently citing drunkenness as an obstacle to their participation.

The problematic relationship between Amerindians and the Eucharist extended beyond concerns about drunkenness. Many colonial writers were horrified to perceive parallels between indigenous cannibalism and the sacrament of communion. As Carlos Jáuregui and Jorge Cañizares-Esguerra have shown, the fact that a number of indigenous groups engaged in ritual cannibalism before Europeans arrived was seen as demonically inspired imitation of the Eucharist.[42] In discussing Mexica sacrifice and the cannibalism associated with it, the Dominican priest Diego Durán, for instance, drew attention to "how well this devilish ceremony counterfeits that of our holy church that commands us to receive the true body and blood of our lord Jesus Christ."[43] Colonial writers disagreed about the precise origin of this horrifying similarity, which they observed not only in Mexica ritual but across the Americas. Like drunkenness, cannibalism was thus tightly linked to idolatry in colonial rhetoric. It was, as Cañizares-Esguerra has observed, a key signifier of demonic activity.[44]

The appropriate consumption of alcohol (in the form of grape wine) and flesh (in the form of transubstantiated wheat bread) was at the center of the Catholic orthodoxy and sensible self-management that Spanish settlers in the New World aspired to represent. In contrast, in the view of Spaniards, Amerindians were characterized by their inability to engage appropriately with this solemn activity and these healthful foods. Their defining vices differentiated them from their Catholic colonizers. Colonial writers stressed that the coming of colonialism simultaneously brought an end to both idolatry and cannibalism because the two were viewed as practically synonymous. And after all, as the learned jurist Juan de Solórzano y Pereira noted in a lengthy tome on colonial legislation, it was perfectly justified to conquer people who ate human flesh, were drunkards, and engaged in sodomy.[45]

## A Community of Cannibals

> *Do you eat the flesh of the Son and drink the blood of the Son of man?*[46]

And yet the boundaries colonialism created are never so stable as to allow sharp demarcation between colonizers and colonized or between the faithful and those beyond redemption.[47] As Marcy Norton has observed, settlers in the Indies were never certain that they could "maintain a Christian and European identity in the colonial milieu."[48] Nor was there consensus that Amerindians were incommensurably and irredeemably distinct from Europeans. After all, bringing Christianity to the Indies was the central justification for Spain's colonial endeavor and the idea that Amerindians were "incompetent" Christians was troubling both doctrinally and morally.[49] Colonial rhetoric reflected such anxieties. Spaniards debated the aptitude of indigenous people for Christianity. Many argued that Amerindians had precisely the same capacity for faith as Europeans did. The discourse of cannibalism that seemed to mark so clearly the differences between Spaniards and Indians in fact demonstrated the diaphanous nature of all such divisions, for it was never quite as evident as Spanish settlers might have desired that they were really all that different from cannibals.

Despite the rhetorical efforts to situate cannibalism solely in the Indies, settlers were uncomfortably aware that Europe too had its cannibals. Although an older scholarship once claimed that cannibalism did not occur "in any culturally significant way" in Europe, in fact cannibalism was present in many different cultural arenas, in literature, in folklore, and, of course, in the Mass, where "it was constantly discussed and represented."[50] Nor was its presence solely symbolic. There is ample evidence that Europeans engaged in cannibalism in a variety of contexts. Spanish texts explicitly discussed the circumstances under which it was acceptable for Christians to eat human flesh, which included cases of extreme hunger and medical need. Stories of cannibalism during sieges and famines were told across Europe.[51] The consumption of human body parts was moreover an established tool within academic and folk medicine. As the Spanish doctor Francisco Nuñez de Oria noted, Europeans consumed "mummia, which is the flesh of dead people," and, even worse, in his opinion, drank fresh human blood as cures for certain ailments.[52] The ongoing wars of religion, in addition, provided contemporaries with ample evidence of cannibalism's currency as a technique of revenge and terror.[53] The uncomfortable existence of cannibalism in Europe, more specifically in Spain, has led scholars to argue that early modern Spaniards focused on New World cannibalism "rather than confronting head on the unthought known" of cannibalism within their own society.[54] Attributing cannibalism solely to Amerindians served as "fictional sublimation" of a historical record that resisted complete erasure.[55] "In reality," notes Tom Cummins, "eating a human body was a practice shared by Spaniards and Indians."[56]

This common history is apparent at many levels within the colonial archive. Its presence far exceeds Bartolomé de las Casas's rhetorical comparisons of Spaniards to wild animals, feasting on the flesh of the innocent Amerindians, similar accounts that Spain's European competitors penned, or even the vivid engravings by Theodore de Bry of conquistadors retailing human flesh.[57] (See Image 2.) Much more concretely, colonial sources admitted that Spanish settlers ate both Amerindians and each other.

A few examples suffice: the Franciscan friar Pedro Simón described in his early seventeenth-century chronicle how Spaniards following the conquistador Ambrosio Alfinger killed and ate their indigenous porters in Venezuela. One man even ate a penis, which Simón condemned as "disgusting and obscene." He however noted that if one was suffering from great hunger, it was acceptable to eat those who were already dead.[58] The German soldier Felipe von Hutten recounted that "contrary to nature," another "Christian" in Venezuela had "cooked part of a boy together with some vegetables."[59] The humanist Peter Martyr D'Anghiera's secondhand account of the early exploration and conquest of the Americas likewise reported a number of incidents of Europeans eating Amerindians.[60] Francisco López de Gómara's history of the conquest recorded both the names of Spaniards who had killed and eaten Amerindians ("Diego Gomez and Juan de Ampudia, from Ajofrín") and the names of Spaniards killed and eaten by their compatriots ("Hernán Darias, from Seville," "Hernando de Esquivel, from Badajoz").[61]

*Image 2*. Spaniards sell human flesh from a market stall. Theodore de Bry, illustration in Bartolomé de las Casas, *Narratio regionum Indicarum per Hispanos quosdam deuastatarum verissima* (Francofurti: Sumptibus Theodori de Bry, & Ioannis Saurii typis, 1598). *Courtesy of the Library of Congress.*

This shared history of cannibalism, which undermined the rigorous distinctions between pious Catholics and idolatrous cannibals, intruded into the sphere in which this distinction appeared to manifest itself most strongly: the Catholic Mass. The very rite that Spanish settlers viewed as the antithesis of cannibalism proved immensely problematic for colonial writers bent on differentiating Spaniards from Indians. European theological and devotional writings offered little help in distinguishing between Christian ritual and indigenous atrocity. As Merrall Llewelyn Price observes, "Anxieties about cannibalism can never be completely absent in the symbolic and literal act of eating the body and drinking the blood of a sacrificial victim."[62]

The materiality of the Eucharistic miracle has for centuries been a central element of theological discourse. Many medieval accounts described communion wafers that became a small child or a hunk of raw flesh or that bled.[63] Images of Christ as a mystical mill or winepress, turning his own body into the flour and wine of the Mass, were popular in both Europe and the Americas.[64] (See Image 3.) The Reformation prompted a proliferation of questions about the mechanics of transubstantiation. Christians wanted to know how Christ's body could be present in all hosts everywhere and whether taking communion caused Christ pain.[65] In the face of Protestant doubt and in some cases pointed accusations of cannibalism, the Council of Trent devoted considerable energy to explicating the implications of this transformation. It stressed, for example, that all

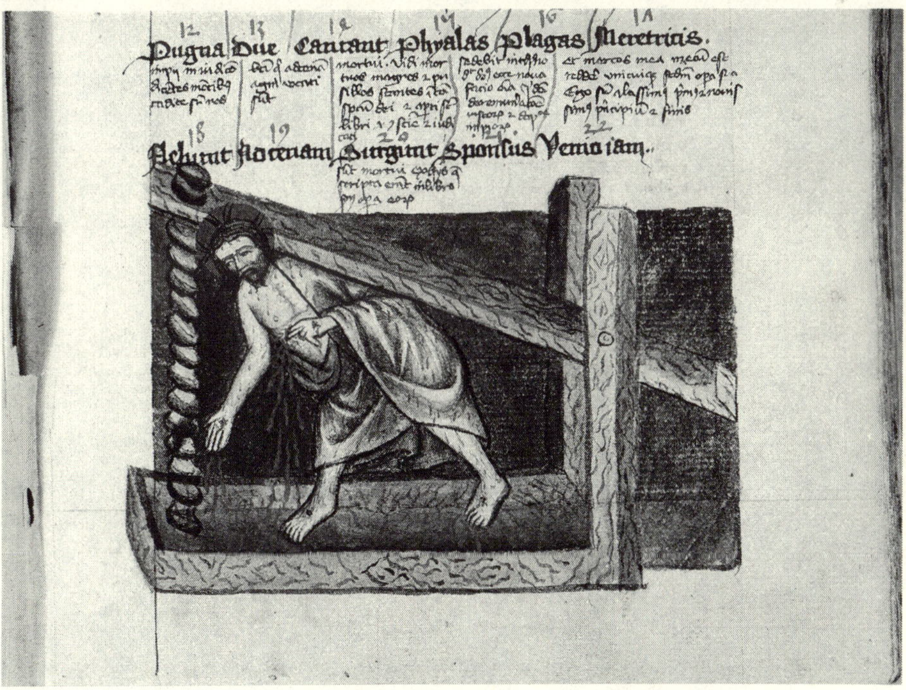

*Image* 3. Christ in the winepress, ca. 1400–1410. Österreichische Nationalbibliothek, Cod. 3676, fol. 14r. *Courtesy of the Österreichische Nationalbibliothek/Wien.*

the pieces of consecrated host left over after the completion of communion contained the body of Jesus, in contrast to Martin Luther, who insisted that only those that communicants ate underwent this mystical change. Tridentine texts were also explicit about the physical nature of the communion experience. "Let your body, Lord, which I have eaten, and your blood, which I have drunk, adhere to my viscera," reads one missal from 1570.[66]

New World texts were no less explicit. The faithful were reminded that Jesus had instructed them to eat "his holy flesh" and drink "his most precious blood." Priests praised the "great delicacy that is the body of Christ."[67] Such ideas were carefully rendered into indigenous languages to enable Amerindians to appreciate them fully. Bilingual *doctrinas,* or primers in Christian teaching, scrupulously translated the central features of Catholic belief, including transubstantiation, into Zapotec, Náhuatl, and a host of other tongues. Clerics did not hesitate to employ direct comparisons between unholy cannibal Indians and saintly Christians. "If those barbarians with human flesh in their mouths put their enemies to flight, what cannot a devout Christian achieve, a son of the church, a soldier in the army of Christ our Lord, carrying in his mouth the flesh of God?" asked the Jesuit Alonso de Sandoval in an evangelical treatise.[68] Spaniard and cannibal, "usually antithetical and supposedly inviolable categories," in fact approached each other in the very ritual that supposedly distinguished most clearly between them.[69]

## Conclusions

*Amerindians "hunger avidly for the body of Christ."*[70]

Was eating human flesh something that set Amerindians apart from Catholics or was it something that united them? The unstable frontiers between colonizers and colonized are revealed with striking clarity in the inability of colonial discourse to maintain a sharp distinction in this apparently most emblematic of arenas. There are many reasons why cannibalism served not only to separate but also to unite Spaniards with the indigenous population. The inherently exploitative nature of all colonial relationships has made cannibalism a potent metaphor in many different colonial contexts. The colonized regularly suspected that those wielding power were cannibals. In seventeenth-century Paraguay, Guarani Indians suspected that the "ordinary food" of the Jesuits who corralled them into missions was human flesh.[71] Andean peoples in the eighteenth century viewed Spaniards as *pishtacos,* fearful beings who sucked the fat out of indigenous bodies. Today, Peruvian highlanders harbor similar suspicions about both foreigners and representatives of the state.[72] Villagers in rural Guatemala insisted that a 1950s Rockefeller Foundation public health program was smuggling children to the United States so they could be eaten.[73] The vampiric colonist has proved an apt symbol of the (neo)colonial relationship. Such stories, writes Luise White, are ways of talking about colonial power.[74]

As White has noted, the nuance and specificity of these stories reflect the historical specificity of different colonial situations. In the case of early modern Spanish America, the Reformation, with its explicit questioning of the very essence of the Eucharist, endowed this vivid metaphor with particular relevance. Spanish colonization occurred at a moment when the unity of Christendom was being reconceptualized in fundamental ways. Christian doctrine seemed no more capable of uniting colonizers and colonized into a single category than it was of bringing harmony to the contending factions in Europe. Or perhaps what united Spaniards and Amerindians was a repellent category mistake whereby, as Protestants charged, Catholics were themselves mere cannibals, no different from the native peoples they sought with such violence to subjugate. Neither option appeared reassuring to colonial actors.

In a treatise on evangelizing Amerindians, the Jesuit José de Acosta defended their capacity to receive the Christian doctrine by insisting that they "hunger avidly for the body of Christ."[75] In the same years, priests were told to quiz indigenous parishioners about whether "you ever eat human flesh cooked with maize, as this is a great and shocking sin."[76] Officials elsewhere instructed a local landowner that her indigenous workforce should be reminded not to eat human flesh. "Tell them," she was advised, "that they must not eat human flesh because the Christians who do this suffer great torments."[77] Colonialism aimed to ensure that Amerindians hungered for the flesh of Christ but not for any other flesh. And what of the Christians who themselves ate human flesh from time to time, as the instruction cited above conceded? They had best keep quiet about it. A sixteenth-century guide for missionaries warned that if any priest found himself compelled to eat human flesh while evangelizing among Amerindians, "upon returning to the company of the faithful he should say nothing, since it could happen that the Christians would expel him from their community, as I understand has sometimes happened here."[78] On such fragile bulwarks did colonial settlers rely in their attempts to differentiate themselves from those they governed.

CHAPTER 5

# "And Greedily Deuoured Them"

## The Cannibalism Discourse and the Creation of a British Atlantic World, 1536–1612

JESSICA S. HOWER

At the start of 1536, London was pulsating with activity: the court of Henry VIII (r. 1509–1547) was teeming with new servants and favorites and Parliament was busily churning out one transformative piece of legislation after another. In January, the death of Henry's first queen, Katherine of Aragon, seemed to momentarily free England from the threat of imminent war with the Catholic powers of Europe that had haunted the kingdom ever since the break with Rome.[1] In early February, chief minister Thomas Cromwell took aim at the "abomination of religious persons throughout this realm" through the Protestant-leaning Ten Articles, the dissolution of the lesser monasteries, and "an Acte extynguysshing the auctoryte of the Busshop of Rome."[2] Near the center of much of it was Anne Boleyn, Henry's evangelically inclined, polarizing second wife and a major part of his dispute with the papacy. Anne had enjoyed a meteoric rise to prominence, and with the death of her predecessor and her latest pregnancy, she seemed poised to exert even more influence. Also part of this changing world of late 1535 and early 1536 was Londoner Richard Hore, "a man of goodly stature and of great courage, and giuen to the studie of Cosmographie."[3] Like Anne, he enjoyed royal patronage, "assisted by the kings fauour and good countenance," as well as by "gentlemen of the Innes of court, and of the Chancerie, and diuers others of good worship, desirous to see the strange things of the world," to undertake "a voyage of discouerie vpon the Northwest parts of America."[4]

The very same courtly atmosphere that empowered Queen Anne and pushed the English Reformation forward facilitated Hore's travel. His was one of the first British Atlantic ventures of the century and, more significantly, the first of consequence since Parliament's 1533 declaration in the preamble to the Act in Restraint of Appeals to Rome that "this Realme of Englond is an Impire, and so hath ben accepted in the worlde, governed by oon Supreme heede and King having the Dignitie and Roiall Estate of the Imperiall Crowne."[5] The voyage lived up to its weighty moment, one in which royal personnel and faction, cultural and intellectual currents, spiritual and ecclesiastical tumult, and theories of sovereignty and supremacy had produced a landmark assertion of empire and, under its auspices, a new church and state at home and a new adventure abroad. Both Anne's much-studied queenship and Hore's overlooked crossing came out of a now explicitly imperial Tudor world, as Parliament's pronouncement harbored implications and applications throughout the Atlantic world. Probing both their fates proves revealing.

Setting out in late April 1536 after taking communion (one of only three sacraments the Ten Articles upheld) with two ships and over 100 men, Hore sailed some two months before nearing Cape Breton, then disembarked on the "Island of Penguin," a place that was exciting both for its nourishing animals and for its name, which sounded enough like Welsh to convince eager Britons of Tudor primacy over at least part of the New World.[6] From there, Hore proceeded to "Newfoundland," traversing the region John Cabot had claimed for Henry VIII's father, Henry VII (r. 1485–1509) in the 1490s. At last Hore spotted "the natural people of the countrey, that they had so long and so much desired to see."[7] But the auspicious start soon turned sour: some of the voyagers promptly "manned out a shipboat to meet them and to take them," but "the Sauages fledde and escaped," leaving Hore's men to rummage through their leftovers. However, before long, "lying there[,] they grew into great want of victuals."[8] Meanwhile, at home, Anne had miscarried, butted heads with Cromwell over foreign policy and monastic assets, and run afoul of Henry and others at court.[9] Two mid-1530s Henrician stars were falling, following very different but nearly concurrent downward paths on opposite sides of the Atlantic.

In Newfoundland, the travelers were starving. In the account of the voyage printed by Elizabethan polymath Richard Hakluyt in 1598–1600, a list of progressively unsavory foodstuffs followed—a "hunger topos" akin to those in early writings about Jamestown in the next century.[10] One of Hore's company evidently resorted to the only meat he could find: while "his mate" bent over to pick a root from the ground, "the fellowe" killed him, "cutting out pieces of his bodie . . . broyled the same on the coles and greedily deuoured them."[11] When another man stumbled upon the scene, the man-eater confessed: "If thou wouldest needes know, the broyled meate that I had was a piece of such a mans buttock."[12] Captain Hore censured the culprit, invoking both scripture and his temporal power to declare it better to perish in body than be condemned forever to the "vnquenchable fire of hell." Though Hore begged God to mercifully relieve their miserable state, the famine persisted.[13] With no other recourse, the voyagers agreed to cast lots to select a victim to eat.[14] As the sailors risked degenerating into the very "Sauages" that they had hoped to find—those "other," barbaric inferiors in the New World—spring had been no kinder to Anne Boleyn. Found guilty of adultery, incest, and high treason, she was executed at Tower Green on the morning of May 19, 1536.[15] Though modern historians have hotly debated the causes for Anne's death, the results are obvious: they ultimately cleared the way for the king's third marriage (to Jane Seymour) and the birth of his long-sought male heir (the future Edward VI), the temporary removal of Anne's daughter (the future Elizabeth I) from the line of succession, further reform of the Church of England, and two serious rebellions against the changes in church and state (the Pilgrimage of Grace in England and Kildare's rebellion in Ireland).[16] Overseas, Hore had better luck: the very night of the cannibal lottery, a well-furnished French ship appeared and, as Hakluyt wrote, "such was the policie of the English, that they became masters of the same, and . . . set sayle to come into England."[17] When the robbed Frenchmen sought redress several months later, Henry took pity on his subjects and "of his owne purse made full and royall recompence vnto the French."[18]

1536 was a watershed year in a watershed decade that has been much studied for its domestic drama. Yet the story was no less sensational or significant overseas. Anne's queenship began to collapse at breakneck speed around the time Hore departed from England; Anne's decapitated body lay newly buried as the crew apparently resorted to cannibalism; and Henry's imperial authority, sovereign in church and state and stretching over a territorially expansive realm that included the British Isles and beyond, reached unprecedented heights as the adventurers limped home.[19] These parallel Atlantic stories were intimately linked by the shared contemporary geography that gave rise to them. In 1536, Henry VIII felt secure enough, powerful enough, and rich enough to indulge his deep-seated desire for empire, a desire that had largely lay fallow since his invasion of France in the 1510s.[20] This shift in circumstance explains his bold support for Richard Hore, his willingness to marry and then dispose of Anne Boleyn, and the means by which he accomplished those ends. Moreover, the significance of these events was not lost on contemporaries. As Anne's death influenced subsequent domestic developments, Hore's adventure, particularly his experience with cannibalism, encouraged further trial and error in the imperial sphere and further engagement with anthropophagy.[21] Taken together, these concurrent, intertwined episodes uncover an early British Atlantic world that has largely been unstudied.

■ ■ ■

The study of cannibalism challenges major conceits in Atlantic history and disrupts the chronological and geographical limits of British studies. The past thirty years have brought seismic changes to imperial history. Scholars of the British Empire have destabilized and nuanced the once-simplistic relationship between metropole and periphery, colonizer and colonized, and official government policy at home and practical reality on the ground, demonstrating the interplay between nation and empire and the limits of European mastery. However, this important work is generally focused on the seventeenth, eighteenth, and nineteenth centuries.[22] Most crucially for the early modern period, Atlantic history has reframed imperialism, unearthing the individuals, ideas, and goods that traveled this oceanic waterway and highlighting the ways that Britain's empire was shaped by its entanglement with the rival empires of Spain, Portugal, France, and the Netherlands.[23] However, British Atlantic scholarship tends to privilege Ireland, Anglo-America, and the post-1603 era.[24] In this narrative, the British are rendered latecomers to the ocean and earlier enterprise elsewhere in Europe, the Americas, or Africa remains obscured.[25]

Complementing this work, the New British History, imagined as an integrative, plural history of the peoples located along the Anglo-Celtic frontier and their global exchanges, has transformed the domestic terrain. But in practice, this effort has fixed on religious pluralism within the British Isles, state-building between the 1603 and 1707 unions, and identity formation.[26] Meanwhile, a penchant for drama, the lengthy reigns of Henry VIII and Elizabeth I, and debates over the Reformation and the exercise of government have overwhelmed the literature on the sixteenth century.[27] Consequently, Tudor studies remain insular, neglecting overseas contexts and leaving their effects on the national dynamic poorly understood.[28]

By tracing notions of cannibalism in sixteenth- and early seventeenth-century British texts, we can challenge these dominant paradigms and bring imperial, Atlantic, and Tudor history together. The physical evidence uncovered at Jamestown in 2013 provides the perfect occasion for such a reassessment, first by further privileging the study of anthropophagy. As numerous scholars have shown, cannibalism—whether practiced, alleged, assumed, fictionalized, wholly fabricated, or some combination thereof and whether described for the benefit of author, audience, or both—played a powerful role in European encounters with the "other," entering the conversation through Columbus.[29] Focusing less on whether man-eating actually occurred and more on what European obsessions with the practice might mean, such work has positioned the practice as central to the cultural and intellectual history of imperialism and informs my approach and methodology. I read texts that describe cannibalism as sources created in a particular context, reflective of and responsive to the particular backgrounds, experiences, and concerns of their creators and readers. Ultimately, colonial sources about cannibalism are useful not solely or even primarily as "fact" or for sleuthing out whether they accurately or reliably "prove" that anthropophagy happened. That is certainly a matter worthy of study, but it is not the only one. The fictions or hybrids of fact and fiction that cannot always be parsed are just as significant and, existing as they do on both sides of the Atlantic and involving both colonizer and colonized, often serve to trouble any simple dichotomy between civilized and savage. I am interested in what some of these British representations and tropes looked like, where and how they were adopted, and what they might expose. Further, and of particular relevance here, Claude Rawson and H. E. Martel have reread well-known accounts of cannibalism by Hans Staden, André Thevet, Jean de Léry, and Michel de Montaigne and connected them to debates over the Eucharist, the French Wars of Religion, and native resistance to European incursion, clearly articulating the ties that bound national to imperial contexts in the sixteenth century.[30] At the same time, the Jamestown findings draw attention to cannibalism in British North America, long overshadowed by instances in Latin America and the Caribbean.[31] Finally, when put in conversation with earlier British cannibalism narratives elsewhere, the discovery of evidence of cannibalism at Jamestown can advance Karen Ordahl Kupperman's efforts to complicate the history of Jamestown as a project.[32] With this lens, the colony becomes a waypoint in a far longer narrative of British imperialism rather than the genesis it is often held up to be and the sixteenth century becomes more than the sole purview of Iberian adventure.

■ ■ ■

Hore's voyage, which produced one of the earliest British tales of cannibalism abroad, ushered in decades of dialogue on the subject in British sources, all written before Jamestown's Starving Time. This dialogue ranged from writings about native "Kennyballes" in Brazil in 1540, to Iberian travel narratives translated into English in the 1550s, to war-torn Ireland in the 1590s. Using these three case studies, I argue that cannibalism was crucial to ventures launched by the British during much of the sixteenth century, each part and parcel of seminal domestic developments.[33] I find that as in the Hore episode, the cannibalism discourse appeared at significant moments of upheaval, when the Tudor crown and its subjects were reshaping the polity at home and looking to expand abroad, two aspects of a single process that were both well served by stories of anthropophagy. Moreover, I suggest that sixteenth-century British engagements with cannibalism were neither simple nor static. The discourse appeared, transformed, and reappeared in sometimes unexpected ways, all highly dependent upon context. Narratives called on the practice of anthropophagy to implicate native-born British peoples, to label and discuss indigenous "others," and to denounce foreign rivals and foes on both sides of the ocean and throughout the century. This chapter reinforces the idea that cannibalism is a valuable unit of analysis and uses it to locate an early and evolving British Atlantic world that is far more long-standing, multifaceted, and multivalent and far less unilinear than the current scholarly literature suggests.

■ ■ ■

On March 7, 1540, a ship called the *Barbara* departed Portsmouth harbor with trade goods and some 100 men.[34] Much had changed in the British Isles since Hore's tragedy four years earlier. Henry VIII was nearly fifty years old. Cromwell was losing influence as the Church of England leaned in a more conservative doctrinal direction after the Six Articles and the king's rejection of his German Protestant bride, Anne of Cleves, and the Crown committed itself to extending Tudor rule in Ireland in the wake of fresh rebellions. In late July 1540 alone, Henry married Catherine Howard, his fifth wife; sent Cromwell to the block; began to rule by broader Privy Council; and dispatched his new lord deputy, Anthony St. Leger, to bring the western island under firmer control.[35] Yet the circumstances felt akin to those of four years earlier: Parliament was again enacting religious reform, the dissolutions continued, marital politics shifted, and Henry was as egotistical, covetous, and bellicose as ever. It was in this context that the king authorized the *Barbara*'s crossing. Fittingly, its captain, John Philips, was guided by "a very excellent goodly carde" that depicted Europe and all "the new founde lande with divers other straunge places."[36] Significantly, this map may have been similar to one drawn for the French, dated 1536 (the same year as Hore's voyage), in which the northern coast of South America bears the word "caniballes" in large capital letters.[37]

The venture began well enough. After stops along the Iberian coast, the ship steered southwest, past an uninhabited "goodly Ilande which they named Phelippe and Jacobbe's Ilande" in a none-too-subtle claim of possession.[38] From there, things went downhill. When it reached Brazil, the *Barbara* struck rocks and was damaged. Then a rival French trader tried to cut the ship's cable and a native ran off with its stores, leading boatswain John Podd and several others to pursue him into the interior.[39] The remaining crew shouted for the missing sailors to no avail.[40] They became convinced that their countrymen had been swallowed up by "the perelles of the countrey and the people," the "Kennyballes."[41] Cannibalism had again struck Tudor Atlantic adventurers, but unlike in 1536, the cannibals were not their countrymen. According to the sailors on the *Barbara,* American maneaters had claimed their first British victims.

The *Barbara* set course for home, but leaks forced it to anchor at Hispaniola, where the crew attacked two Spanish ships, plundered their rich cargoes, and piloted a Seville-based vessel home. After suffering through storms and sickness, the battered crew landed in Devon in August 1540 with only thirteen men left fit for duty.[42] When news of their escapade reached the Habsburg court, Charles V pressed Henry to indict the survivors on charges of piracy.[43] Imperial ambassador Eustace Chapuys promised swift retribution "to obviate such evils" and to "get it enacted that no armed ship shall sail for Brazil or such countries without giving security not to attack the Emperor's ships."[44] Although a trial took place, spreading word of the voyage and the sailors' encounter with cannibals, no record of the outcome exists.[45]

Though the journey of the *Barbara* was a grisly and embarrassing fiasco, there was also great promise—the *Barbara* had shown that the "Kennyballes" lived amid brazilwood and other attractive resources and that the danger they presented could be mitigated by local guides whom the crew reported as eager to aid the British. The voyage had also indirectly led the adventurers to a prize of Iberian sugar and hides. This paradoxical description of great New World prospects alongside its most barbarous offerings would become a common pairing in early modern travel narratives by the late sixteenth century, as exemplified by the writings of Walter Ralegh in the 1590s, some fifty years after the *Barbara* reports. For him, El Dorado always lay just beyond Amazonian warriors and their cannibalistic neighbors.[46]

Although modern historians overlook the *Barbara* episode, presumably because of its apparent isolation and failure to gain the British a toehold in America, it resonates with significance. The 1540 adventure produced what may be the first eyewitness British account of assumed native cannibalism in the New World, an account that five crew members substantiated before the High Court of Admiralty. It demonstrates continued Tudor activity in the Atlantic in the first half of the sixteenth century and attests to the ways domestic developments both encouraged voyaging abroad and fostered a powerful yet changing discourse about cannibalism. That discourse functioned to excuse maritime error, to "other" native inhabitants, to legitimize Tudor incursions at indigenous and Iberian expense, and to promote a (perhaps misplaced) sense of British superiority and ascendancy over both groups that was essential to the consolidation efforts of king and council. Over the course of 1541–1542, these developments on both sides of the Atlantic bore fruit: Henry VIII assumed the title of king (rather than mere lord) of Ireland to reflect the extent of power he desired over the island, initiated the Anglo-Scottish "Rough Wooing" Wars for primacy over his northern neighbor and a single monarchy throughout the archipelago, invaded France in yet another attempt to make good on his historic royal claim there, and set off a proxy war in Newfoundland that added an American dimension to these explicitly British and explicitly imperial fights.

■ ■ ■

Despite the efforts of Hore and Philips—captains who visited the Americas, claimed to encounter cannibalism, and then spread word of their experiences at home in the 1530s and 1540s—the British did not dominate the Atlantic world or its literature in the sixteenth century. Travelers from continental Europe were more numerous and more prolific writers. However, their experiences were enormously useful for Tudor authors and audiences. Indeed, some of the most influential publications to promote sixteenth-century British imperialism were derived from Spanish, Portuguese, Dutch, and French pens, works that were translated into English with new prefatory or other material and were intended to spur Tudor enterprise abroad. A momentary chronological shift backward in time reveals just how vital these texts could be, especially in the context of the cannibalism discourse. The *First English Book on America,* a 1520 translation of a Dutch text, included both the first use of the word "America" and the first descriptions of New World cannibals in English. In British minds, then, images of "Armenica" and of "they [that] ete also on[e] a nother" were linked from very early on.[47] Ultimately, this pairing of practice and place mediated by translation endured as a means of promoting British imperialism. It reappeared some thirty years later, at a pivotal moment in the aftermath of the *Barbara.*

The death of Henry VIII in 1547 left behind a nine-year-old boy king shackled with a costly war with Scotland, courtly factionalism, and an uneasy Church settlement. For many historians, the accession of the young Edward VI (r. 1547–1553) and the twelve years that followed constituted a "mid-Tudor crisis," a tumultuous period of destabilizing minority and female rule, religious zealotry and persecution, rebellion and alien Spanish influence that mercifully ended with the death of Mary I (r. 1553–1558) and the accession of Elizabeth I (r. 1558–1603).[48] Yet this interpretation overdramatizes the period, diminishes the impact and lasting significance of the Edwardian and Marian eras and masks a fundamental continuity and shared source of strength: imperialism. Under the supposedly "evangelical" Edward and "bloody" Mary, the Crown and its subjects fostered new theories and projects on both sides of the Atlantic, including the coining of the phrase "thempire of greate Briteigne" amid the Rough Wooings in 1548.[49] In developing this imperial ideology and practice, mid-Tudor actors drew from experience gained under Henry VII and Henry VIII and set new precedents for the Elizabethans. In the 1550s, courtier Richard Eden played a major role in this process, and he did so through a discourse of American cannibalism in translation.

Eden, the Cambridge-educated descendant of cloth merchants and clerics based in East Anglia, rose to prominence as a scholar and scientist and became a close ally of leading Edwardian statesmen John Dudley, Thomas Smith, and William Cecil.[50] In 1553, he completed his first major work, *A treatyse of the newe India.* The *Treatyse* was a translation of part of Sebastian Munster's *Cosmographia* (1544), one of the most important descriptions of the world then in print. As he explained in his dedication to Dudley, Eden wrote out of duty to God and to his "natyue countrey & countreymen, which haue of late to their great praise (whatsoeuer succede) attempted wt newe viages to sereche ye seas and newe found landes," hopeful that a history of Spanish and Portuguese feats might "further theyr enterprise."[51] For Eden, the Tudor state had already begun to wade into Atlantic waters and Munster's work, laced with tales of New World cannibalism as one of its central tropes, was the perfect prod to push it even further.

As an edition and translation of Iberian exploits, Eden's book was unlike the recollections that Hore or Philips brought home. Yet this new literary venture reflected a similarly tumultuous domestic atmosphere. Its intended reader, John Dudley, Earl of Warwick and later Duke of Northumberland, had just pulled off a series of major coups. Between October 1549 and February 1550, Dudley had toppled the existing minority government (a protectorate administered by the king's uncle, Edward Seymour, Earl of Hertford and later Duke of Somerset), seized the regency for himself, withdrawn English troops from their costly and futile effort to conquer Scotland, and refocused attentions at home. There, he sought to quell the popular unrest that had reached a breaking point in the 1549 rebellions, reduce the Crown's debt, centralize power in the Privy Council, consolidate his supreme hold on the Church, and push further Protestant reform. Now, with these programs in the works and acting with Cecil's advice, Dudley was considering a new plantation scheme in Ireland and new journeys to search for a northern passage to the East.[52] Eden intended his *Treatyse* to contribute to these expansionary efforts overseas.

Eden's translation painstakingly detailed "that cruel & fearse people which eate mans fleshe," fattening children for slaughter, salting and pickling them, and sparing women so they might birth a new generation of meals.[53] In their villages, the cannibals tied still-bleeding human heads to posts, mixed human and animal meat together, and repurposed human arm and leg bones as arrowheads.[54] Met with such barbarity, Spaniards had fled the vicinity.[55] In failing to conquer, the translator implied, Spain had relinquished its sovereign claim to the territory. The horror thus served Eden's purposes: it warned of the hazards that lay ahead, yet it proposed that the British, who believed themselves to be superior in faith, honor, and legitimacy to the Catholic Iberians who had fallen victim to cannibal wrath, could seize the opportunity to set forth the "true Relygion in perpetual combatte agaynste learned heretykes" and partake in a "great aboundaunce of golde" and spices the New World had to offer.[56] The book might well have succeeded, but it was poorly timed. In 1553, the year it was published, Edward VI died, Dudley was executed for plotting to install Lady Jane Grey on the throne, and the Tudor inheritance fell to Mary I, Edward's half-sister and the Catholic, half-Spanish daughter of Henry VIII and Katherine of Aragon. The Tudor realms faced potentially mammoth changes in church, state, and foreign policy.

With his associates now awash in charges of heresy and treason, Eden returned to translation, imperial promotion, and telling tales of cannibalism—a shrewd, calculated move, which succeeded and demonstrates continuity and consistency across the Edwardian and Marian regimes, a tumultuous period in British History. Eden must have been sure enough of the persistent, pervasive relevance of Atlantic empire to the Tudors to risk his career and reputation on it, as he chose to employ the same skill set and message that had endeared him to the Edwardian court. Moreover, the discourse of American anthropophagy played an equally central role in this second work, *The decades of the newe worlde,* a translation of Peter Martyr's *De orbe novo decades,* Gonzalo Oviedo's *Natural hystoria de las Indias,* and numerous other complementary works, published in 1555 with a new laudatory dedication to the Crown. In fact, Iberian adventure felt even more relevant in light of Mary's marriage to her Habsburg cousin, Prince Philip (later Philip II of Spain, r. 1556–1598), in July of 1554. Their subsequent co-monarchy bred a fierce xenophobia that urged national autonomy and global competition with Spain. These feelings spread among some English and Welsh and even some Scottish and Irish people.[57] Responding to fears that Philip was consolidating his power at court, reaching for the Tudor crown, and turning England into a pawn of Madrid and Rome when he selected the texts, his work described a "wylde and wanderynge" people who were expert archers with poisonous arrows and were spreading "lyke a pestiferous contagion" "to hunte for mannes fleshe."[58] As translator, Eden seemed to relish the more specific passages in his sources, the ones that described how the cannibals ate "the intralles and extreme partes" first, then moved on to the fleshy bits.[59] Yet, in their wake, "these monstrous bludsuckers," the text emphasized, had left uninhabited thousands of acres that were full of foodstuffs and gold.[60] Moreover, Eden related that although the cannibals had proven to be an intractable, warmongering hindrance to the Spanish, they could be defeated by force and all other natives could be brought "from theyr wylde and beastly rudenes to ciuilitie and trewe religion."[61]

Though Eden took care to praise and even defend the Spanish for rescuing some "cruell Canibales" from their "horrible licenciousnesse," his book, which was tinged with Hispanophobia and anti-Catholic sentiment, unabashedly reflected its domestic context.[62] England, he wrote in his preface, is "decayed and impouerysshed," while Spain grows rich on New World wealth.[63] Here, in the land of cannibals, lay the key to national survival and greatness at a critical moment, and the very presence of man-eaters would both justify and smooth the way for Tudor victory. He pled, "O Englande, whyle tyme is gyuen thee, circumcise thy harte. Put to onely thy good wyll, and thou mayste fynde grace and fauoure to recouer thyne aunciente bewtie whiche hath so longe byn defaced."[64] This time, the courtier's manipulation of American anthropophagy, shaped to fit his unique circumstances, worked. As historian Gillian T. Cell put it, the *Decades,* "more than any other single book, stimulated English curiosity about America" just before Elizabeth I ascended to the throne.[65]

■ ■ ■

We can connect Eden and his cannibal discourse to the adventures of David Ingram in the 1560s, Martin Frobisher in the 1570s, and Humphrey Gilbert in the 1580s. Each author commented on the prospect and practice of cannibalism on the western side of the Elizabethan Atlantic world, giving audiences his own take on this evolving narrative.[66] But something shifted when the Spanish Armada set sail in May 1588. With England's home shores at risk, all available ships were pressed for defense of the domestic realm, leaving the Roanoke colonists and Newfoundland fisheries abandoned, the searches for the

Northwest Passage halted, and the enmity with Scotland (temporarily) smoothed over. Although the immediate threat passed with the wreck of Philip II's fleet and providential triumphalism filled Tudor writings, the 1590s were characterized by unease and a modest turn inward. Sometimes dubbed "the nasty nineties" by scholars, Elizabeth's last decade was strained by poor harvests and plague, worries over the succession and the economy, political turmoil and infighting in the Privy Council, war with Spain, rebellion at home led by the Earl of Essex, and religious dissension under Archbishop of Canterbury John Whitgift. The British Isles had to take priority.[67]

It was amid this turmoil at home that the cannibalism discourse enjoyed sustained promotion in another British Atlantic venue that had occupied the Tudors since the start of the dynasty in 1485: Ireland. Significantly, then, this was after the explosion of that discourse in sixteenth-century literature on the Americas. This timing disrupts a neat, linear theory of westward expansion from an Irish laboratory where Elizabethans established a "pattern" of rule for export to the New World.[68] In 1594, Hugh O'Neill, Earl of Tyrone, rebelled against the Tudor crown, beginning the Nine Years' War. Strapped for resources, O'Neill turned to Philip II and the pope for support, couching his struggle in a powerful, anti-British imperial rhetoric of "faith and fatherland" and drawing in both Gaelic Irish and the disaffected Anglo-Irish, or "Old English," descendants of settlers who had arrived in the twelfth century.[69] As aid from the European continent proved wanting, the Irish resistance faltered and peace came within days of the queen's death in 1603. As contemporaries writing about the war while it was unfolding and in its immediate aftermath, British observers Edmund Spenser, Barnaby Rich, John Davies, and Fynes Moryson all turned to alleged occasions of anthropophagy in order to defame the rebels and delegitimize their cause, justify the brutality of Elizabeth's forces, and pitch schemes for the future of Ireland. These contributors shifted the cannibalism discourse toward war-torn Ireland, for different reasons and with different effects, at the end of the Tudor century and the start of the Stuart era.

Contemporary with a Crown report from early March 1596 that mentioned that the Irish "traitors" were employing "cannibals" in their service, Spenser's *View of the Present State of Ireland* (written ca. 1596, published in 1633) incorporated two episodes of anthropophagy into its dialogue on the isle.[70] First, Spenser related the wartime execution of "Murrogh Obrien" whose old "foster mother, tooke up his heade, whilst he was quartered, and sucked up all the blood running thereout, saying, that the earth was not worthy to drincke it," in what was said to be an ancient practice.[71] Spenser then described the rebellion in Munster, where the land had turned from plentiful to barren and the Irish had been reduced from eating corn and cattle to consuming carrion and shamrocks before finally "devoure[ing] one an other" in a hunger topos like Hore's.[72] Nearly two decades later, as part of his *Itinerary* (1617), Moryson set down a similar account from the Nine Years' War, relating "a most horrible spectacle of three children . . . knawing with their teeth the entrals of their dead mother, upon whose flesh they had fed twenty dayes past" and a group of old women who were executed for killing and eating little children.[73] Like Spenser's cannibals, these Irish had been "driven to unspeakeable extremities."[74]

Spenser's and Moryson's accusations were certainly damning, but they were also anecdotal and comprehensible, even excusable, in the contexts of famine, cultural tradition, and war. While Spenser used cannibalism to aid the colonial cause, situating it alongside other descriptions of Irish barbarity, critiques of current policy, and his own suggestions, Moryson was different, at least superficially, and appeared to be motivated by an altruistic desire to travel and record tales from Naples to Constantinople. Yet his *Itinerary* offered a similar anecdote from the Nine Years' War in Ireland, illustrating the "lamentable effects [that] followed [the] rebellion" and suggesting that the Irish had brought such horror upon themselves by their insubordination.[75] The cannibalism discourse aptly served all these purposes: it promoted British superiority, it justified Tudor intervention, and it demonstrated that Ireland was not a lost cause.

Ulster colonist and soldier Barnaby Rich, a self-styled expert on Ireland, its true nature, and its importance within the British world, took a different approach. In 1610, he published *A new description of Ireland*.[76] Rich, who defended the Tudor presence and its strong hand, emphatically deployed cannibalism to censure the Irish as inherently cruel. He presented none of the situational explanations that Spenser or Moryson offered, no wartime exigency or hatred of foreign rule to excuse them.[77] Instead, Rich positioned the Irish as even more barbaric than "the most barbarous sauages that neuer knew ciuility." According to Rich, they were devoid of law and religion, nomadic, and "licentious," using the same word Eden had used to describe New World cannibals half a century earlier.[78] All of this made the Irish prone to rebellion and "bloudy executions," as O'Neill had shown.[79] But unlike his contemporaries, Rich never actually accused the Irish of anthropophagy—a significant departure. Rather, he used the practice as a tool of comparison, writing that "the Canibals, deuourers of mens flesh, doe leaue to bee fierce amongst themselues, but the Irish, without all respect, are euer most cruel to their very next neighbours."[80] Jacobean solicitor-general John Davies used a similar technique in his 1612 tract, determining that the Irish were "little better than cannibals, who do hunt one another, and he that hath most strength and swiftness doth eat and devour all his fellows."[81] This, he charged, was among the "true causes why Ireland was never entirely subdued" under Elizabeth I.[82] Addressing a new generation of planters in Ireland who were under Stuart rather than Tudor command, Rich and Davies demonstrate the power and relevance of cannibal discourse for British audiences by the 1610s. It had become the ultimate tool of national flattery and imperial rebuke.[83]

■ ■ ■

When Davies's book reached print in 1612, it found an audience increasingly familiar with another even more terrifying experience of cannibalism in the British Atlantic, one that brings this story full circle. That year, Jamestown colonist and secretary William Strachey penned his *Historie of Travaile into Virginia* and published his infamously strict *Lawes Diuine, Morall and Martiall* in England.[84] Both texts were intimately tied to the Starving Time, attempts to save the floundering project by attracting new colonists and creating order among current ones. During that terrible winter of 1609–1610, Virginia's colonists had allegedly turned to eating one another to survive, in the vein of Brazil's "Kennyballes," Iberian America's "Canibales," and Ireland's rebels but most reminiscent of Hore's sailor nearly seventy-five years earlier. Although Jamestown is certainly the most notorious and well-known example, it was part of a much broader, much longer British discourse of cannibalism in the Atlantic world in which adventurers, colonists, officials, and commentators used tales of anthropophagy in measured, calculated ways that reflected highly significant changes in both the national and imperial landscapes. Although the cases examined here are only a limited sample of Tudor texts that invoked the practice, they suggest how the study of cannibalism can uncover a new early modern Atlantic history.

CHAPTER 6

# Imperial Appetites

## Cannibalism and Early Modern Theatre

MATT WILLIAMSON

The Starving Time in Jamestown constituted an event of pivotal ideological significance in the history of British imperialism. Poorly supplied, badly organized, and showing little ability to grow their own food, the colonists in Virginia had experienced difficulties since their arrival in 1607. In 1609 and 1610, following worsening relations with the Native population, the colony reached a crisis point. By the time new supplies arrived in March 1610, only 155 of the original 245 inhabitants remained.[1] Although the majority of deaths were a consequence of disease rather than starvation, as Robert Appelbaum has noted, hunger was nevertheless rife, and contemporary observers assumed it was the key cause of death.[2] Most sensationally, the absence of food was such that on at least one occasion a colonist resorted to anthropophagy. In the years that followed, a series of accounts were written by John Smith, George Percy, and William Strachey, among others. These accounts claimed that settlers dug up "dead corpses outt of graves" and "licked upp the Bloode which had fallen from their weake fellowes."[3] One colonist was said to have "murdered his wyfe Ripped the childe outt of her woambe and threw itt into the River and after chopped the Mother in pieces and salted her for his foode."[4] Rumors of cannibalism spread through London and were the subject of heated debate and furious rebuttal on the part of the Virginia Company. The intensity with which these events were discussed is testament both to the fascination cannibalism evokes and the precariousness of England's nascent colonial project. At a time when England's empire was insignificant compared to that of Spain or the Ottomans, events at Jamestown were the focal point for discussions of the nature and viability of England's colonial expansion.

In addition to sparking debate, these events provided material for the London theatres. A significant example is John Fletcher and Philip Massinger's *The Sea Voyage*, originally performed by the King's Men in June 1622. In part inspired by Shakespeare's *The Tempest* (1611), the play depicts various groups of pirate-colonists who explore two islands, one defined by extreme natural bounty, the other by absolute want. Central to the action of the piece is the depiction of a group of shipwrecked would-be colonists who find themselves faced with starvation and who engage in a failed attempt at cannibalism. Although Claire Jowitt and Teresa Walters have argued that the play is a response to the 1622 massacre in Jamestown, this is questionable, given the length of time it took for news of that event to reach London.[5] However, the text engages with accounts of the earlier Starving Time and without doubt its later performances acquired a more pronounced resonance as details of the massacre emerged.[6] Gordon McMullan notes that "the magical elements of *The Tempest* are conspicuous by their absence from *The Sea Voyage.*"[7] In place of the supernatural, Fletcher and Massinger portray "the possibility of starvation in paradise" and concentrate "on the problems of practical government by human resources."[8] Although Anthony Parr has argued that "the very abundance of analogy tends to suggest that, like *The Tempest,* this play refutes any attempt to tie it exclusively to a particular place or venture," Jowitt emphasizes the relevance of the New World, arguing that "the presence of European women on board Portuguese and French ships is significant in locating this play in a Western rather than an Eastern context, since the former was concerned with permanent settlement and the latter with temporary trading posts."[9] However, in order to understand the extent of the play's engagement with and ambivalence toward the colonial project, it is necessary to pay particular attention to the significance of its central episode of cannibalism. In doing so, it becomes possible to discern the degree to which cannibalism is associated not simply with the barren landscapes of a failed colonial project but also with unruly and fundamentally European appetites.

As instances of early modern European subjects engaging in cannibalism in a New World setting, both *The Sea Voyage* and the events of the Starving Time provide significant examples of the trans-Atlantic nature of cannibal encounters in this period. Early work on the issue of cannibalism placed great emphasis on the question of whether or not cannibalism actually occurred and generally tended to read early reports of cannibalism as part of a process of legitimation through which European colonizers justified their subjugation of Native peoples. In *The Man-Eating Myth,* William Arens asserted the absence of "adequate documentation" for socially sanctioned anthropophagy in any existing society.[10] And, as Rachel Herrmann has argued, "Long before English colonization began, fantasies of cannibals infused textual and visual representations of the New World."[11] Increasingly, however, critics have acknowledged the degree to which cannibalism was associated with the Old World as well as the New. Louise Noble highlights the tradition of medicinal anthropophagy, noting that "paradoxically, while charges of cannibalism were being levelled at the geographically distant Other, cannibalism was being practiced at home."[12] Maggie Kilgour situates cannibalism within the Christian ritual of the Eucharist.[13] And David Goldstein has noted the significance of "the founding myths of the Greco-Roman tradition, as well as early ethnographic descriptions by Herodotus and Pliny of tribes who ate human flesh."[14] The presence of these myriad modes of cannibalism means that even when it is figured as a characteristic of the Natives of the New World, anthropophagy can be deployed as a way of commenting on Europe. As Goldstein has argued, "Within the word 'cannibal' . . . lies buried a trove of conflicting and symbolically rich etymologies that connect the Old World with the New through a rapt fascination with the taboo of person-eating."[15] This joint tradition has obvious relevance for a play in which the Native population of the New World is essentially absent.[16] But it also provides a significant way to move toward an understanding of *The Sea Voyage*'s cannibalism as a product not simply of its colonial setting but also of the colonizing subjects themselves.

Indeed, the play repeatedly associates cannibalism with the hunger and appetites of a group of specifically European characters in a way that assumes a particular significance in the context of England's colonial and domestic development. In contrast to the Spanish and Ottoman Empires, England's overseas expansion was predicated on an increasing demand for imports that stemmed from a change in the nature of its agricultural production. As Robert Brenner has argued, in a period defined by recurrent economic crises throughout Europe, "the English economy was able to sustain ongoing development on the basis, above all, of the transformation of its agrarian social and property structure in a capitalist direction."[17] Brenner's emphasis on the "capitalist direction" of the economy is significant. Extensive theoretical and historical work has explored the nature of the transition from a feudal to a capitalist mode of production, but Brenner's model is of particular utility for the extent to which it stresses the role that improvement of agricultural production, land reorganization, dependence on the market, competition, and class struggle played in the formation of the system we now define as capitalism.[18] This model enables us to recognize the partial and emergent nature of capitalist praxis in this period and the wide-ranging significance of its effects. Shifts in the structure of agrarian social relations prompted mass economic polarization and recurrent periods of dearth, contributing to the creation of a nascent proletariat that depended on wage labor and the market for subsistence. The result was a rapid increase in demand for food that laid the foundation for imperial expansion. Like the majority of England's overseas projects in this period, the colonization of the Americas operated along relatively traditional lines. The Virginia Company was a joint-stock company that, as Brenner has noted, received "a monopoly on the trade with that portion of the American mainland located between 34 degrees and 40 degrees north latitude, and control of land allocation and utilization."[19] Work for the company was primarily carried out by indentured laborers, a sharp difference from the market-dominated social relations of the English countryside. Yet England's dependence on overseas trade and colonization meant that Virginian laborers' ostensibly more traditional work remained inextricably connected to the rise of capitalist social relations in England.

By reimagining the events of the Starving Time as a product of unruly imperial appetites, *The Sea Voyage* links New World settlement to unrestrained Old World consumption. The play participates in a feeling of profound anxiety about the dependence of England's trading companies on imports rather than exports. *The Sea Voyage* was contemporaneous with the publication of a series of pamphlets that discussed the wisdom of using British currency to purchase commodities in the East Indies and the Levant. The debate emerged in the context of the economic crisis of 1622–1623 and formed the basis of what would later be termed mercantilism.[20] Thomas Mun, a prominent member of the East India Company, sought to justify a high volume of imports on the ground that those commodities could be developed and reexported to a European market. But Mun's emphasis on the importance of a balance of trade reveals a persistent anxiety about the fact that imports could also be consumed, prompting "wantonesse and riot" instead of national prosperity.[21] In *The Sea Voyage*, that unrestrained excess is embodied in the depiction of cannibalism. But in order to understand this, it is first necessary to situate the play's cannibal episodes in the context of an evolving cultural and dramatic tradition. To that end, I will consider the broader dramatic significance of cannibalism on the early modern stage, placing it in the context of economic polarization, the decline of traditions of hospitality, and social mobility. I will also explore the specific way *The Sea Voyage* deploys cannibalism, situating the play in the context of the Jamestown colony in Virginia and considering the wider significance of that project at a time when the Virginia Company was the object of increasingly pronounced criticism. This analysis makes it possible to consider the relation of the theatre to political debate in the earliest stages of British imperialism and to scrutinize the particular characteristics cannibalism could exemplify on the stage.

## Hunger, Appetite, and Revenge: Old World Cannibalism

Cannibalism pervades the early modern theatre. In tragedies such as *Titus Andronicus* (1592–1593) and *The Bloody Banquet* (1609) it becomes a tool of revenge: characters unknowingly or unwillingly devour the bodies of their relatives and lovers.[22] In the romance play *Pericles* (1607), famine forces a starving population to engage in anthropophagy.[23] And in texts such as *Timon of Athens* (1607), the depiction of hospitality and excessive consumption is infused with cannibalistic undertones.[24] In part, these plays seem to accord with the basic distinction Goldstein has identified between Old World and New World cannibalisms. Accounts of the former "emphasize the physical act of eating, while in visual and verbal depictions of New World cannibalism the act of eating occurs as an afterthought or a leftover of the ritual killing that precedes it."[25] This trend in the representation of Old World cannibalisms receives a specific inflection on the stage. The playing companies relied on both aristocratic patronage, which ensured protection from anti-vagrancy laws, and public appeal, because ticket sales provided the primary source of profits. It can be argued that cannibalism's primary function is entertainment, a means of appealing to the desires of its audience. But at the same time, during the early seventeenth century, a period of sweeping social change, the use of cannibalism in the theatre is a trope that both operates within and comments on England's changing socioeconomic structure.

In the first instance, cannibalism functions as spectacle. Above all, it is related to what Thomas Cartelli describes as the theatre's need to "satisfy the audience's desire for release from normative constraints and its wish to explore vicariously abnormative or heterodox states of mind and feeling."[26] A key example is Shakespeare's *Titus Andronicus,* a text that was written early in the playwright's career and participates in the contemporary vogue for revenge tragedy. Set in a fictional period of Rome's history that draws on elements of both the republic and the empire, it depicts factional conflict between the emperor, his foreign queen, and the titular general. In a play that is littered with bodies and features scenes of mutilation and rape, cannibalism provides the text's climactic act of barbarity. Titus cooks the queen's sons in a pie and after serving them to her reveals their severed heads, declaring "Why, there they are, both baked in this pie, / Whereof their mother daintily hath fed, / Eating the flesh that she herself hath bred."[27] A central aspect of the horror of the scene is the incestuous implication of a mother feeding upon the "flesh" of her own sons. But no less significant is the way the flesh has been consumed. To feed "daintily" in this period could signify simply "elegantly," but it could also imply "delicate attention to the palate."[28] The dramatic power of the scene is derived from a basic opposition between the ostensible refinement of the feast and the brute reality of its contents. The emphasis on this final spectacle attests to the play's attention to the various appetites of its audience and the attempts of the playing companies to satisfy the vogue for spectacle and revenge that characterized much of the early modern theatre. But even when deployed as titillation, the representation of cannibalism derives its dramatic impact from the implicit opposition of civility and barbarity.

The lurid attraction of cannibalism could also be deployed in a way that linked it to a material basis in hunger and famine. This was particularly the case in times of crisis. William Shakespeare and George Wilkin's *Pericles* was first performed in 1607, shortly after bad harvests and dearth had prompted a mass uprising in the Midlands.[29] The play is episodic in structure, depicting the travels of the eponymous prince through the Mediterranean, where he encounters a wide variety of societies ruled by monarchs who range from benevolent kings to incestuous tyrants. At the end of the first act, in a scene generally ascribed to Shakespeare's collaborator, Pericles arrives at the city of Tarsus to discover that the population has reached such extremes of hunger that they have been forced to eat each other. This cannibalizing hunger is figured as the source of the fundamental upheaval in the hierarchical structures of Tarsan society. The city's ruler describes how:

> Those mothers, who to nuzzle up their babes
> Thought nought too curious, are ready now
> To eat those little darlings whom they loved.
> So sharp are hunger's teeth that man and wife
> Draw lots who first shall die to lengthen life.[30]

Hunger is presented as the source of perverted appetites that threaten the natural order of mothers and children and husbands and wives. The text invokes characteristic tropes of famine, reflecting the emphasis on familial cannibalism in works such as Nashe's *Christ's Tears over Jerusalem.*[31] But these images of social disorder acquire a particular significance in the context of the social upheavals that preceded the play's probable date of performance. The depiction of the uncontrollable hunger famine conditions produce provides a way to question the strength of traditions of civility, foregrounding the degree of material well-being that is necessary for maintaining bonds of kin and loyalty.

Famine itself, however, is never purely a matter of misfortune in the early modern period. The underlying assumption of contemporary accounts is almost invariably that it is a punishment for sinful behavior. Consequently, cannibalism produced by hunger has a particular ethical inflection. A key example is the work of the Puritan preacher William Gouge, in which famine is "a judgement," one of "three sharp mortall arrowes of the Lord which he useth to shoot as judgements against children of men."[32] Gouge's work is striking for the extent to which moral issues intersect with social ones. Famine is a punishment sent to afflict "the wickednesse of a sinfull nation."[33] Thus, consideration of sin entails consideration of the state of the nation. *Pericles* adopts a similar stance. It implicitly presents the city's disruptive cannibalism as a consequence of the appetites that preceded hunger. The play characterizes plenty as a force that drove the citizens of pre-famine Tarsus to satisfy ever more exotic appetites and repeatedly links their later hunger to these practices. Cleon contrasts their desire for "inventions to delight the taste" with the simple bread that hunger later prompts them to demand and notes that the city's tables were "stored full, to glad the sight, / And not so much to feed on as delight."[34] The notion that excessive consumption might increase appetite recurs in the dietary literature of the period. The *Homyly Against Gluttonie and Dronkennes* claimed that "he that eateth and drinketh unmeasurably kindleth ofttimes such an unnatural heat in his body, that his appetite is provoked thereby to desire more than it should."[35] And George Hakewill cautioned that "*powring* down strong drink and inordinate devouring delicious meats, ariseth oftner from the greedinesse and vncontent of the eie, then from any reall want, or desire of the appetite."[36] God might punish such excess: "If we in eating and drinking exceed, when God of his large liberality sendeth plenty, he will soon change plenty into scarceness."[37] In plays like *Pericles,* these excessive, expanding appetites are not simply morally questionable; they risk inviting an inversion of that plenty so that appetite changes seamlessly to hunger. An excess of plenty thus risks producing, in the final instance, the most problematic appetite of all: an appetite for human flesh.

This emphasis on appetite raises the possibility that cannibalism can be used to comment not just on singular episodes of famine and dearth but also on processes of socioeconomic change more generally. This is particularly evident in the literature of hospitality, which repeatedly describes guests who metaphorically or literally consume their hosts. The paradigmatic example is Shakespeare and Middleton's *Timon of Athens,* which depicts the downfall of a wealthy Athenian whose profligacy leads him to be surrounded by flatterers. They feast at his expense and receive extravagant gifts, the costs of which eventually and predictably lead to his bankruptcy. The play repeatedly figures the parasitical actions of Timon's guests as cannibalism and, significantly, associates the consumption of the host's body not just with the erosion of his resources but also with the accumulation of debt. The cynic Appemantus declares, "What a number of men eats Timon and he sees 'em not! It grieves me to see so many dip their meat in one man's blood, and all the madness is, he cheers them up too."[38] The "meat" and "blood" that his guests consume immediately invite parallels with the last supper and the Eucharist. Timon, the host who invites his own destruction, is figured as a Christ-like martyr who "cheers" men on to devour him. But the cannibal dimension lends a pronounced element of vulnerability to that position. The literal food and drink the guests devour become an extension of Timon's body and the image of consumption simultaneously insists on the finite nature of his resources, implicitly satirizing his reliance on credit and its power to produce ostensibly unlimited funds. Although Timon declares that "to Lacedaemon did my land extend," it is evident that he has used his land not as a resource but as collateral for loans: it is "all engaged, some forfeited and gone."[39] Timon's unrestrained borrowing enables the unrestrained appetites of his guests. The host's desire to satisfy the appetites of his guests forces him to rely on practices of usury that were characteristic of the emergent capitalist system.

Even when cannibalism is more overtly figured as a characteristic of the Native Other, it retains this capacity to function as a comment on European social and economic practices. In Jonson's *A Staple of News* (1626), for example, the cook Lickfinger describes his comic plan to send an expedition of cooks to the New World so they can convert the cannibals into "good eating Christians."[40] The text implicitly parodies the attempts of colonists to impose a Christian civility on the Natives of the New World. The very name "Lickfinger," with its implicit emphasis on sexual and culinary pleasure, emphasizes the prevalence of Old World appetites. But above all, it is significant that the power of Lickfinger's cookery is demonstrated through its supposed ability "to make such sauces for the savages,"

> And cook their meats with those enticing steams,
> As it would make our cannibal-Christians
> Forbear the mutual eating one another,
> Which they do do more cunningly than the wild
> Anthropophagi, that snatch only strangers,
> Like my old patron's dogs there.[41]

Like Montaigne's "Of the Cannibals," which claims that "there is more barbarity in eating a man alive, than in eating him dead," Jonson deploys New World cannibalism as way of satirizing an emergent capitalist economy.[42] His text participates in a wider tradition that figured non-Native cannibalisms as the modi operandi of European society. But in Jonson's play, the power of this image derives in large part from its inversion of the previous, parodic dichotomy between colonizers and colonized. Jonson uses cannibalism in a manner akin to the estrangement technique of Brechtian theatre: the elements of horror and barbarity it implies function as a way of satirizing the civilized barbarity of European society.

Cannibalism can thus seem to operate as a recurring trope that in its most basic form consists of pure spectacle. It was a means by which the theatre shocked and enticed its audience, creating the emotional impact necessary for the sale of tickets. Yet the theatre's use of this trope was also defined by a repeated emphasis on wider themes of hunger and appetite. This tended to distance cannibal acts from purely ritualistic violence, instead emphasizing their basis in socioeconomic realities. At these moments, cannibalism became a means of exploring a world in which, as the fishermen of *Pericles* declare, "the great ones eat up the little ones."[43] Cannibalism became the quintessential image of all against all, blatant disregard regard for others, and the collapse of traditional forms of charity that contemporary moralists condemned but that stubbornly persisted in early modern society. The very element of spectacle that prompted playing companies to depict the cannibal act became a tool of critique. There is a degree to which the use of this trope reinforced the othering binary of colonial thought: to consume to excess was to reduce oneself to the perceived condition of the native inhabitants of the New World. But the relative infrequency with which native cannibalisms were associated with these monstrous, inherent appetites complicated this construction. Cannibalism on the stages of the early modern theatre was most often not the property of an ostensibly uncivilized Other but rather an index of what those who were ostensibly civilized could become or even of what they might already be.

## Cannibalism and *The Sea Voyage*

The uneasy connections among hunger, appetite, and cannibalism acquire particular significance in the colonial setting of Fletcher and Massinger's *The Sea Voyage.* The play was produced contemporaneously with the 1622 uprising of Powhatans against Virginian colonists and only two years before the final dissolution of the Virginia Company. Although it is unlikely that news of the attack had reached England at the time the play was performed, criticism of the colony and its management was widespread. The Virginia Company was gripped by severe factional infighting and faced a crippling lack of investment.[44] *The Sea Voyage* constituted an intervention into colonial discourse at a moment of crucial importance, and its representation of cannibalism was central to this process. Although the play draws on the wider repertoire of cannibal associations that characterized early modern theatre, it is notable for its pronounced emphasis on the significance of the land the colonists explore. The action of *The Sea Voyage* occurs on two islands, one of which is plentiful, the other barren and devoid of sustenance. After the play's opening storm, a crew of French pirates are forced to land on the latter island. There they encounter two Portuguese nobles who have been stranded and are reduced to a state of famished desperation. The nobles successfully steal the pirates' ship, abandoning them on the barren island. As hunger begins to affect the French pirates, they attempt to kill and eat their captive, a young woman named Aminta with whom their captain has fallen in love. Critical analyses of *The Sea Voyage* have offered conflicting interpretations of its colonial setting. Jean Feerick reads the play as "a sustained meditation on how alien soils affect elite Europeans."[45] But for Michael Neill, it is simply "an exotic stage on which to play out domestic issues."[46] Attention to the play's central episode of cannibalism reveals a more complex picture. The play is defined by the interaction of colonizing subjects with colonized land in a way that embodies the transatlantic nature of both anthropophagy and colonialism in the early seventeenth century. Cannibalism in *The Sea Voyage* is the product of a foreign land that is resistant to development and the appetites of would-be colonizers.

In order to understand the precise way *The Sea Voyage* interacted with the theatre's wider engagement with cannibalism, it is necessary to consider how the literature of the period and this particular play constructed a New World setting. The early modern experience of the New World was mediated through textual accounts of the potential productiveness of the land, which was variously envisaged as a space of abundance, a barren location defined by want, or a space that needed Europeans to cultivate it if it was to release its natural plenty. The emphasis on plenty is a dominant theme of colonial propaganda; many accounts drew parallels between the New World and the bounty of the Garden of Eden. Hakluyt's *Principal Navigations* is replete with descriptions of the Americas as a land that is "the fairest, frutefullest, and pleausantest of all the worlde, aboundinge in honye, waxe, venison, wilde fowle," where there existed such "great store of vynes, all as full of grapes as coulde be, that if any of our followes went on shoare they came home laden with them."[47] However, in the early seventeenth century, imperial adventure involved not just luxury goods and prosperity; it also involved extreme hardship. The images of plenty in colonial propaganda frequently proved to be inaccurate, and early English attempts to settle in the Americas were markedly unsuccessful. When the Roanoke colony of 1587 was left without supplies due to Britain's war with Spain, the colonists disappeared. Even the more successful Jamestown colony was, as John Wood Sweet has noted, "plagued by persistent disease, starvation, and poor discipline," particularly during the Starving Time.[48] By locating *The Sea Voyage*'s central episode of cannibalism in a land that was the precise opposite of the plenty that appeared in contemporary propaganda, Fletcher and Massinger implicitly situated their text in the context of debates about the viability of the colonial project itself.

From the very beginning of *The Sea Voyage,* hunger is enacted onstage.[49] Stranded on the barren island, the upper-class Sebastian condemns the position he finds himself in:

> Nor meat nor quiet;
> No summer here, to promise any thing;
> Nor Autume, to make full the reapers hands;
> The earth obdurate to the teares of heaven,
> Let's nothing shoot but poysoned weeds.
> No Rivers, nor no pleasant Groves, no beasts;
> All that were made for man's use, flye this desart;
> No aëry fowle dares make his flight over it,
> It is so ominous.
> Serpents, and ugly things, the shames of nature,
> Roots of malignant tastes, foule standing waters;
> Sometimes we finde a fulsome Sea-root,
> And that's a delicate: a Rat sometimes,
> And that we hunt like Princes in their pleasure;
> And when we take a Toad, we make a Banquet.[50]

While contemporary colonial propaganda sought to establish the New World as a new Eden, *The Sea Voyage* delivers an image of a fallen world of "serpents," an earth that is "obdurate to the teares of heaven." This irredeemable nature places the island in explicit opposition to a colonial discourse that, as Patricia Akhimie has noted, "frequently imagined the globe as a series of potential country estates, waiting to be claimed and cultivated."[51] In the play, the island is presented as resistant in every way to the project of colonial improvement. It is not just devoid of sustenance, it does not produce harvests for "the reapers hands" and lacks even the seasonal change that might make possible the transformation of the land. The references to rats as the object of hunts, seaweed as a "delicate," and a Toad as a "banquet" present the island as the inversion of the aristocratic lifestyle that writers such as Walter Ralegh and John Smith imagined might be established in a New World context. In this context, hunger is a visceral critique of plans for colonial settlement. It is the most overt manifestation of the land's physical resistance to the project of improvement and a fundamental constituent of the text's repudiation of conventional images of New World plenty.

Hunger constitutes an overt threat to the identities of the colonists it affects. When the pirate captain Albert and his crew first encounter Sebastian and Nicusa, the two stranded Portuguese nobles, the nobles are described in terms that question their humanity. Aminta, the crew's female prisoner, draws attention to the "sunk eyes" of the two aristocrats and notes that they "are crept in, as if they had been frighted!"[52] Albert wonders whether they are alive or are merely "wandring shaddows."[53] The image joins the effects of hunger to the idea of the supernatural. They are "shadows" in the sense that they are subject to the physical effects of starvation, but the word imbues them with a ghost-like quality. In much the same way, John Smythe had described how "sicke and starued Souldiors" returning from the Low Countries were reduced to "miserable and pitiful ghosts or rather shadowes of men."[54] But in *The Sea Voyage,* the characters who are subjected to this degenerative process are Portuguese aristocrats, not common soldiers. The text establishes hunger as a force that can corrupt identity, making the elite monstrous and reducing them to the same status as the "shames of nature" that inhabit the island.[55] Sebastian responds to the pirates' questions by asserting the power of his rank. He tells them that "Onely our miseries make us *seem* Monsters."[56] Nevertheless, his immediate shift to duplicitous behavior when he steals the pirates' ship while they search for gold implies that the nobles' famished condition has affected more than their outward appearance; it has also affected their morals. The result is to emphasize the degree to which an aristocratic identity is reliant on a certain standard of material well-being and, more important, a public perception of that well-being.

Yet the fate of Sebastian and Nicusa was determined not by the barren nature of the island but by their former shipmates' greed. Sebastian recalls how, with the "cursed Gold enticing 'em," his crew set upon him and one another, causing their initial shipwreck. In much the same way, it is the pirates' unbridled desire for gold that enables Sebastian and Nicusa to steal their ship and leave them stranded on the barren island. In this way, the play reworks accusations that recurred in accounts of the Starving Time, particularly among those who sought to locate the failure of the project in the inadequacies of the colonists. Although these accounts were published shortly after the performance of *The Sea Voyage,* the fact that they were preceded by the account of the Virginia Company, which strenuously denied rumors of cannibalism induced by hunger, makes evident the large degree of public knowledge of events in Virginia. In *Purchas, His Pilgrimes,* Samuel Purchas reported that one group of colonists who had obtained corn from trading with the Indians decided not to return to the colony. Instead, they "*made a league amongst themselves to be professed Pirats, with dreames of Mountaines of Gold, and happie Robberies: thus at one instant, they wronged the hopes, and subuerted the cares of the Colonie, who depending vpon their returne, fore-slowed to looke out for further prouision.*"[57] In a similar manner, John Smith claimed that the colony failed because his fellow settlers refused to work: "There was no talke, no hope, no worke, but dig gold, wash gold, refine gold, loade gold, such a bruit of gold, that one mad fellow desired to be buried in the sands, least they should by there art make gold of his bones."[58] Both in Jamestown and on the early modern stage, hunger could be read as a consequence of this earlier greed, whether in practical terms because of the settlers' inability to collaborate or plan for the future or in moral terms that mirror those that *Pericles* presented as responsible for the fate of Tarsus. Excessive appetite, these authors suggested, gave rise to hunger and want.

The same dynamic can be discerned in the play's representation of cannibalism. Ostensibly, it appears to be a consequence of the hunger that followed from the island's barren landscape. The text deploys what Herman Pleij has described as a "hunger topos" that was typical of contemporary accounts of famine. The sailors do not mention cannibalism until they have considered a variety of tainted foodstuffs.[59] They first consider trying mud and bark and then medical supplies. Only after that do they consider eating human flesh. This progression mirrors what occurred in accounts of the Starving Time. For example, George Percy claimed that "having fed upon horses and other beasts as long as they lasted, we were glad to make shift with vermin, as dogs, cats and mice."[60] In *The Sea Voyage,* the shift between unacceptable foods to human flesh is initiated when Franville asks the surgeon:

> Wher's the great Wen
> Thou cutst from *Hugh* the saylers shoulder?
> That would serve now for a most Princely banquet.[61]

The "wen," a reference to a lump, a protuberance, or a tumor, is transformed into a "princely banquet."[62] The play implicitly contrasts the enthusiasm of the characters onstage with the repulsion the audience would feel in response to images of corrupted flesh and the ingestion of part of another body. This was undoubtedly intended to elicit both laughter and disgust. The element of disgust is in part contained by the playwrights' use of dramatic irony. While the audience would have been well aware that the absent captain, Albert, had already secured a promise of food for his starving companions, the play situated cannibalism as an act of desperation arising from necessity.

However, when the sailors decide to eat Aminta, their female captive, instead, the representation of cannibalism acquires a very different inflection. Aminta becomes not just sustenance, but a delicacy. She is "young and tydie" and will "eate delicatly / Just like young Porke a little lean."[63] The audience's reaction of disgust is thus anticipated at precisely the same moment when the sailors turn from eating human flesh as a matter of necessity to eating human flesh because of desire and pleasure. Moreover, Aminta is described as "unrosted" and "unsod"; the latter term implies that she is a virgin and the former, more literally, signifies that she has not been boiled.[64] She has been turned into an ingredient. The playwrights thus introduce an implicit element of difference between the more sophisticated appetites of the sailors and contemporary accounts of cannibalism among Native tribes, which tended to stress the simplicity of their customs. Later, they discuss the possibility of salting her body, with some declaring "we shall want Salt" and others arguing, "Tush, she needs no powdering."[65] Powder, in this period, could signify both "cosmetic in the form of powder" and "a preparation used in food or cooking as a seasoning." The pun made explicit the various ways that women could be consumed: as objects of sexual desire or as literal food.[66] But the reference to "powdering" the body is also significant in the context of later reports on events in Virginia, the majority of which noted that the man who ate his wife salted her body in order to preserve it. As Robert Appelbaum has argued, "The mutilation of the corpse, along with application of the culturally 'cooked' process of salting the body parts—in other words, daring to act on barbarous impulses with all the Providence that civility demanded—is perhaps what most offended his executioners."[67] In precisely the same manner, *The Sea Voyage*'s representation of cannibalism moves beyond the trope of European identities degenerating into colonial Other identities and toward a parody of the very elements of sophistication that notionally distinguished the two. The play presents cannibalism as a product of the European appetite for delicacies, not just the hunger inflicted on the pirate-colonists by a barren land.

An emphasis on appetite, rather than hunger, was also characteristic of contemporary accounts of anthropophagy during the Starving Time. For those who were sympathetic to the Virginia Company's propagandist aims, it was necessary either to refute reports of cannibalism or to distance anthropophagy from the issue of starvation. For example, while William Strachey acknowledged the fact that a man had killed and eaten his wife, he claimed that he did not do so "to satisfie his hunger" and placed great emphasis on the ample quantities of food that were later found in his home.[68] In contrast to these accounts, the conjunction of appetite and cannibalism in *The Sea Voyage* was a way to critique colonial expansion, not to legitimize it. Indeed, a significant motivating force behind the awakening of the sailors' cannibal appetites is their frustration with the failure of their colonial project. Parr argues that although in *The Sea Voyage* hunger affects characters across the social spectrum, those who attempt to engage in cannibalism are those who are "modelled on the younger sons of minor gentry who hoped to find in the colonies the wealth and status denied them at home, and who proved in many cases to be maladjusted and workshy."[69] The expectations of these aspiring characters serve to aggravate the hunger the barren land inflicts on them and becomes the source of their cannibal desires. Franville declares:

> True we were bound yee all know,
> For happy places, and most fertill islands,
> Where we had constant promises of all things,
> She turn'd the Captains minde.[70]

Aminta, the young woman with whom their captain has fallen in love, is a fitting object for the men's cannibalistic appetites because they believe she is responsible for their plight and the consequent failure of their imperial ambitions. Fueled by his romantic attachment to

Aminta, the Captain has abandoned their plans for colonial exploration, in an effort to discover the location of her missing brother. Robbed of the ability to fulfill their colonialist desires, the men shift their attention to the body of Aminta. The language the men use to describe the devouring of Aminta is the language of the colonial project. They plan to "cut her throate, / And then divide her, every Man his share," and they worry that her "hinder parts . . . will not fall to every Man's share."[71] As Wrightson has noted, joint-stock companies constituted a key model of colonialist expansion in the early modern period as "associations of capital, open to any investor," in which trade "was conducted by the directors on behalf of the company, and the proceeds were shared among investors."[72] These companies were not only "a great advance in the capitalist organization of English society" but were also the business model theatre companies such as the King's Men used.[73] Fletcher and Massinger link the implicit connections between imperial projects, cannibalism, and theatre to an instance of actual anthropophagy in Virginia. They deploy a depiction of colonists' tainted appetites as a way of exploring the destructive potential of imperialist expansion.

In *The Sea Voyage,* the representation of the cannibal act is accentuated by the metatheatrical emphasis the play places on the colonists' actions. The element of distance between audience and characters is severely compromised by the degree to which characters in the play justify cannibalism by referring to the textual legacy of cannibalism in early modern culture. Morillat declares he has "read in stories—," while Lamure responds "Of such restoring meates, / We have examples; Thousand examples."[74] The fact that Lamure's comments are an interjection to Morillat's sentence, amplifying the implied textual presence of cannibalism, creates the impression of a communal literary tradition of cannibal practices they intend to act on. As Parr has noted, audiences in the Blackfriars would undoubtedly have possessed "a sense of familiarity with the issues that a play about voyaging would be likely to raise, and an expectation that the standard *topoi* of 'colonial' writing—wilderness, promised land, cannibalism, gold hunger, savage customs—will be deployed to create a deft and topical entertainment."[75] Yet the degree to which the play uses the existence of these topoi to justify the practice of anthropophagy seems to blur the line between passive audience member and active character. The result is to emphasize the degree to which the difference between a lurid appreciation of and the enthusiastic practice of cannibalism is simply a product of material circumstance. The barren islands of the failed colonial project provide a space for activating a tradition that was not only widespread but to which the play itself was contributing.

## Conclusion

To a degree, *The Sea Voyage* can be seen as indicative of wider tendencies in the representation of cannibalism on the early modern stage. In the theatre of this period, cannibalism is a complex trope that operates as an uneasy combination of hunger and appetite. Whether as metaphorical image or as represented practice, the consumption of human flesh accrues connotations of both want and excess that give it a fundamental power as a way of conceptualizing processes of polarization in early modern society. However, in contrast to the vaguely moralistic and satirical dimension of cannibalism in the theatre more generally, Fletcher and Massinger bring a degree of specificity to their representation of cannibalism that more explicitly associates it with the structures and impulses of a specifically capitalist form of colonial expansion. In *The Sea Voyage,* cannibalism constitutes not simply a satirical portrayal of the flawed nature of colonial propaganda; it also manifests a fundamental unease about the nature of colonial expansion itself. The force that drives the colonists to attempt to kill, cook, and eat Aminta is not hunger alone but hunger in conjunction with appetites that, through the text's emphasis on her potential status as a delicacy and an object of colonial "sharing," are clearly presented as originating in the society the sailor-pirate-colonialists have come from. In conjunction with the text's wider emphasis on the fragility of European identity, this comic scene serves to raise the worrying prospect that frustrated imperial hopes could make manifest the troubling undercurrents in the colonizing society. Hunger makes possible the activation of the unnatural appetites that lurked within contemporary European civilization.

The play is also significant for its metatheatrical emphasis on the potential for cannibal stories to provide a model that audience members might actually act on. The result was a marked sense of complicity. The play foregrounds the extent to which its own success is reliant on satisfying the dramatic appetites that gave its characters a cannibalistic model to follow. This complex reaction to the colonial project is perhaps unsurprising. As is well attested, the King's Men were themselves a joint-stock company and the careers of its actors and playwrights, although notionally reliant on the support of their royal patron, were in practice fundamentally invested in London's emerging capitalist economy. It might be argued, therefore, that cannibalism provided a significant image for Fletcher and Massinger not just because of the horror it aroused but also because of the element of fascination it invariably generated. Cannibalism, at once repulsive and darkly attractive, provided a way to explore the playwrights'—and their audience's—anxious complicity with the capitalist appetites *The Sea Voyage* ostensibly condemned. Through its emphasis on the ambiguity of the dividing line between text and practice, *The Sea Voyage* insisted on the possibility that these appetites might exist within audience members.

CHAPTER 7

# Retelling the Legend of Sawney Bean

## Cannibalism in Eighteenth-Century England

JULIE GAMMON

The sensational and gruesome account of a murderous family of cannibals living in a Scottish cave has circulated in print, song, and drama for over the past 300 years.[1] Although the details of the many narratives differ slightly, the same common themes emerge: Sawney Bean was born near Edinburgh in the late sixteenth century to agricultural laborers. Being too idle and unwilling to work, he ran away with a woman of poor character to a deserted part of Galloway. They lived in a cave overlooking the sea for over twenty-five years without ever entering a town or village. They had eight sons and six daughters who, through incest, then produced eight grandsons and fourteen granddaughters. The Bean family survived by robbing travelers, then murdering them and removing their bodies to the cave, where they dismembered and pickled them. The Beans were thought to have been responsible for over 1,000 murders, and while they went undetected for years, it was claimed that many innocent local innkeepers were executed in the belief that they were responsible for the unexplained disappearances. The family was eventually caught when a young man managed to escape from the cave, but not before he witnessed his wife having her throat cut and the women drinking her blood while the men removed her entrails. King James VI of Scotland (who later became James I of England) was alerted to the survivor's bloody account and personally took 500 troops and bloodhounds to search the area until the cave was located. When the soldiers entered the cave, they saw how "such a number of arms, legs, thighs, hands and feet of men, women and children" were "hung up in rows like dry'd beef, and with a great many laying in pickle."[2] The family was captured and taken to Edinburgh, where they were executed twenty-four hours later without being tried. The executioners cut off the men's penises, then removed their arms and legs. They were left to bleed to death. They forced the female family members to watch and then they burned them at the stake.

Academic and popular interest in the story of Sawney Bean and his family has largely centered on trying to prove or disprove whether or not the family of cannibals ever really existed.[3] Even a recent publication by Blaine Pardoe, which claims to be the most fully researched account of the story, concentrates on mining the archives for evidence to find whether or not Bean was a real person.[4] Despite the fact that the Galloway tourist industry feeds off the fantastical story by offering tours of the supposedly genuine Sawney Bean cave and Bean continues to feature in several accounts of the worst Scottish criminals in history, the academic consensus now is that the story was fabricated.[5] There are no archival records relating to Bean, to mass disappearances of the Galloway population, to the supposed executions of innocent innkeepers, or to the involvement of King James VI. Louise Yeoman astutely points out that it is unlikely that James VI would not have recorded his involvement in the hunting and capture of a gang of cannibals responsible for many murders.[6]

While the story of Sawney Bean was sensational and shocking for eighteenth-century audiences, as a tale of cannibalism it was certainly not unique. Stories of cannibals were told to horrify, amuse, and entertain readers. A fascination with men (and women) eating men (and women) existed in the popular imagination not because people did not believe it possible but because they were confident that it did occur. Many accounts of anthropophagy associate the practice with exotic, uncivilized tribes; for example, tales from the New World described a practice linked to warfare or pagan religions. But the truth is, alongside these narratives there also existed accounts of cannibalism, both historically and contemporarily, that occurred much closer to home. This chapter will provide a wider context for the stories of cannibalism that circulated in England in the eighteenth century. First, it will demonstrate how the tale of Sawney Bean served a particular sociopolitical purpose by providing a convenient way to characterize the rebellious Scots as greedy, stupid, and brutish. The Sawney Bean narrative drew on a trope that linked Scottishness with cannibalism. Moreover, cannibalism was shown to have a direct association with gender disorder through its links to witchcraft and the disruption of the patriarchal family. Writers used tales of cannibalism to attack both individual and tribal or communal behaviors that lacked restraint and civility and used them to target groups of people (e.g., bailiffs and booksellers), regions (e.g., the Scottish Highlands, Ireland, Devon), and individuals. In addition, the figure of the cannibal provided an enduring and versatile metaphor in English culture for the detrimental effects of excessive greed in a rapidly developing society, and Sawney became a convenient shorthand for conveying this shift. The cannibal was not, therefore, an entirely alien figure but a form of bogeyman (or possibly bogeywoman) who could be located in a variety of settings as a comment on the levels of disorder in contemporary society.

■ ■ ■

The first known written accounts of Sawney Bean's crimes appeared in England in the early eighteenth century, over 120 years after they were alleged to have taken place. The earliest report of the story is hard to pinpoint. Captain Charles Johnson recounted the tale in *A General and True History of the Lives and Sections of the Most Famous Highwaymen, Murderers, Street-Robbers, &c.,* first published in London in 1734 and then again in Birmingham in 1742; most modern authors recognize this as the earliest published account.[7] Johnson himself cited other earlier texts as his "authority" on the story but, in keeping with contemporary publishing behavior, he provided no bibliographic details. A nineteenth-century author, John Nicolson, indicates that Johnson may have based his account on a chapbook from 1719, but this remains unverified.[8]

The appearance of the Sawney Bean story in England in the turbulent aftermath of the 1707 Act of Union between England and Scotland was no coincidence. The combination of economic conflicts and a rising Jacobite threat exacerbated an anti-Scot sentiment south of the border that was enhanced by a negative stereotype in print. Evidence can be found that tales of cannibalism were used to directly attack those involved in orchestrating the Act of Union between the English and the Scots. The reputation of the second Duke of Queensberry, the central Scottish supporter of the union, was severely damaged by a lurid tale that claimed that his "idiot" son had broken free from the rooms where he was kept locked in the house. He then supposedly seized and killed the kitchen boy, roasted him on a spit, and was found eagerly devouring him when the family returned from the signing of the act.[9] The horror associated with the image of human flesh being turned and roasted over a fire was directly analogous to the images of Amerindian cannibalism that had been reproduced on maps since the early sixteenth century.[10] Murray Pittock points out that narratives were already widespread in early modern England that associated the Scots with greed and opportunism due to the long history of conflict between the countries.[11] Many Englishmen had regarded the Act of Union with trepidation, viewing the Scots as "poor and pushy" neighbors.[12] It was believed that the Scots would demand access to rich English resources such as labor opportunities and economic trade yet would be unwilling to pay their full share of taxation. The famine in Scotland that had decimated the population during the 1690s (the mortality rate was estimated at between five and fifteen percent of the population, and twenty percent in the Highlands and upland areas) was regarded as a major precipitating factor for the Act of Union and the English were nervous about potentially high levels of immigration from north of the border.[13] The risk of disorder generated by the pro-Stuart uprisings that had been taking place in Scotland, Ireland, and Northern England since the Glorious Revolution of 1688 had produced a climate of fear in England. The discourse that represented the "savages or aborigines" from the Scottish Highlands as a threat to English security and prosperity continued into the 1830s.[14] The story of Sawney Bean developed into an eighteenth-century colonial fiction in which a narrative that confirmed the barbarity of the "other" (in this case, the Scot) was used as political propaganda to justify colonization and subordination. Bean's rapacious appetite for people served as a metaphor for the uncontrolled hunger of the Scots that needed to be tamed by the civilized English, a task that would arguably need to be accomplished with more urgency following the Act of Union.

Although the first records of the story emerged in the first half of the eighteenth century, it was not until the 1770s that the narrative became popular. Four undated pamphlets appear to have been published after 1764.[15] In addition, the story of Sawney Bean appeared in 1773, in the first edition of the *Newgate Calendar*, a compilation of stories of notorious criminals that had been circulating through the century. The first edition included condensed versions of criminal biographies, but although most of these were real, the calendar also included fictional stories if it was believed that the tale had a moral value for the reading audience. The publication of these numerous accounts of the tale of Sawney Bean coincided with a period of intensified Scotophobia in England. The legacy of the final Jacobite rising in 1745, during which Scots rebels had reached as far south as Derby before being crushed, still simmered in the English mind as a symbol of the disloyalty of Scots. In addition, in the early 1760s, the government of the deeply unpopular Scottish nobleman, the Earl of Bute (a favorite of George III), significantly reinforced perceptions of Scottish greed because of his heavy taxation policies.[16] His name, "John Stuart," also directly referenced the Jacobite rebels and kept their legacy alive. One of the most strident critics of Bute was John Wilkes, who began publishing the *North Briton* as a direct attack on the government and its policies. Wilkes summed up the ongoing English animosity toward the Scots:

> The restless and turbulent disposition of the Scottish nation before the union, with their constant attachment to France and declared enmity to England, their repeated perfidies and rebellions since that period, with their servile behavior in times of need, and overbearing insolence in power, have justly rendered the very name of Scot hateful to every true Englishman.[17]

Martyn Powell notes how there was a "plethora of anti-Scottish toasts, squibs, caricatures, effigy burnings and even physical violence" by the 1700s.[18] The circulation of accounts of Sawney Bean in England during the final decades of the eighteenth century contributed to this xenophobic discourse.

The *Oxford English Dictionary* dates the first use of the term "Sawney" as an abusive English term for a Scot to 1704, a date that highlights two key points. First, negative stereotypes of the Scots circulated in England prior to the Act of Union in 1707; and second, the choice of the invented cannibal's first name in the eighteenth-century crime pamphlets was deliberate.[19] By the eighteenth century, the name "Sawney" had become a shorthand term of abuse for a Scottish person in England, just as "Paddy" was for an Irish person in the nineteenth century. Evidence abounds that negative imagery of the Scots were produced throughout the eighteenth century.[20] The famous caricature "Sawney in the Boghouse" that was widely circulated in England after 1745 emphasized the supposed savagery and stupidity of the Scottish people. In the cartoon, the Scot is shown as incapable of understanding "modern" civilized society as he stands with his feet in two adjacent toilet pans and urinates on the floor. In many of these cartoons "Sawney" is dressed as a Highlander, drawing direct parallels with the images of Sawney Bean that were produced alongside the cheap broadside and chapbooks that repeated his story later in the century.

Printers gradually extended their representations of Sawney Bean to include other "uncivilized" Scotsmen more broadly. The same volume of *The Newgate Calendar* that contained the gruesome account of the deeds of Sawney Bean reported the crimes of "another" Scottish cannibal. Nicol Brown was executed in Edinburgh in 1754 for murdering his wife. Brown was hanged and gibbeted for the brutal act of holding his wife against the fire until she died after a long history of domestic violence. In addition to this horrific crime, the *Calendar* recounted how witnesses had also accused Brown of acts of cannibalism at his trial.[21] They claimed that they had watched a drunken Brown as he cut a piece of flesh off the leg of the body of a gibbeted felon, then cooked and ate it. It is interesting to note, however, that in the several accounts of Brown's trial and execution in the English press in 1754 and 1755, no mention is made of the incident of man-eating. Instead, his extreme cruelty toward his wife is the sole focus of these stories.[22] It was not until the 1780 version of the *Calendar* that any reference to the cooking and eating of human flesh appeared. The *Calendar*'s authors' embellishments of Brown's story (a practice they did in other cases) served to further emphasize the murderer's brutality. In so doing, they tapped into a contemporary interest in the cannibal that exemplified extreme violence while also highlighting an existing link between Scottishness and cannibalism.

Sawney Bean's story, in other words, was not unique or new; it was a representative example of print media that identified non-Englishmen with acts of cannibalism. Accounts of Scottish cannibal families living apart from the mainstream and committing brutal crimes featured in books written by Scottish and English historians before and during the early modern period. For example, *Holinshed's Chronicles,* published in the 1580s, told of a cannibal called Tristicloke (sometimes recorded as Christie o' the Cleek, using a variety of spellings) who lived in 1341 and stole and killed women and children to consume.[23] Likewise, the *History and Chronicles of Scotland,* published in the same decade as *Holinshed's Chronicles,* recounted the story of a cannibal in Angus in 1460. In this tale, readers learned of "a certain thief that with his family lived apart in a den . . . who would kill young persons and feed on their flesh."[24] An association between outlaw families and cannibalistic survival in Scotland thus predated the story of Sawney Bean, possibly indicating that the author of the original account drew on these earlier narratives from Scottish history. Eighteenth-century authors associated the ancient Celts with man-eating. One text claimed that the Attacotti were a tribe from Argyllshire who resorted to cannibalism until they were "civilized" by the Romans and enrolled in their army.[25] Authors from the early modern period onward thus constructed a narrative of the relationship between the Scots and man-eating at particular historical moments. An eighteenth-century audience likely saw the accounts of Sawney Bean as exemplifying such tales.

So far, this chapter has focused almost exclusively on narratives of Scottish male cannibalism that were disseminated in England. However, although the main protagonist in the story of Sawney Bean was a man, the significant role women played in the story is important in understanding perceptions of gender and cannibalism. Sawney's wife, daughters, and granddaughters are described as just as involved in the terrible crimes as the men. When the young couple was supposedly caught by the clan, the man watched the female family members cut his wife's throat before "falling to sucking her blood with as great a gust as if it had been wine." The women then "ripped up her belly and pulled out her entrails."[26] In eighteenth-century narratives, women were often accused of lacking self-control and giving in to greed. The Bean women's ravenous behavior horrifically exemplified the extremes of this sin.

In some accounts of the Sawney Bean narrative, the authors develop the role of Bean's wife in the story by giving her an identity. Interestingly, she is named "Black Agnes," a woman whose morals were supposedly as loose and disreputable as those of her husband. However, the use of this name for Sawney's wife also contributes to the theory that the tale was invented by the English to discredit the Scots. Black Agnes was the name given to a famous fourteenth-century Scottish heroine, Agnes, Countess of Dunbar, who in 1338 had successfully defended Dunbar Castle against the English after enduring a ten-year siege.[27] For an eighteenth- and nineteenth-century audience, however, the name Black Agnes was no longer associated with an act of extreme female valor. Instead, it was linked to extraordinary forms of disorder as Black Agnes became associated primarily with the figure of Sawney Bean. All the members of the Bean clan were depicted as "enemies of mankind," but in the accounts of their punishments, the female family members were treated differently. Whereas the men were dismembered and left to bleed to death, the women were forced to watch this take place before they were then all burned at the stake, a punishment usually reserved for heresy or treason. Through their violation of patriarchal norms, the female cannibals represented a different threat to the social order than the male offenders did.

The characters of Sawney Bean and his family exemplified the stereotype of the cannibal as symbolizing a lack of civility. The vitriolic anti-Scottish narrative that led to the construction and dissemination of these stories is evident from the context in which the stories circulated. For centuries, the Highland Scots had been depicted in England as comical, alien, and dangerous. The Elizabethan theatre had emphasized this negative stereotype with Shakespeare's *Macbeth* (1606), perceived by audiences as one of the most anti-Scottish representations. By the eighteenth century, specific political tensions increased the association of the Scots with ignorance and superstition. However, it is important to note how other representations of cannibalism in eighteenth-century England had an important currency in emphasizing forms of immorality and barbarity that went beyond the tensions that existed around the creation of Great Britain.

■ ■ ■

On rare occasions, the British public was brought into direct contact with supposedly "real" exotic cannibals. These incidents both provided amusing stories for the reading public and promoted a sense of fear and otherness. In 1701, the *English Post* reported on the public curiosity surrounding a monstrous giant from "the Indies" who had been brought to London by a ship's captain and sold as a freak-show exhibit. The paper stated that it was "reported that he was a cannibal or man eater," but this information was disclosed only to justify the sailors' fears in approaching the giant, who was said to be sixteen feet tall and covered in hair. The article focused on amusing its readers by reporting that the sailors had given the giant a cask of wine to drink that it downed in one go, then fell over drunk. This was what had enabled them to move him from the ship to the shore.[28] The "actual" cannibal therefore was depicted as a monstrous figure who presented little threat once he was removed from his natural habitat (similar to the character in "Sawney in the Boghouse"). If the giant man-eater had been loose in the hostile terrain of the Indies, he would have been perceived as foreign and dangerous to travelers, but brought to England he became an unthreatening, exotic exhibit. More common than the focus on the "ridiculous" nature of this figure, however, was the tendency of writers to draw parallels between the behavior of foreign tribes that were known to resort to cannibalism and the barbarous nature of groups closer to home.

The otherness of the "Celtic fringe" and its association with cannibalism was a feature of early modern English narratives. Some analyses of the Sawney Bean story have pointed to a similarity between this and the tales that circulated in early modern England of cannibalism committed by the indigenous populations of the new colonies. Fiona Black argues that the remote Scottish Highlands were part of a "shared space" with the newly colonized lands in the minds of the English.[29] As the home of the majority of witchcraft trials in the early modern British Isles, Scotland had become associated with magic, superstition, and devil worship.[30] Storytellers compared the isolated and hostile terrain in which Sawney's cave was thought to be located to the imagined landscapes of the new worlds. English audiences perceived the inhospitable and impenetrable geography and culture of the Highlands as alien. Early eighteenth-century newspaper reports doubted the abilities of the English to civilize foreign tribes. An anonymous author in the *British Journal* in 1724 bemoaned the Iroquois practice of fathers teaching their sons that killing and eating their enemies was a source of pride and honor because this tutelage meant that cruelty was a habit that was passed down from generation to generation.[31] The writer also criticized the savagery of Peru, where women from enemy tribes would be captured and forced to bear children that the captors would then eat. Once the enslaved women from other tribes had passed child-bearing age, the captors would eat them too. Such negative commentary questioned the moral values and concepts of family that applied in these contexts in much the same way that the incestuous nature of the Bean clan provoked outrage. The implication is that travelers' stories of exotic tribes who practiced cannibalism were refashioned into a form that could be used to construct the image of the savage within the British mainland. By extension, aspects of the story of Sawney Bean could be transposed onto other societies the English sought to establish their superiority over.

The English also defined the Irish as "savage" and thus also violent, greedy, and lacking in intelligence. Following the Irish rebellion of 1641, reports of Catholic barbarities circulated in both official and popular discourse as justifications for Thomas Cromwell's colonial program. Peter Hill gave a deposition to Parliament in 1643 that stated that "since the Rebellion began, but especially for a year and above now last past, it hath been a very common and ordinary thing for the Irish to murther and devoure and eate the persons of such English as they could light upon, and when they could light upon none of them, then to kill, devoure and eat one another."[32] Such stories survived in popular myth and surfaced again later in the seventeenth century and after.[33] Jonathan Swift's famous satirical piece *A Modest Proposal* (1729) drew mockingly on the links between Irishness and cannibalism by indicating that a proportion of Irish babies should be sold to rich men and women to be consumed as a way of controlling population levels and combating poverty among the Irish peasantry.[34] Swift's implication was that, given the repressive English policies toward Ireland that had resulted in the rise of starving beggars, the tradition of the Irish as "baby-eaters" could be of significant socioeconomic value. The participation of women in acts of cannibalism added another level of horror for contemporary audiences. Irish women in particular were criticized during and after the rebellion for eating children. Clodagh Tait notes that in one part of Ireland, it was claimed that a number of old women had been executed in the eighteenth century for the crime of eating children.[35] Reports of the savage and bloodthirsty Irish resorting to man-eating continued. In 1798, the *Times* reported that after a rebellion at Wexford, "if the rebels did not eat the flesh of the loyalists, in the thirst of cannibals they licked their blood."[36] During the Seven Years' War (1754–1763), the British drew direct comparisons between the French and Indians, regarding the allied groups as equally brutal and bloodthirsty.[37] During the French Revolution, frequent accusations of cannibalism were levied at the savage mob from the 1780s onward, and by the nineteenth century, Napoleon was presented in British nursery rhymes as a child-eating bogeyman.[38] In the early 1700s, accusations and representations of cannibalism suggested the savagery—defined in various ways—of non-English Scots, Irish, and Celts, among others. By the late eighteenth and early nineteenth centuries, associating other societies with cannibalistic practices had become a way for the English to emphasize the superiority of the British Empire.

That said, there were circumstances where writers acknowledged that the English themselves could and did engage in forms of cannibalism. Early modern writers recognized that eating people because of desperation and starvation, although an abhorrent practice, occurred in extreme situations. In the early seventeenth century, rumors abounded in England that the Jamestown settlers had practiced cannibalism during the Starving Time of 1609–1610. Even though the Virginia Company rejected these claims, narratives of cannibalism that circulated in England, which had previously accused only the Indians of such practices, recognized that even Englishmen could be driven to such horrific practices. Likewise, accounts of starvation cannibalism among sailors and the shipwrecked was a common theme of popular literature.[39] Such texts showed that even when those in dire circumstances were rescued before they were driven to eating each other, discussions might take place over who should be eaten and when, as though this were a rational, if somewhat shocking, reaction to starvation.

Accusations that English people could turn to cannibalism were not restricted to events overseas. In Renaissance Europe, narratives of witchcraft frequently associated witches with eating infants or body parts at the witches' sabbaths. Such accounts also traveled to England, most famously in the Lancashire witch trials of 1612, where a fourteen-year-old girl testified that she had witnessed the accused women boil and roast small children before consuming them.[40] A wider context to these accounts can perhaps also be inferred from the stories that spread in England in the several years leading up to the witch trials that acts of cannibalism had taken place in the American colonies during the Starving Time. The key involvement of women in food preparation and cooking seemed to present ideal opportunities to consume human remains. During the English Civil Wars, both sides of the conflict spread propaganda that attacked prominent figures by claiming that they were known to eat human flesh. Graphic satires from the 1640s claimed that Archbishop William Laud feasted on the ears of his enemies and that royalist officer Sir Thomas Lunsford devoured children.[41] Brutal stories from the Thirty Years' War in early seventeenth-century Germany were reshaped into English accounts that could be used to target enemies in the Civil Wars as cannibals. This provided a useful precedent for the later creation of the Sawney Bean narrative, whose original author likely drew heavily on both historic and exotic accounts of anthropophagy. As Mark Stoyle has indicated, although the stories from the Civil Wars were treated with skepticism, they continued to circulate in print for hundreds of years. In the case of Thomas Lunsford, such stories shaped his legacy in the popular imagination as a "bogeyman."[42] The British cannibal (real or imagined), therefore, became a figure to be both feared and despised, for both his excessive behavior and his lack of civility mirrored practices in other "primitive" societies.

Concepts of anthropophagy in the eighteenth century acknowledged that cannibalism could be driven by either the techniques of warfare (exocannibalism) or by famine or hunger (starvation cannibalism). Tales of these types of cannibalism accounted for many of the reports in the contemporary press. Less understandable, however, were acts of individual cannibalism in Europe, especially England. Reports in eighteenth-century English newspapers referenced European cases of criminal cannibals. In 1772, a number of sources reported on the execution of a man in Germany who had confessed to killing several young lads "for no other reason but to gratify his unnatural and inhuman passion for eating human flesh."[43] The following decade the shocking story arrived from Hungary of the execution of forty-five cannibals and 150 others who were still in prison. The reporter wrote with horror of the decision of the emperor, who did not believe such men could be cannibals, and who planned to establish a commission "to examine the proceedings against them." These (all male) cannibals, it was asserted, killed their pregnant wives in order to eat their unborn babies or murdered and devoured their mothers and fathers.[44] In 1866, Dr. R. S. Charnock, an anthropologist, concluded that "it would doubtless be going too far to assert that in modern times any European nation or tribe has been addicted to cannibalism," yet "many solitary cases have however occurred in different parts of Europe."[45] Charnock explicitly rejected the idea that cannibalism could occur in civilized nations as an embedded cultural practice. Instead, acts of man-eating needed to be understood as behavior that was caused by criminality or insanity and was restricted to individual actions.

Such beliefs were not new in the nineteenth century. Reports in the eighteenth-century press of "home-grown" cannibals attributed such behavior to lunacy. Stories of men eating living (or dead) cats and dogs led to the perpetrators being described as cannibals. Although this was not cannibalism, the writers' disgust reflected an eighteenth-century dietary taboo whereby cats and dogs were seen as representative of their masters and mistresses, which meant that eating them would be deemed "akin to cannibalism."[46] The conduct of the men who consumed cats was explained away in reports as the result of either drunkenness or a ridiculous bet, but Robert Darnton's seminal text has skillfully indicated how such behavior could be interpreted as a more significant form of social protest.[47] Reports of the consumption of body parts of executed criminals (possibly for medicinal purposes) were also common in eighteenth-century folklore.[48] In 1746, the *London Evening Post* reported that a man had removed the liver of a criminal who had been executed in London, broiled it, and devoured it. The article questioned whether the man was trying to be like a cannibal or whether he had acted out of contempt for the criminal or for the sentence that had been imposed against him. The journalist expressed how "the inhabitants are much displeased by both his banquet and taste" to emphasize the popular horror and condemnation of such behavior.[49]

Although purportedly factual accounts of English cannibals were rare in the eighteenth century, popular literature demonstrates a level of public fascination with the threat of humans eating other humans. One notorious early eighteenth-century ballad exemplified such fears. It centered on the figure of an evil stepmother who murdered her stepdaughter because of jealousy and greed and then served her remains to her natural father by hiding them in his dinner.[50] Although in this instance, the woman involved was not actually the cannibal, she facilitated an act of cannibalism. In the nineteenth century, the cannibal facilitator became a significant figure in popular culture as Mrs. Lovett the piemaker in the story of Sweeney Todd.[51] A pamphlet published in the 1720s told a horrific story of human cannibals who had been discovered living on the outskirts of London. The sensational tale claimed these people had converted human bones into household implements and that they had large boiling cauldrons of human remains.[52] The publication of spurious tales and extreme incidents reminded a reading and listening public that acts of cannibalism could—and did—occur anywhere.

Often the term "cannibal" was used in the eighteenth-century press as shorthand for excessive greed and depravity and the impact of these failures on others rather than as a direct reference to the consumption of human flesh. For example, bankers were often labeled as cannibals. In the aftermath of the collapse of the South Sea Bubble, those who prospered from the misfortunes of others, such as the "Lombard Street Cannibal," were vilified by a reporter who noted that it was hoped that up to 30,000 pounds might be retrieved from him for distribution to those who had lost so much.[53] Bailiffs were also commonly targeted in newspapers; *Applebee's Weekly Journal* commented that as many as six bailiffs were being held in custody in London after their excessive behavior had led to the deaths of people from whom they had retrieved money and goods. Interestingly, the report does not use the word "murderers" to describe the bailiffs; it describes them as cannibals.[54] In these cases, the word "cannibal" was used as a synonym for those who were thought to be greedy and to prey on human misery. Cannibalistic behavior, therefore, was not just something foreign; it also represented a threat to civilized society.

British cannibals shared similarities with their more exotic counterparts due to their "tribal" behavior. In a letter to the *Weekly Journal* in 1727, one author complained about the "Cannibal Tribe of Booksellers" that made it impossible for him to make a living from getting his work published.[55] Disorderly behavior from those lower down the social scale was also frequently compared to the conduct of cannibals. The smuggling and wrecking gangs that operated in coastal communities were negatively portrayed for their "cannibal cruelty so scandalous to human nature."[56] In eighteenth-century England, man-eating had an equivalent in the greed displayed by particular groups in the population who figuratively "picked over the bones" of others who had experienced misfortune and tragedy.

■ ■ ■

No other accounts of cannibalism attracted the level of public interest in England that the story of Sawney Bean achieved. Although we cannot ascertain how many people read the tale in the eighteenth century, the survival of the story and its transmission in different forms beyond the century are testament to its popular appeal. This final section examines the retelling of the Sawney Bean legend in the eighteenth century in different contexts to indicate how a narrative of cannibalism could be used for different purposes. The cultural resonance of the tale of Scottish cannibalism crossed the Atlantic in the late eighteenth century, according to Daniel Mandell. He has explored how references to "Sawney" in a vicious broadsheet published in southern New England in the 1790s that aimed at Native Americans in the region used the word "Sawney" so the readership would automatically associate Native Americans with the criminal, incestuous behavior of the Scot Sawney Bean.[57] In addition, Pittock points to the direct parallels that were drawn between Sawney's stupidity in "Sawney in the Boghouse" and perceptions of Africans during the colonial era as too "uncivilized" to use the lavatory.[58] Although the story of Sawney may have originally been informed by early modern narratives of cannibalism in the New World, by the late eighteenth century it had become a useful analogy for any community the English perceived as backward-looking, ignorant, and potentially dangerous.

However, for an eighteenth-century audience, the familiar tone of the story of Sawney Bean made the idea of the home-grown cannibal appear dangerous. The versatility of accusations of cannibalism as a means of constructing "bogeymen" or marginal groups is further evidenced by the reissuing of the story of Sawney Bean with different protagonists in the later eighteenth century. A chapbook produced in 1789 told a tale that sounds strikingly familiar to the one that opens this chapter, this time about John Gregg and his family of Clovelly, Devon. Gregg ran away from his agricultural laborer parents with a woman of ill character and they lived in a cave on the seashore for over twenty-five years without entering any town or village. They had eight sons, six daughters, eighteen grandsons, and fourteen granddaughters, "begotten in incest." They robbed and murdered over 1,000 people and ate their bodies to survive. The chapbook is virtually identical to the Sawney Bean story; only the dates, names and locations have been changed. Again, there is no evidence from other records that John Gregg ever existed. A local historian of Devon has suggested that the story was published by the lord of the manor, who was running a smuggling gang and wanted to keep travelers away from the area, but this is disputed by Ian Maxted, who claims that printers looking to capitalize on popular interest in sensational crime stories often produced fake histories such as this one.[59]

Only a few years later, at the turn of the nineteenth century, another account of a tribe of Devonshire cannibals surfaced in a pamphlet. The story of John M'Claud also largely plagiarizes the Sawney Bean tale, although it does not include the claims of incest in the Gregg and Bean accounts to explain the growth in size of the cannibal gang. This story instead describes them just as formed of a "company of profligates." The M'Claud tale takes place near Exeter in Devon, even though it uses a noticeably Scottish name for the cannibal.[60] The work that told the tale of John M'Claud included a report of a Hungarian cannibal (Joseph Franks) who had recently been caught and executed as part of a gang. The short narrative on Franks provides little detail other than the remoteness of the location where the gang were operating.[61] So far scholars can only speculate about why the focus shifts to Devon in these later cannibal narratives. Local concerns about high crime rates (and a correspondingly high rate of executions) may have generated fears regarding a "crime wave" that pointed to levels of social disorder that purportedly were comparable only with those of London.[62] Smuggling was seen as out of control along the Devon coast, where authorities were ill-equipped to deal with the scale of the problem.[63] The savagery and lawlessness of the Devonians was becoming legendary, and smugglers in particular were perceived as greedy because they avoided paying taxes and pursued wealth through illegal means. The universalism of the Sawney Bean story as a shocking tale of incestuous sex, murder, and man-eating meant that it had the potential to be transposed to any remote coastal area that could be perceived as "uncivilized," and this applied both within Great Britain and in the wider world.

Blaine Pardoe suggests that the publication of the Gregg and M'Claud texts in Scotland may have been published as retaliation for the perceived anti-Scottishness of the Sawney Bean tale, but he acknowledges that there is little evidence to substantiate this. Indeed, there is no evidence that the story of Sawney Bean circulated in print in Scotland until the nineteenth century.[64] However, *Harlequin Highlander; or, Sawney Bean's Cave* was performed as one of the four grand spectacles that appeared at the Edinburgh circus from 1790 to 1800. Kim Baston notes that although the production originated at the Royal Circus in London, English performers traveled to Edinburgh to present Scottish "history" to a Scottish audience. The spectacle included equestrian performances, acrobatics, songs, music, and a loose storyline. Books of the song lyrics were available for purchase at the time of the productions.[65] *Sawney Bean's Cave* opened with the principal character, the "Harlequin Highlander," being confronted by Sawney, a band of robbers, and three "old hags" (drawing a direct link with the witches in *Macbeth*), who gave the Highlander the choice of joining the robbers or dying. Although the cannibal narrative is not explicit in the play, the chained skeletons of murdered travelers located around the cave inferred a link to the earlier accounts of Sawney's crimes with which the audience appeared to have had some familiarity. This production may well have appealed to an Edinburgh "lowland" audience that probably shared many of the prejudices about their Highland neighbors that circulated in England.

It must be remembered that the majority (if not all) of the cannibal episodes that feature in this chapter were not "real." There is no evidence that Sawney Bean, John Gregg, Sir Thomas Lunsford, or Nicol Brown ever existed or if they did, that they ever actually engaged in man-eating. Instead, the popularization of fictitious accounts points to a public appetite for characterizing forms of unruly behavior in the most extreme terms. This undoubtedly intensified in the later eighteenth century as travelers' tales from the New World, accounts of shipwreck starvation, and the horrors of revolutionary France fed into the public imagination. The republishing of Sawney Bean's story in different forms and plagiarizations of the tale in pamphlets about John Gregg and John M'Claud in the final two decades of the eighteenth century was no coincidence; publishers recognized the appeal of such tales and their utility for attacking certain forms of behavior. Tales of the exotic savage who resorted to cannibalism could be translated into a moral warning about untamed greed much closer to home.

CHAPTER 8

# Honor Eating

## Frank Lestringant, Michel de Montaigne, and the Physics of Symbolic Exchange

ROBERT APPELBAUM

At first glance, Frank Lestringant's *Cannibals* (first published in French in 1994) appears to belong to the tradition of what Michel de Certeau called "heterology," or the study of writing about "the Other."[1] Lestringant's text takes the reader from the origin of the idea of New World cannibalism in the journals of Christopher Columbus to the mid-nineteenth-century perspectives of writers such as Jules Verne and Gustav Flaubert. Central to Lestringant's study, as it is to de Certeau's, is Montaigne's essay "Of the Cannibals," in which, according to de Certeau, a key instability lies in the use of the words "savage," "barbarian," and "barbaric" and the so-called Other is always at arm's length, a figure of indeterminacy. But Lestringant's study is not a heterology. It is rather a literary history of a fantasy or, to put it another way, the history of heterology itself, where the key theme is the degradation of the fantastic idea of the cannibal in French literature. At first the trope of a challenging natural nobility, imagined as embodied in the light-skinned and worthy nations of South America, the cannibal eventually becomes a pathetic, animalistic, slavish being, barely articulate, embodied in the dark-skinned captives originally hailing from sub-Saharan Africa, forced into cannibalism by economic necessity. As the idea of the cannibal degrades in Western literature, so a degradation in the West itself becomes apparent, according to Lestringant, when European countries come to dominate the world order, aided by convenient attitudes of racial superiority and a smug faith in the idea of progress. But a subsidiary idea also comes to the fore: when cannibalism becomes imagined as a characteristic of desperate peoples, it also becomes imagined as a desperate measure to which the most civilized of people might revert because it signifies the ghastly primitive impulse of life itself, from whose power no one is immune.

There is an important omission in Lestringant's work: the concept of the Noble Savage. The Noble Savage survived in Western mythology in a way that the Noble Cannibal did not.[2] The story of American Indians was largely behind it. Here is what Benjamin Franklin wrote on behalf of Native Americans in an essay published in 1784:

> Savages we call them, because their manners differ from ours, which we think the Perfection of Civility; they think the same of theirs. . . . Perhaps, if we could examine the Manners of different Nations with Impartiality, we should find no People so rude, as to be without any Rules of Politeness; nor any so polite, as not to have some. . . .
>
> Having few artificial Wants, they [Indians] have abundance of Leisure for Improvement by Conversation. Our laborious Manner of Life, compared with theirs, they esteem slavish and base; and the Learning, on which we value ourselves, they regard as frivolous and useless.[3]

Franklin's idea of Native Americans impacted countless literary adventure stories, for example James Fennimore Cooper's *The Last of the Mohicans* (1826), westerns in print and on the screen, and science fiction in print and on the screen. In many *Star Trek* episodes, crews encounter noble primitives and in *Star Trek: The Next Generation,* the enemy Klingons are refashioned into a noble warrior race. The 2010 Oscar nominee and blockbuster *Avatar* is essentially a noble savage story. In France, some of the writings of Diderot can be said to foster the myth of the Noble Savage, especially his *Supplément au Voyage de Bougainville* (1772). And among the great anthropologists of the twentieth century, Claude Lévi-Strauss can be seen staring the myth in the face in *Triste Tropiques* and arguing that it is not so mythic. He observes that "contemporary anthropology supports the theses of the eighteenth-century *philosophes.*"[4]

But Lestringant insists on ignoring this strand of thought. Anthropophagy and the cannibal, noble or degenerate, real or imagined, is his theme. The loss of respect for the noble eater of human flesh, according to Lestringant, is something to be lamented. It leaves us, at least until the time of the development of modern anthropology, with a horrible decadence. Lestringant chooses his evidence selectively; after 1700, he tactically chooses texts to support his thesis about decadence, ignoring counter-examples he sometimes feels compelled to acknowledge (like Diderot's work) and he ends his analysis uncertainly.

I nevertheless draw attention to Lestringant's text because despite some faults, two decades after its original publication in French it is still thought provoking and is still a model work of literary and intellectual history. Unlike other scholars of his time, Lestringant does not decry early moderns for their stigmatization of Native Americans as cannibals. On the contrary, he applauds them for having found a way of dignifying the natives. But Lestringant is not a cannibalism skeptic. He accepts that ritual cannibalism was probably an abiding feature of American life.[5] When Lestringant traces how the idea of the cannibal developed in the sixteenth century and then degenerated in subsequent eras, he finds plenty of mythopoesis and plenty of often-comical error in descriptions of foreign cannibals from the very beginning, but he does not dismiss them as pernicious delusions for that reason. Instead, he finds a worthy imaginary construction in which the cannibal becomes "both foil and bogeyman, by turns an immoveable enemy and—more frightening still—an alter ego."[6] The cannibal becomes that which cannot be absorbed into European writing; he (and it is usually he) is too dangerous.

I also draw attention to this text because I wish to experiment with an idea that is implicit in Lestringant's work: the idea of symbolic exchange. In early representations the cannibal is often shown to be engaged in a form of it. For Lestringant, this is one of the main reasons why the cannibal can be respected. I see this notion implicitly at work in his analysis, but I also adopt it from my reading of theorists such as Georges Bataille, Jean Baudrillard, René Girard, and Jacques Derrida and from anthropological studies of gift giving and sacrifice. Cannibalism is potentially a model of symbolic exchange. As he reads through writers such as André Thevet, Jean de Léry, and Montaigne and then goes on to eighteenth- and nineteenth-century writers, Lestringant repeatedly raises the prospect of symbolic exchange. Lestringant asks this question: Regardless of whether cannibalism exists among primitive peoples or if it exists in the mind of Europeans, reporting on what they take to be cannibalistic behavior, what purposes does it serve? The answer yields a fundamental distinction: on the one hand is cannibalism undertaken to satisfy a hunger for human flesh, a bare if horrifying need, exacerbated by conditions of scarcity; on the other is cannibalism undertaken to serve a ritualistic and moral purpose—in other words, a response to a demand for symbolic satisfaction under conditions of material abundance. Cannibalism may have a use value in some instances, but cannibalism may also have an exchange value, and this exchange value may have nothing at all to do with use.

Of course, I am using the words cannibals and cannibalism as if they were universal categories. But it is one of the strengths of Lestringant's work that it shows how the terms shift over time and space to indicate different categories of referents. At first, they might be dog-headed men inhabiting islands in the Caribbean who eat human flesh without ceremony. But in French writing, soon enough, they lose all reference to ancient myths, they become people who look pretty much like Europeans, and they are moved from the Caribbean to Brazil and other parts of mainland America. For the most part (there are exceptions), these continentals are held to practice a cannibalism of symbolic exchange in which instead of greed for flesh, ritual requirements are the motive. But eventually, cannibals, no longer Americans, are found in other parts of the world and turn dark. They become figures of isolation. They are held to live on islands or in the isolated regions of deepest Africa. And they are incapable of symbolic exchange because they live in poverty, with few resources or technologies, little language, and no leisure to engage in a healthy symbolic life. They represent pre-civilized Malthusian man as a kind of beast, so delivered over to his needs that he is capable of eating away at the survival of his own species. Putting him on remote islands or in Africa (where in fact there is little if any record of actual cannibalism) writers indulge themselves in the racism of the conqueror.

Anthropology, again, would rescue the cannibal from such disrepute, according to Lestringant. But he doesn't say how, when, or why. The book ends abruptly. We are left face to face with the ambivalent complacency of Jules Verne and the dismissive nihilism of Gustave Flaubert, who once described supposed cannibals he had seen at a sideshow in his native Rouen as near-animals, "uttering inarticulate cries" and "crouching like monkeys around a cookpot."[7]

An excellent supplement to Lestringant's analysis is Jennifer Brown's *Cannibalism in Literature and Film,* which begins its analysis with the eighteenth century and finishes with the present.[8] Taking up where Lestringant leaves off (and focusing on English-language rather than French texts) she documents what became the future of cannibalism in art. But Brown's book is another heterology: another study showing how the motif of cannibalism is a writing of "the Other." No doubt she is right, since that is what documents about cannibalism almost always do (I don't know of any authentic autobiographies written by cannibals). But Lestringant's analysis poses another challenge. The challenge is especially clear in his analysis of Montaigne's "Of the Cannibals," which is the most important chapter of his book. Before Montaigne, thinking is clumsy; after Montaigne, degradation sets in; but in Montaigne a climax comes, where the cannibals are at their best and Western observers are at their worst. And being at their best means showing themselves as people who engage in what I call honor eating—that is, using a biological function to transcend biology and enter into a timocratic system of symbolic exchange.

That is not, of course, how Montaigne would put it, or even Lestringant. But the concept is operative in both the sixteenth-century essayist and the twentieth-century literary historian. Commercial exchange was much on Montaigne's mind, as Philippe Desan has shown.[9] It is less on Lestringant's mind, although he acknowledges the work of Desan and others, but it is implicit even in the basic distinction his thesis relies on between the free-willed cannibalism of Renaissance Brazilians and the cannibalism by constraint of modern sub-Saharan Africans.[10]

The most famous achievement of Montaigne's essay is not that it distinguishes Brazilians from other primitives but that it uses the model of Brazilian cannibals to rebuke the history of Western culture. The rebuke is well known but bears repeating. "What we actually see in these nations," writes Montaigne—who usually refers to the cannibals as "these nations"—"surpasses not only all the pictures in which the poets have idealized the golden age, and all their inventions in imagining a happy state of man, but all the conceptions and the very desire of philosophy itself."[11] If Plato had known about those nations, Montaigne implies, he would have revised even the wishes of philosophy—and hence, the history of philosophy. This is a rebuke against *thought* and *desire,* based on empirical observation: "what we see," in this case a people who organize themselves and thrive according to natural impulses without the input of art or artifice or even law. That in itself implies a critique both of the past and of contemporary Europe.

It may be hard for a modern reader to follow Montaigne's next step of appreciation, but it is necessary if his picture of anthropophagy and its symbolic dimensions is to be understood. "They have their wars with the nations beyond the mountains, further inland," writes Montaigne. That does not bother the Frenchmen, though. Montaigne considers war an inevitable "disease" resulting from the character of human society, so he does not condemn the cannibals for being perpetually enmeshed in it, especially seeing that they handle war so well.[12] "It is astonishing what firmness they show in their combats, which never end but in slaughter and bloodshed; for as to routs and terror, they know nothing of either."[13] When the Brazilians fight, they go all out. There is no cowardice or strategic duplicity in their wars; they don't ambush, they attack. Brazilians never retreat, scatter, or give chase. They stay until the war making is finished, and this, in Montaigne's mind, is as honorable as it is astonishing. It is part of Montaigne's ethics of war that, when it is fought out of necessity (and if necessity is not the motive for war, then Montaigne is against it), it should be *fought,* without sly maneuvers, trickery, or care for mercenary advantage.[14] War should be war: not a game, not an exhibition, not a land grab, and not a commercial enterprise. In all these respects Montaigne thinks the Tupinamba worthy. They are a timocratic society not only in name but also in practice.

Yet then of course comes anthropophagy:

> After they have treated their prisoners well for a long time with all the hospitality they can think of, each man who has a prisoner

> calls a great assembly of his acquaintances. He ties a rope to one of the prisoner's arms, by the end of which he holds him, a few steps away, for fear of being hurt, and he gives his dearest friend the other arm to hold after the same way; and these two, in the presence of the whole assembly, kill him with their swords. This done they roast him and eat him in common and send some pieces to their absent friends. This is not, as people think, for nourishment, as of old the Scythians used to do; it is to betoken extreme revenge.[15]

The reference to the Scythians is something Lestringant has anticipated: in the mythology of anthropophagy, if any cannibal is to be celebrated for having noble motives, then another sort of cannibal is usually referred to who has base motives, mere fierceness of need. Scythians, or a people who live just beyond Scythian territories, are legendary choices.

But then comes the critique of European modernity. After complaining about how the Portuguese cruelly execute their prisoners, making them suffer as they die, Montaigne talks about economic exploitation, religious persecution, and the ongoing civil wars in his own country:

> I am not sorry that we notice the barbarous horror of such acts, but I am heartily sorry that, judging their faults rightly, we should be so blind to our own. I think there is more barbarity in eating a man alive than in eating him dead; and in tearing by tortures and the rack a body still full of feeling, in roasting a man bit by bit, in having him bitten and mangled by dogs and swine (as we have not only read, but seen within fresh memory, not among ancient enemies, but among neighbors and fellow citizens, and what is worse, on the pretext of piety and religion), than in roasting and eating him after he is dead.[16]

So here are three distinctions: at one extreme, the Scythians who are cruel because of need; at the other extreme, the Europcans, who are cruel because of an excess of greed, hatred, and religious hypocrisy; and in the middle, the kind moderation of the Brazilians. Only the Brazilians practice anthropophagy, however barbarously, within a closed, self-moderating system of honor eating.

Lestringant argues that Montaigne is able to put cannibalism in this middle region of what I am calling honor eating because of a doubly pertinent context. The Brazilians' actions seem to be justifiable because their warrior ethics mirror the ideal warrior ethics of feudal Europe: the cannibals fight for honor, they punish for honor. There is nothing they *want* from one another, either greedily or sadistically, in the sense of a use value except honor and its ally, revenge. The rituals of vengeance, which include adopting the foreign warrior into one's own nation, possibly giving him a wife and allowing him to procreate, and, in the end, almost certainly allowing him to stand up and express defiance even as he is being prepared for execution and consumption, keep the cannibal practice within the realm of what is actually thus a form of moderate uselessness, even if it can also be characterized as extreme. Unlike less-impressive savages, the Brazilians are not really hungry for flesh, and unlike Europeans, they are not hungry for land, money, or spite. All they want is honor, and they are eager to use violence to achieve it.

But Lestringant also argues that the Brazilians' cannibalism seems to be justifiable because it is a form of sacrifice; it reminds the European of the Eucharist, which has cannibalistic overtones.[17] Europeans during the lifetime of Montaigne were of course fiercely debating the Eucharist, even in Brazil, but at the very least, if the Brazilians revered the sacrificial body of their victims even a little, they were little different from Catholics who partook of the body and blood of their Savior weekly.[18] In Tupinamba rituals, in this reading, the warrior about to be eaten actively sacrifices himself, gives himself up for a common good. This surrender is admirable; it is proof of natural nobility. By partaking of the flesh of the executed enemy-hero, the Brazilians partake of his brave spirit. The ritual encourages this doubly significant sacrifice, giving both the killers and eaters of flesh something to take pride in.

The theory of symbolic exchange somewhat complicates the matter, however, in view of both the honor in honor eating and the sacrifice in the honor of being eaten. The theory of symbolic exchange, as developed in both anthropology and social philosophy, rests on distinctions between material use value and signifying exchange value, where exchanges of both kinds signal equivalences and reciprocities.

To a degree, this distinction jibes with Montaigne's analysis, particularly in his favoring of exchange over use.[19] Scythians use other humans for food, Europeans use other humans for self-aggrandizement, but the Tupinamba don't *use* other humans at all; they engage in a ritual with them and against them. To the extent that symbolic exchange is not an exchange of useful commodities but is rather a circulation of social values, the Brazilians are perfect merchants of meaning. And yet the Tupinamba *use each other up*. The distinction between use and exchange is unstable in this respect. "I don't use my enemy," the noble cannibal might say, "but I use him up. I don't eat him out of hunger, but I eat him." And where is the difference? To this Montaigne (and Lestringant) might reply that if the Tupinamba use each other up, they do so, both victimizers and victims, *voluntarily*, in the interest of honor. In other words, honor eating takes place in response to honorable self-sacrifice, and the type of symbolic exchange in which the Brazilians engage is really a form of sacrifice. But this idea too has its problems. How do I give myself up if in the first instance I have to be forcibly *taken*?

Let us think a little more about symbolic exchange. The idea gains special prominence in two key works by Jean Baudrillard, *The Mirror of Production* and *Symbolic Exchange and Death*. Baudrillard is arguing against the economistic prejudices of traditional Marxism, where "production" (placed in inverted commas here, since it is for Marxists a term of art) is held to be the governing principle of all human society. In *Symbolic Exchange and Death*, Baudrillard proposed that late twentieth-century Western society had entered a postproduction stage, the era of the simulacrum, of postmodern replication.[20] He applied notions of symbolic exchange (and death) to the virtual world of postmodernism, with a view toward articulating a post-Marxist politics waged against a postproduction capitalism. But Baudrillard takes a beginning from the analysis of "primitive" societies (Baudrillard makes no excuses for using the word "primitive"; rather the word "society" troubles him). Primitive societies, in classic Marxist theory, are societies that attempt but fail to engage in "production"; they never accumulate more than their people need over the short term and they never succeed in extracting a profit from labor that could be used for the "primitive accumulation" of capital.

But Baudrillard thinks this analysis is short sighted. Instead of being societies of scarcity, Baudrillard imagines the primitives as forming societies of abundance—but an abundance of meaning rather than wealth. The surplus of material well-being that we call wealth has nothing to do with the surplus of meaning on which primitive societies may thrive.

"Primitive 'society' does not exist as an instance apart from symbolic exchange; and this exchange never results from an 'excess' of production," Baudrillard writes. In the course of symbolic exchange, "*exchange excludes any surplus.*" "Exchange is based on non-production, eventual destruction, and a process of continual *unlimited* reciprocity between *persons,* and inversely on a strict *limitation* of exchanged *goods.* It is the exact opposite of our economy based on unlimited production of goods and on the discontinuous abstraction of contractual exchange. In primitive exchange, production appears nowhere as an end or a means: the meaning occurs elsewhere."[21]

Baudrillard is relying, of course, on the distinction between the *gift* and the *commodity* that Marcel Mauss first proposed.[22] There are commodities in "primitive" societies, and there are usually markets or market mechanisms in which they are exchanged, sometimes through bartering and sometimes (especially among more settled and agricultural societies) through currency such as shells, beads, and coins. The Tupinamba, as Westerners observed, used feathers as form of currency and had developed elaborate markets where different groups traded with one another. But astride the exchange of goods, preindustrial societies commonly feature economic activity that Baudrillard calls symbolic exchange, based on the exchange of gifts. Gifts may be goods, like bundles of corn, but they are not exchanged as such, and commonly gifts involve less material or useful phenomena, like ceremonial gestures. Anthropologist C. A. Gregory provides a succinct explanation of the phenomenon: "The distinction between gifts and commodities manifests itself as a difference between the exchange relation established: gift-exchange establishes a relation between the transactors, while commodity exchange establishes a relation between the objects transacted." Gregory even provides a formula for the difference between the two:

Suppose two transactors, *A* and *B,* exchanged two things, *x* and *y.*

When *x* and *y* are commodities this exchange appears as one transaction as follows:

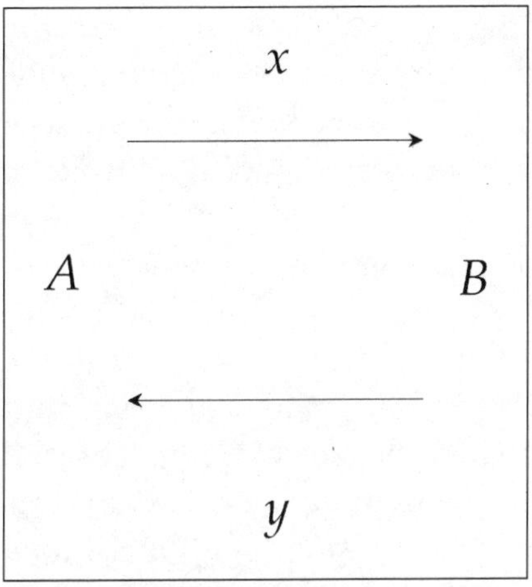


Courtesy of Robert Appelbaum

However, when *x* and *y* are gifts this exchange appears as two transactions, as follows:

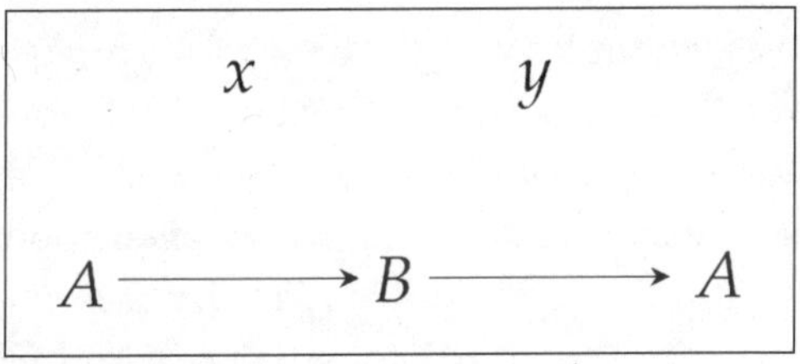


Courtesy of Robert Appelbaum

The first exchange establishes an equivalence between two goods. Even without the intervention of specie, exchange simply establishes an equivalence of value between two sets of utilities, *x* and *y*, and the transaction is complete, with no further consequences. But the second exchange establishes an equivalence between two subjects, *A* and *B*, an equivalence this time between two transactors who are "mutually indebted to each other." To give a gift is to put one's giftee in debt, for the giftee is now required to reciprocate with another gift.[23] And so on.

Gift giving is an endless chain of reciprocal gestures. But reciprocity itself can entail non-equivalent relations of power and prestige, and gift-giving can thus serve as an endless chain of domination of one giver to another. *A* can give a very big gift to *B* that *B* can never repay entirely, so when *B* repays *A* (whether through a service, labor, a good, a person such as a daughter in marriage, or a ceremonial gesture such as a feast) he signals the largess and social dignity of *A*, to which *B* can never aspire.

Food is an especially common sort of gift. But among the peculiarities of the food gift is that it may entail ritualistic observance and deference as well as opportunities for consumption. A bushel of corn may be consumed and then reciprocated with a basket of fruit or some other kind of gift, such as a hunting tool. But the gift of food may also entail a mutual ceremony of consumption. I give you food, but you are supposed to invite me over to eat some of it. Or else I put on a feast for you, so you and I both share in my largess. One of the signs of your appropriate reception of the gift is that you eat it with me in your capacity as my guest. Your obligation may be repaid in part simply by your appropriate reception of it. And in an unequal society, it is precisely your deferential reception that repays a good part of your obligation, for your reception signifies the power I hold over you for now. Mauss gives examples of this form of exchange, which leads not only to reciprocity but also to waste and irredeemable obligation (the guest becomes a *vassal*) in his discussion of the potlach.[24] Seth Mallios similarly points to the problems of food exchange in early colonial Virginia, where Native Americans seem to have provided food expecting in return not only future gifts but also deference.[25]

In any case, in the hands of some observers, including Montaigne and for that matter Bataille and Baudrillard, a gift-giving economy can seem superior to the modern commodity economy. It can make symbolic exchange into a form of life that is in many ways superior to material economic exchange, indicating what humanity really is, or can be. For this is the golden age remembered so nostalgically by classical writers from Hesiod to Ovid. Or if you are Bataille or Baudrillard, this is at least an example of how humanity can free itself from the restrictions of capitalism and indeed is already free from them, if it would only come to know itself better. We live, argues Bataille, in order to *give,* not in order to *accumulate* and *use.*[26] But working anthropologists have not shared this point of view. They have cast a colder eye on preliterate societies. Marcel Mauss himself, thinking about the powers of obligation and deference, insisted that nothing romantic or nostalgic should be made of the picture of primitive gift-giving he developed. In the opening statements of *The Gift,* Mauss writes that the study of gift-giving systems like the potlatch in Northwest America is a study of

> prestations [*sic*] which are in theory voluntary, disinterested and spontaneous, but are in fact obligatory, interested and calculated. The form usually taken is that of the gift generously offered; but the accompanying behavior is formal pretense and social deception, while the transaction itself is based on symbolic aggression and economic self-interest.[27]

So where a writer like Montaigne might see a form of nobility in potlatch gift-giving (after all, it corresponded ideally with the feudal system of aristocratic patronage from which he as a nobleman descended), Mauss insists that nobility of this kind is just another word for egotism. And where Bataille or Baudrillard might see a form of Nietzschean self-fashioning in the economy of gift-giving, Mauss would be inclined to see just another form of hegemonic inequality—although, in another context, Mauss also extols the spirit of symbolic exchange. "We can and must return to archaic society and to elements in it," he writes in his conclusion. "We shall find in this reasons for life and action . . . the joy of public giving."[28]

Significantly, if Mauss is right and the economy of the gift (whatever its joys) is at bottom a form of pretense and deception, masking material interest and the will to power, the concept of sacrifice, which is so important to Baudrillard, Bataille, Lestringant, and Montaigne, can be correlated with it only with difficulty. Does cannibalism among the Tupinamba really include the gift of death, the self-giving of sacrifice, or the relinquishment of a beloved? Montaigne believes it does and the theory of symbolic exchange helps explain his belief. The defeated warrior *gives himself up.* All accounts of the ritual seem to agree with this. Instead of being compelled to be eaten, the defeated warrior is encouraged to volunteer himself and to take pleasure in this volunteering, which is accomplished in a spirit of both cooperation and defiance. But the self-interest and pretense of the ritual gift still needs to be accounted for and still another step of analysis would need to be undertaken in order to confirm it. As it happens, Mauss was also (with his partner Hubert) among the first to study ritual sacrifice systematically.[29] And once again, his theory puts into question the romantic or nostalgic notions that might be attached to Tupinamba behavior, for the Hubert and Mauss theory denies that sacrifice can derive from an exogenous source such as an enemy warrior may be taken to be. The Hubert and Mauss theory assumes that sacrifice properly so called is always a *relinquishment* and therefore sacrifice cannot involve the *expropriation* of something or someone that doesn't already belong to the sacrificer without intervening ritualistic transformation. Like Abraham, one can sacrifice one's son; like Samson or Christ, one can sacrifice oneself; but one cannot sacrifice a stranger.[30]

But let us look now at how Brazilian cannibalism, in Montaigne's analysis, and as seconded by Lestringant, is configured as a form of exchange. For Montaigne, and very possibly for the Tupinamba themselves, cannibalism is a *social* exchange, undertaken between two rival clans. Consider a hypothetical rivalry between two clans, the clan of the Rio and the clan of Sao, and the fate of two warrior adversaries, Jorge and José, Jorge representing Rio and José representing Sao. Jorge is defeated in battle and taken from Rio to Sao. The dotted line imagines his incorporation into Sao society, which involves rituals of punishment, humiliation, and honorifics, where the victim is in effect consecrated as a special being. Then comes X, the moment when Jorge is killed and consumed. X marks the completed exchange, the delivery of a symbolic value to the clan of Sao. To get that X is to receive value in exchange for killing and consuming a victim, what Montaigne calls "extreme revenge." That X remains with the Sao community, which apparently distributes the value according to custom. And then of course there is the story of José, who is treated in just the same way by the Rio clan, which captures him, incorporates and consecrates him, and eventually gets its symbolic value out of him. And the value, presumably, is equal. X equals X. A dead and eaten warrior from one clan equals a dead and eaten warrior from another. I call this exchange "traffic."

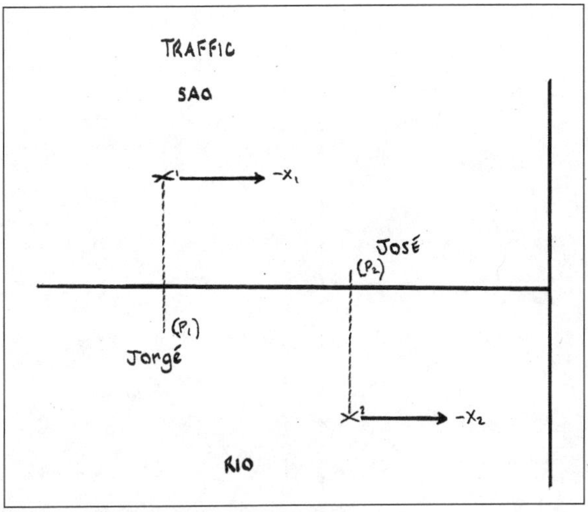


Courtesy of Robert Appelbaum.

What is imagined here is an endless reciprocity. Even if the killing and eating of José is *not* exactly equal to the killing and eating of Jorge, since they may be of different ages or may for other reasons boast more or less prestige than another, the logic of symbolic exchange is perfectly exemplified except for the fact that instead of *giving* a form of *taking* is involved. For Sao to take Jorge from Rio, to convert him into the value X, and then to consume this value, is to place Rio in a position of inverse debt to Sao, which *must be repaid, even if the payment is unequal.* This is the "debt" of revenge. Sao in effect obliges Rio to revenge the death of Jorge, just as Rio obliges Sao to revenge the death of José.

This sort of mutual culling of rival clans or tribes, with or without cannibalistic culmination, has not been uncommon in preliterate societies. Although the actual numbers and their significance can be debated, it is now widely accepted that both hunter-gatherer societies and small-scale preliterate agricultural societies, such as the Tupinamba, were often very violent and frequently involved themselves in skirmishes and raids against neighboring societies that might aptly be called "war."[31] Tupinamba clans and villages raided one another and, if Montaigne is right, engaged in open combat. And such warfare has little to do with the religious model of ritual sacrifice.

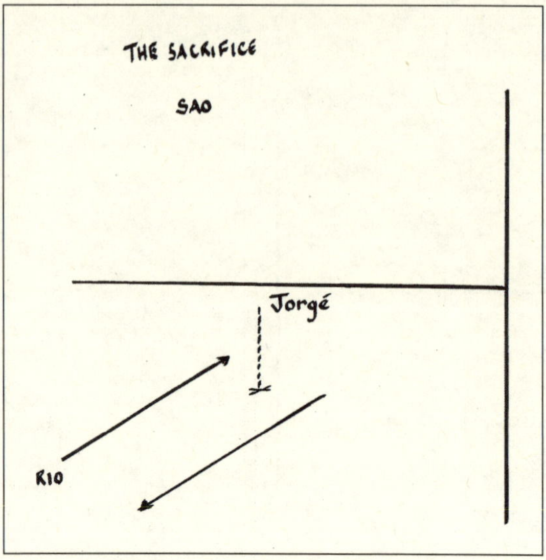

"The Sacrifice." Courtesy of Robert Appelbaum.

As I have said, in a sacrifice, as it is usually understood, it is not an outsider who is victimized on behalf of a group, but rather an insider. A sacrifice, Hubert and Mauss say, is primarily a form of relinquishment and "consecration." The victim, taken from the profane world of his or her society and given up to the larger needs of the society, is consecrated by the ritual of violence—made sacred, set apart. The death of the sacrificial victim restores a link between the sacred and the profane. The parties involved have had their "condition" modified so that a form of allegiance is renewed or a kind of curse is removed.[32] Although there may be many varieties of sacrifice and many gradations of consecration, it would not seem logical to claim that when, as among the Brazilians, an enemy is killed or executed, a "sacrifice" has been made, since nothing has been given up, nothing consecrated, nothing divinely restored.

To perform a sacrifice, by this reasoning, the Sao would have to execute and consume not Jorge but José, their own clansman; José, being selected, would be consecrated and destroyed. But that is precisely what the clan does not do. In ritual cannibalism, the enemy is killed and eaten and a profane if crucial value—revenge—is expressed.

Although it may still be plausible to argue that the existence of the Eucharist made early modern Catholics more at ease with cannibalism than they otherwise would have been, it does not seem plausible that the Eucharist model of the sacrifice was on their minds when they considered the ethics of American anthropophagy. For in South America, an outsider was victimized; in Christianity, the ultimate insider was the perennial victim.

But there is still another dimension to the killing and eating of the enemy rival, for the rituals of captivity and anthropophagy modify the social status of the enemy. The Brazilians do not mirror the model of ritual sacrifice insofar as the giving of the self to warfare and the giving of the victim to the ritual needs of his captors is an expression not of care but of hostility and an exaction of "extreme revenge." (As we will see, the extremeness of the revenge is crucial.) There is nothing of the Eucharist in this. There is nothing of the same relinquished for the benefit of the same. But the Brazilians mirror Christianity and other religions of sacrifice at least in this: when the victim is taken into the enemy camp, his enemies then *adopt* and *consecrate* him. They make him into one of them, with the distinct, sacred status of a sacrificial enemy victim, at once insider and outsider, both a member of a community and a defier of it, as if the victim were a version of Derrida's reading of the Greek *pharmakon:* a drug or scapegoat at once therapeutic and toxic.[33]

We seem to be at a crossroads here (or maybe even at an aporia) between a cycle of consecration and a cycle of vengeance. I have said that a clan gets a value, X, when a victim is executed and consumed, and I associated this value with a symbolic advantage that may well be divine. But I have also said that getting this value means achieving vengeance. And the mechanics of vengeance involves a serious problem. For when a clan gets X, a credit, it also gets a –X, a deficit. In return for the vengeance, the clan makes itself vulnerable to an attack; in fact, it invites an attack and a quest for vengeance in return for vengeance. Cycles of vengeance, as Girard and many others have taught, have no logical end—except the very kind of unambiguous sacrificial killing that the Tupinamba did *not* undertake.[34] As in the related logic of gift-giving, an endless chain of reciprocity, a deadly chain in this case, is established. But when we consider the X and –X as a pair of values, we again have to note that they may well be subject, like other forms of gift giving, to uneven distribution. Not all clan members get X or –X equally. In some accounts, the champion who kills his victim is specially honored by the ritual. Some accounts add that the champion is the one member of the community who does not consume the victim. Finally, in most accounts it appears that the champion will now be the preferred victim of the rival clan, especially of the family members of the victim.[35]

Montaigne begins to explain this phenomenon by alluding to the relation between vengeance and valor. Wars in Brazil, according to Montaigne, have "no other foundation than the sole jealousy of valor." Here, jealousy—coveting something the other has, but in the case of valor coveting something one can get only by a violent transaction with the coveted other, where one *gives* up one's fear of death, and gives up one's body, if necessary—is that mimetic desire Girard speaks of elsewhere: I want what the other *is,* but only insofar as I take it at once for a model and a rival, a goal and an obstacle, an epitome to emulate and a vehicle to kill—a *pharmakon* again.[36] Montaigne intimates that American cannibals are fighting for the dignity of being one another. Extreme revenge, in other words, comes not just in achieving the X of an execution but in achieving the –X of exposing oneself to attack and execution, for that is genuine valor and the ultimate payoff of having a rival executed. It is a form of taking that is also a giving. As Montaigne writes at one point, "there is not one who had not rather be killed and eaten than so much as ask not to be."[37] For if he asked for pity and release, he would taking himself out of the exchange. He would, among other things, find himself where he has been given a non-exchangeable gift, his own life, and is therefore unable to take anybody else's.

Philippe Desan suggests that in Montaigne's eyes, war, in effect, is the only form of work the cannibals do. For Montaigne's cannibals, again, live in a golden age when even providing for nutritional needs—hunting, fishing, farming—is play. Fighting for the sake of valor is the only job that burdens the cannibal. But the ritual of anthropophagy is also play: it is a form of representation that follows a script, obeys a number of rules, and dedicates itself as much to expenditure as to acquisition. Eating the flesh of one's enemy is, in Montaigne's words, to "betoken" (i.e., *representer*) an extreme vengeance.[38]

It is precisely because they could be associated with a golden age that the Brazilians could stand as a rebuke to the European. Lestringant underestimates this dimension of Montaigne's argument. Montaigne's cannibals epitomize a society that has yet to undergo either the deprivations of a hostile nature or the corruptions of civilization. From my own readings of ethnographical literature, I believe Montaigne was wrong. There seems to have been a number of functional uses in Brazilian cannibalism, including nutrition and thus a taste for human flesh and ritual uses that Montaigne was ignorant of.[39] Moreover, the Brazilians were not innocent of history and there are stories of Tupinamba raids on neighboring tribes (that spoke a different language) where slaughter and then cannibal feasting seems to fulfill a naked will to power rather than a ritual function. After all, the Tupinamba had migrated to the Brazilian coast and had conquered the region. But Montaigne imagines them as innocent, living a life without natural constraints, in a golden age without a past. Freed from history and need, the cannibal is all play.

Lestringant may thus also underestimate the importance of Montaigne's location of the Tupinamba, his positioning of them not in a story of the migration of Amerindian peoples and the settlement of many of them in agricultural communities but in a golden age without history or scarcity of any kind. But Lestringant is right to show that once the Enlightenment takes hold and then the nineteenth century's doctrine of progress, the idea of a golden age had less and less relevance. Humanity, it was thought, was becoming more enlightened, more free, more powerful over both nature and itself. In such a world, the free play of the valorous cannibal had no place—no place to be and no place even to be imagined. For ritual cannibalism cannot be improved upon; it can only keep repeating itself. Or to put it another way, symbolic exchange had to be effaced in the interest of *homo oeconomicus.* A main reason why the cannibal could no longer be admired was that the cannibal defied the premises of capitalist economy. Consuming without use, exchanging without profit or gain, the noble cannibal was outside the history of progress—or at best, he was *prior* to it.

One can ask whether Montaigne's picture was at all accurate. Lestringant does not care one way or the other, since his study is of an imaginary construct. Montaigne *imagined* the cannibals in a certain way and what he imagined would have a great deal of influence. But was Montaigne really right about the cultural values and valor of "those nations"? One may inquire into the two halves of savage nobility as Montaigne imagined it: on the one side, perpetual warfare, fought with great valor for no purpose other than honor; on the other side, perpetual cannibalism, marking the consummation of revenge. One may inquire into the neatness of Montaigne's view, where one type of cannibalism fits so neatly with the other, and all of it adds up to a golden age. It seems likely that the reality of warfare and cannibalism was a lot messier than Montaigne allowed. On the one side, war could at least on occasion have been a lot more brutal and vicious or a lot more clumsily motivated than Montaigne allowed. Were the Tupinamba really inspired only by "honor"? Were there never any lesser or more personal motives involved? And on the other side, was cannibalism really so complementary to warfare and so methodically performed? Were both warfare and cannibalism really so *symbolic*? We will probably never be able to answer such questions.[40]

But in asking them we can see a little better what was at stake in Montaigne's essay—along with what is at stake in Lestringant's analysis. It is conventional to suppose that Montaigne thinks of cannibalism as a barbarous surplus, an unspeakable act that is justified only insofar as it is "not worse" than what supposedly civilized Christians do to one another and better than what the fabled Scythians once did. Certainly we have seen Montaigne use this idea. The implication is that anthropophagy is an *excess*, an *extreme* measure in the Tupinamba system of justice that really isn't needed. To have captured, consecrated, and then killed an enemy would seem to be enough: a death for a death, revenged. To eat the dead is redundant, especially if no use at all is attached to it and no pleasure. But if Montaigne's view of Brazilian cannibalism is correct, the excess of anthropophagy is, paradoxically, as necessary as it is superfluous. Cannibalism is adoration coupled with repudiation, incorporation of the worthy rival coupled with a dehumanization of a mortal enemy, an admiring imitation and a contemptuous annihilation of one and the same subject.

In his own way, then, Montaigne anticipates that perennial theme of the theory of symbolic exchange—that in spite of the principle of reciprocity that governs it, it inclines toward excess and self-destruction. Cannibalism is an excess, not to mention (to us) a horrible thing. But it is a necessary excess. It completes a quest for symbolic satisfaction. Yet it also reopens the symbolic chain, and requires a reciprocal quest for satisfaction from the partner-enemies in the affair. It finishes a quasi-judicial process: left with the body of the captive, the revengers dispose of it by making the body their own. Yet the disposal of the body in this way is gratuitous; it has no "use."

Neither Montaigne nor his interpreter Frank Lestringant actually believe that there is something "honorable" about eating an enemy. But they find it useful to point out that by Tupí standards, honor eating is honorable indeed, both because it satisfies conditions of symbolic exchange and because it exceeds those conditions in an incalculable excess.

CHAPTER 9

# Conspicuous Consumptions in Atlantic Africa

## Andrew Battell's Fearsome Tales of Hunger, Cannibalism, and Survival

JARED STALLER

Andrew Battell of Leigh, in Sussex near Stratford-on-Thames, departed England in 1589 as a crewman aboard Abraham Cocke's privateering expedition headed for the south Atlantic seas then controlled by Spain. Battell returned to Leigh sometime between 1607 and 1611 with tales of adventures that ranged geographically from the West African coast of modern-day Liberia to the Atlantic African islands, Brazil, and Argentina. The vast majority of his time was spent in West Central Africa as a prisoner, trader, shopkeeper, and soldier in the region from Angola to Loango in modern-day Gabon. In Leigh, the Anglican churchman Samuel Purchas befriended and interviewed Battell. Purchas was writing a history of religion designed to encapsulate all of human history and all manner of religious diversity around the world. Emulating the great travel-narrative compilers Richard Hakluyt of England and Giovanni Battista Ramusio of Italy, Purchas sought out recently returned sailors such as Battell to add eyewitness data to the extensive body of written travel narratives he relied on as primary sources for his history of religion. The massive tome was first published in 1613 as *Purchas his Pilgrimage;* it underwent three revisions and republications in 1614, 1617, and 1626.[1] In 1625, Purchas published *Purchas, his Pilgrimes,* which he claimed reprinted his informants' narratives in their own words.[2] Andrew Battell's account was called "The Strange Adventures of Andrew Battell" (hereafter "Strange

Adventures").[3] Although there are very serious reasons to question whether "Strange Adventures" faithfully reproduced Andrew Battell's words, the text is one of the few extant eyewitness accounts of Angola and Loango in the 1590s. It has been extensively used by scholars who have been interested in it, in no small part, because Battell lived among a group of alleged African cannibals called Imbangala for sixteen months in 1600–1601. His fearsome tales of hunger, cannibalism, and survival shed light on varieties of conspicuous consumptions in Atlantic Africa around 1600.

In their studies of the Imbangala, Africanist scholars frequently repeat Battell's stories about their conspicuous consumption of humans by killing or enslaving them and of the palm trees they cut down to obtain palm wine (as the Europeans called it) within a social ethic of "unabashed greed and selfishness."[4] This analysis adds to earlier studies of the Imbangalas' ingestions of palm trees and human flesh by analyzing them in comparison with Andrew Battell's descriptions of foods he ate. For this analysis, I will expand the term "conspicuous consumption" from Veblen's definition of it as the habit of people in a capitalist system to accumulate wealth and then display their discretionary economic power to attain or maintain membership in a particular social class.[5] I will unhinge the term from class analysis and define it more broadly as any consumptive activity done with the intent that others take notice. Using this definition, all published descriptions of eating in "Strange Adventures" were explicitly conspicuous because Battell wanted his readers, or at least Purchas, to know what he or his African acquaintances ate at given moments. What becomes most obvious with a careful investigation of Battell's mentions of food is that he does not often speak at length about what or how Africans ate. He mentions a few African food ceremonies, such as the fact that people in Loango were not allowed to watch the king eat or drink. But by far the highest density of food-related stories in "Strange Adventures" described times when he claimed to be hungry, even starving.

Battell's narrative is stuffed with overt references to eating food or human flesh and to the sometimes mortally perilous activities that a person without food must be willing to perform. He even presented the dread of food scarcity as greater than anxieties about other potentially terrifying activities, such as armed conflict. Most noticeably, he described the fear of hunger as being more acute than the terror of living among alleged Imbangala cannibals. However, closer analysis of Battell's claims about hunger demonstrate a complexity beyond experiences where food was scarce or entirely lacking. Typically he related that he had access to food but still felt famished because the available food was low in quantity or, more likely, of a sort that he might not have preferred to eat. By narrating what he was compelled to eat to survive, "Strange Adventures" makes conspicuous Battell's consumption of what he considered to be undesirable foods. This consumption allowed him to cast himself as a survivor of fearsome circumstances, including starvation. His alleged calmness in the face of physical dangers contrasts with and underscores his anxieties about hunger, which adds narrative weight to stories of surviving those circumstances. Emphasizing fears about food insecurity had the effect of increasing the number of Battell's heroic actions that a reader might notice.[6]

The stakes of these conspicuous consumptions are quite high for African, and Atlantic, history. Mining the "Strange Adventures" for instances of hunger and eating yields important data on how European travelers constructed knowledge about Africa by contrasting their own food consumption with that of the locals. The hero Battell ostentatiously ate little or barely edible foodstuffs while overcoming great trials while the Imbangala pastoralists he lived among were allegedly notorious consumers of human flesh and palm wine even in the midst of implied food security that was based on desirable supplies of meat from cattle herds and stolen crops from agricultural villages. The juxtaposition of tales of Battell being forced to consume little or unfamiliar food juxtaposed with Imbangala cannibalism rehearsed older European ideas of Africa as an inhospitable place of savagery and applied those ideas to the new context of increasing slaving.

Two caveats are necessary before launching into Andrew Battell's "Strange Adventures." First, I will write with a confidence about Battell's description of food and eating that is, to some degree, at odds with the fact that it is not certain that these are his words.[7] "Strange Adventures" was a text that was co-produced between Andrew Battell, Samuel Purchas, and an unnamed transcriber who was most likely

Purchas's son (also named Samuel). However, even given this uncertainty about authorship, we can be reasonably certain that the details about food and eating derive from Battell without much (if any) alterations from either Purchas. While the elder Purchas routinely altered his texts over time, he typically corrected other sorts of details such as updating geographical or economic numbers and distances, revising his own sermons within the text, or engaging well-known controversies such as the location of the font of the Nile River. He also heavily revised Battell's data about the Imbangala. However, other facts Battell related remain consistent in every reprinting from 1613 to 1626 and there is little reason to suspect that Purchas was interested in correcting details about food.[8] Second, specialists who study African history are likely to find my coverage of the Imbangala to be a bit too generic and my focus too centered on Battell to consider this chapter to be African history. This is correct; my engagement with the Imbangala will adhere rather faithfully to Battell's problematic descriptions of them. An extensive body of scholarly literature investigates this group and I will point to more nuanced studies in the endnotes. However, the scholarly literature agrees on the particular point I am engaging: the conspicuous consumption of Imbangala groups committed to slave raiding. Certain groups of Imbangala did live by terrorizing, raiding, and enslaving the local Mbundu populations, and one prominent feature of their culture was the greedy and wasteful method they used to obtain palm wine. With that in mind, I offer this study of Andrew Battell as an analysis in a specific African historical context (focused mostly on Angola), whereas a study of alleged human flesh eaters somewhere in the North Atlantic, for example, might yield similar but not entirely congruent arguments about food, hunger, survival, or cannibalism in relation to conspicuous consumptions.

## Andrew Battell's Fearsome Tales of Hunger and Survival

Andrew Battell sailed in 1589 with an English captain named Abraham Cocke on a trading expedition to South America, doubtless intending to break the blockade against foreign shipping in the Atlantic waters that Spain claimed exclusively. Cocke was part of a commercial family from the very active shipping village of Stratford in Sussex. The expedition, which included two ships with crews, must be considered a privateering journey if Battell's details are to be believed. Little more needs to be said about Cocke. He disappeared and presumably died off the coast of Brazil within a year of his departure. Much more needs to be said about Andrew Battell's personal history, but unfortunately, "Strange Adventures" gives almost no clues about his background and scholars have not found any evidence about him beyond the published materials Samuel Purchas produced. After his long journey, Battell returned to England sometime between 1607 and 1611, befriended Samuel Purchas shortly thereafter, and died sometime before Lent of 1619. His enduring legacy from nearly two decades of travel in South America and West Central Africa results from the density of his extraordinary adventures, including captivities, fevers, wars, slave-raiding expeditions, encounters with "monsters" (gorillas, manatees, and so forth), living among the Imbangala, and recurring intense hunger.

The Andrew Battell described in "Strange Adventures" was a heroic figure who overcame all manner of trials and tribulations and remained a faithful Anglican amid Catholic and African "superstitions" (as Purchas called non-Protestant beliefs). Like all heroes, he overcame his fears to survive and sometimes thrive in the South Atlantic seas. While I remain cautious about any hero's braggadocio, Battell's mentions of fear might give a hint about his upbringing. He regularly mentioned being afraid, being anxious, or suffering (perhaps without fear) in contexts where he lacked food, was adrift at sea for long periods, was deathly sick, or languished in Portuguese prisons in Angola. However, "Strange Adventures" relates many instances when Battell participated in armed violence without mentioning any fear. He also noted repeatedly that he was valued for his musketry skill by Portuguese governors at Luanda, the Imbangala chief, and a king in Loango. He was given command of Portuguese troops while fighting in the Angola interior wars of the 1590s (discussed below), an amount of responsibility that a common sailor would almost never receive. These contrasting attitudes toward fear combined with his bravery during armed violence and his expertise with a musket hint that Battell may have had a gentleman's upbringing that trained him to handle a firearm and prepared him for war. His descriptions of himself are quite similar to those of Anthony Knivett, another English sailor who traveled at the same time. Scholars know more about Knivett's background. He was chosen to go on a similar privateering expedition precisely because of his shooting expertise.[9] If Battell was not overstating his shooting ability, then perhaps Abraham Cocke chose crewmen like him because he knew that armed conflict was inevitable on his privateering mission. However, unlike common soldiers, who might be less ready with a firearm but more accustomed to food scarcity, young men from comfortable backgrounds could be more likely to feel distressed about the unfamiliar anxieties and pangs of hunger.[10]

Cocke's two ships sailed out of the Thames River on April 20, 1589, and arrived in Plymouth to provision on April 26. After taking on the necessities, Cocke tried to sail out into the Atlantic, but a storm forced them to remain at Plymouth for several days before they finally set out on May 7. Cocke sailed first for the Canary Islands, off the shores of southern Morocco, before turning the expedition southeast toward the African mainland. Battell complained that the boats stalled along the West African coastline and many of the men on board fell ill with scurvy, which suggests the shortage of healthy food that often plagued ships in that era, although sailors would not have known the etiology of the disease. Cocke put in at Cape Palmas (in modern Liberia), where the crew recuperated and took on food. However, they hurried away when the local villagers (unnamed in the text but most likely Glebo) tried to take one of their ships, injuring some of the crew in the process. Cocke continued heading southeast, a course Battell claims was dictated by deceptive winds and currents, until he reached São Tomé Island in the Gulf of Guinea, well to the south. In fact, the winds and currents in that region were very well known; Cocke's continuation southward for the relatively prosperous sugar and slave island of São Tomé instead of westward toward Brazil is evidence of his piratical intentions.

Having deviated so far east of the normal course to Brazil, and apparently failing to obtain great trade at Cabo das Palmas, Cocke's crew set ashore on the islet of Rolas, about a mile off the southeast coast of São Tomé Island, because they were in "distress of wood and water."[11] There Battell and some other crew members found oranges and plantains but no good water. They burned the village on Rolas (Battell gave no reason why, but perhaps they burned as they looted the stores of oranges and plantains) and sailed north to São Tomé, which had an abundance of freshwater streams. Cocke's ships sailed up the entire east side of the island again, indicating that they were looking for more than water since freshwater streams are visible along the coastline.[12] They eventually approached the colonial capital on a north-facing bay, where soldiers at the Portuguese Fort São Sebastião fired on them. Cocke then turned his ships even farther east, headed for the African mainland in the vicinity of modern Gabon, before circling back the next day and trying to obtain fresh water on the west side of São Tomé. However, the members of Cocke's crew who went ashore there were ambushed. One sailor was killed and another wounded. After this attack, Abraham Cocke finally set course for southern America.

Without explaining where the crew took on enough provisions to successfully cross the Atlantic, Battell claimed that once the expedition had crossed the Atlantic, Cocke stopped his two ships to take on water and food and to rest his crew on Ilha Grande, sixty miles south and west of Rio de Janeiro. After twelve days, a Portuguese merchant captain also stopped on the same island to gather food and water. Cocke's crew captured him and discovered that he was involved in lucrative trading in the Plate River estuary to the south (present-day Uruguay and Argentina). Although Cocke decided that he wanted to participate in this Plate River trade, he sent half of his crew back to England. The captured Portuguese captain led the remainder of the crew, obviously including Battell, to a Portuguese convict (*degredado*) who had been exiled to Ilha Grande. This *degredado* sold plantains to them so they could continue to the Plate River because their other supplies had run out. Battell noted that they sailed toward Argentina for thirty-six days, eating only this "hard allowance" until they eventually arrived on Seal Island at the mouth of the Plate River (five miles south of Punta del Este, Uruguay).[13] Thirty-six days seems like too long to sail roughly 1,040 miles and might indicate that Battell's memory of the journey was altered by the monotony of eating only plantains. On Seal Island, they lingered for an additional thirty days as they formulated a strategy for obtaining trade goods in Buenos Aires, the principal Spanish port in the region. Battell described Seal Island as only half a mile long. It had no fresh water and beaches so full of seals and walruses that the crew had to beat them back with oars in order to put in. He tells us, "Upon these seals we lived for thirty days, lying up and down in the river, and were in great distress of victuals."[14]

What might Battell have meant when he said they were in great distress of victuals? If Seal Island truly had no fresh water, then the crew must have found a source somewhere on the mainland. Could they not also have scavenged for food items on shore? In fact, the journey from Ilha Grande to Seal Island would have carried them close to the shoreline of Brazil and Uruguay and taken them through fish-rich waters. All those seals were eating something, after all. So why would the crew have had to live for a month on only plantains and another month on only seal meat? I do not question Battell's claims about food and water scarcity in general, but I do think that his claim was more about the types of food available. Plantains and seal meat were foreign to the Europeans aboard Cocke's ships, and their experience of distress might have related more to being forced to survive solely on strange foods than to having access to food familiar enough to provide some measure of psychological comfort during this trying episode. On this point I think that Mary Black-Rogers's analysis of "varieties of starving" as narrated by French fur-traders who interacted with Native American groups in Canada is instructive; she emphasizes that starving was a term with varied meanings depending on the context. "Starving" within the context of religious practice might have linked it to pity to invoke charity or it might have signaled specifically coded language that pertained to those trading scenarios as a way to drive down the price of foodstuffs.[15] Battell's "distress" likely operated similarly as a word that signified more than the stomach pains and groans from lack of food. The distress certainly heightened the tension in "Strange Adventures." Battell noted illness and a lack of food in virtually every episode going back to the time the expedition was in Cape Palmas, and in every case the remedy for those privations was the acquisition of foreign food: oranges, plantains, and seal or walrus meat. The hunger and distress in the narrative emphasizes the traveler as a survivor of tribulations and a consumer of foods that were considered exotic, even undesirable, in the homeland.

After this lean month on Seal Island, the crew determined to take their boat upriver to surprise and attack one of the trading vessels that called at Buenos Aires. However, their raiding expedition was driven back by a storm and the crew found themselves on an island that Battell called Ilha Verde, which the modern editor of his account, E. G. Ravenstein, surmised must be Flores (just off Punta Carretas, the site of modern Montevideo). Already weakened from the distress of the month on Seal Island, Battell complained that on Flores the crewmen were "all discomforted from lack of victuals."[16] Cocke turned his empty-handed expedition out of the Plate River and headed north toward Brazil. They arrived at the island of São Sebastião (now called Ilhabela, in the vicinity of São Paulo), not too far from Ilha Grande. The "famished" crew rushed onto São Sebastião to fish or gather fruit in the woods. Indigenous people lurking in the woods captured five of the crewmen. To avoid this attack, Cocke sailed out to sea and was not heard from again. The Amerindians transported Battell and four others nearly 200 miles to Rio de Janeiro and handed them over to the Portuguese authorities.[17] The Portuguese imprisoned them for four months before sending Battell and another man across the Atlantic to (São Paolo de) Luanda, the fortified center of the military occupation of adjacent parts of what is now Angola. The moral of Battell's capture on São Sebastião is obvious: even when famished, one must be wary of impending calamity. Battell's carelessness while foraging cost him nearly a decade and a half of time spent in Angola and Loango, making this particular eating episode on São Sebastião one of the most conspicuous of his entire narrative.

## Andrew Battell's Fearsome Tales of Captivity, Violence, and Cannibals

If Battell's recollection of time can be believed, he arrived in Angola in 1590 or 1591. From Luanda, the Portuguese sent him up the nearby Kwanza River to a Portuguese military outpost called Massangano, the outer staging ground for Portuguese attempts to capture territory in the region. After two months, they sent him back to Luanda, where he fell ill. He claimed that he was laid up for eight months with very poor care, since the Portuguese in Luanda "hated me because I was an

Englishman." There are no complaints about food in his description of this time.[18] Once he recovered, he was put to work by the captain of Angola, João Furtado de Mendonça, who was trading in the Congo River to the north for ivory, palm oil, and grain.[19] Captains were the highest political authority in the Portuguese and (at that time) Spanish domains (the Iberian crowns were joined from 1580 to 1640). Often, and certainly in Angola, captains were in the business of enriching themselves. Chapter one of "Strange Adventures" ends with Battell released from prison and military service but compelled to work for Furtado de Mendonça in the ivory and palm oil trade.

Chapter two of "Strange Adventures" focuses on dangers in battle more than on the fear of hunger. In fact, Battell remarks with no detail that he spent two and a half years trading for Furtado da Mendonça between Luanda and Loango, located on the coast well to the north of the mouth of the Congo River, which likely indicates that he had adequate food and personal security. After those two years of trading, he attempted to abscond on a Dutch ship but was found out by Portuguese crewmen. They turned him over to the Luanda authorities, who sent him back to the outpost of Massangano, where he lived a "most miserable life for six years without any hope to see the sea again."[20] Battell is unclear about the details of his misery.

The drama in "Strange Adventures" increased when Battell convinced *degredados* in the fortification there, four gypsies and seven Portuguese, to escape from Massangano with him. Once again, Battell the hero traveler survived by eating non-European foods. On the first night of their westward flight toward the Atlantic coast they roasted maize, the only food they had been able to steal from the fort. However, they had absolutely no water on that first night or on the second day. Their conditions were so bad they could not travel the second night and instead had to "dig and scrape up roots of trees, and suck them to maintain life."[21] On the third day, the twelve thirst-weakened men seized an African traveling alone and forced him to take them to the nearest village. There they intended to secure drinking water by force but were in such a pathetic condition that the village chief offered them water and kind words and implored them to spend the night. Battell's group believed these overtures would lead to betrayal, so they continued their journey to the coast.

After another two days of travel, they joined a group of Africans who claimed to be heading north to the Kingdom of Kongo. When they realized that they were being led back inland, Battell's group tried to turn westward toward the Atlantic. However, the Africans stood in their way and a confrontation ensued. Although Battell and the *degredados* were able to flee toward the coast after firing their muskets, the Africans pursued them and injured two of the company. On the seventh day after fleeing Massangano, Battell's group approached the village of the Duke of Mbamba, near the coast in a territory between Luanda and the Kingdom of Kongo, leading to one of the most dramatic episodes in "Strange Adventures."

Mbamba was allied with the Kingdom of Kongo, and, perhaps unsurprisingly, the villagers sent a force out to confront the noticeable group of twelve European *degredados.* When they saw the large force approaching, the seven "faint-hearted Portugals" hid themselves in thickets. Battell and the gypsies tried to run away, but not being able to outrun men on horses, they scurried into a small wood. Once the emissary from Mbamba and his men caught up to them, they fired a volley into the wood and the five men were separated. Battell thought that if the Africans caught him in the woods, they would surely kill him. He preferred to make a bold last stand, risking his life. He claimed, "I came presently out of the wood with my musket ready charged, making none account of my life."[22] The emissary, who thought the entire party was still together and that Battell's companions were lurking behind the trees, promised not to hurt them if they yielded. Battell related, "I, having my musket ready, answered the captain that I was an Englishman, and had served six years at Massangano, in great misery" and being alone would rather die than be hanged.[23] Impressed by Battell's "resolute mind," the emissary promised to spare his life if Battell turned over his weapon, which he did. Although Battell's life was spared, the Duke of Mbamba turned him over to Portuguese officials and he was once again jailed in Luanda, this time for three months.

Following this recapture, Battell was permanently banished to the region of the Portuguese conquest wars of the interior after 1596, the year that Luanda tried to control surrounding African chiefs and *sobas* (lords). For the next three years he served well as a solider but was eventually wounded in the leg. He returned to Luanda in 1599 to recuperate. Because of his good service in the wars, Furtado da Mendonça engaged Battell again as a merchant. This time he sailed south to trade with Africans near Old Benguela, at the mouth of the Cuvo River. In his account of these years of fighting and trading, Battell made no mention of fear of enemies or of hunger. During one of these trips to the south, Battell encountered and ultimately lived among the Imbangala slavers. After he had lived with the constantly mobile Imbangala band for sixteen months, they passed within a few days' journey of Massangano, at which point Battell left them and traveled to the fort with another group of African slavers. He stayed again at Massangano for perhaps a year, then in 1602 the new captain, João Rodrigues Coutinho, summoned him for wars he was planning to the south of Luanda. In these wars under Coutinho (who died shortly after undertaking them) and his successor, Manuel Cerveira Pereira, Battell was allegedly given command over a contingent of Portuguese soldiers and fought in the bloody battle against a powerful leader, or Soba, named Soba Cafuxe on August 10, 1603. After defeating Cafuxe, Pereira, who by then had become the captain, gave Battell permission to return home to England. Battell worried that if he remained in Luanda the offer of freedom might be rescinded, so he journeyed north through the Kingdom of Kongo, apparently headed for Loango. His anxieties proved correct because Pereira recalled him before he could secure transportation off the continent.

Andrew Battell's last account of conspicuous food consumption in Angola comes from this period, 1606 to 1607, after Pereira compelled him to return to Luanda. Pereira had served his three-year term as captain in Angola and was being recalled to Portugal. The custom in Angola was that upon their arrival new captains would grant amnesty to convicts. Battell believed in 1606 that the new captain, Manuel Pereira Forjaz, would arrive imminently. He decided to dodge Pereira, who had not yet left Luanda, and live in the wilderness, hoping to return to the city after the arrival of Forjaz, when he might be given amnesty and be allowed to return home. Since Battell was technically in Pereira's service he could not travel to any Portuguese-controlled lands or in those of allied Africans for fear that he would be captured and sent to Luanda. Instead, he attempted to survive in the bush with two servant boys, his musket and powder, and enough food for ten to twenty days. Battell began traveling north, but he soon heard that Forjaz had been delayed and would not arrive in the near future.

Battell was, in his words, "put to his shifts" at this point, as he was faced with the dreadful choice of returning to Luanda to be hanged for deserting (for the third time) or trying to survive in the African bush with his meager supplies.[24] He and his servant boys remained in the woods between the Bengo and Dande Rivers for a month.[25] After that, he traveled to Lake Lalama (he called it Casansa), which he claimed had the greatest variety of wild game in Angola. For six months he lived on dried fish and dried meat from game such as impala, water buffalo, and roebuck that he hunted. He even described catching a four-foot-long lungfish that was skipping on top of the water.[26] Sometimes one of his servants could trade dried fish for maize at a nearby village. Once again, when he faced the prospect of death (being hung in Luanda), the hero Battell survived the anxieties and trials of his situation by eating food that was exotic to his English readers. And once again, although he had access to an abundant quantity and variety of foreign foods, Battell claimed that life as an exile in the wilderness was difficult. "Thus after I had lived six months with the dried flesh and fish, and seeing no end of my misery, I wrought means to get away," he wrote.[27] Desperate to finally escape both the woods and the fear of being captured, Battell and his servants crafted a small three-oared boat out of light wood and fashioned a sail from an old blanket. They sailed down the nearby Bengo River and into the Atlantic north of Luanda, a journey that was quite dangerous in their makeshift craft. After one night of sailing north, a sailor friend picked Battell up at sea and deposited him in Loango, where he spent roughly three years in relative comfort before escaping on a Dutch ship bound for England.

Battell's dramatic accounts of his tribulations in Angola juxtapose the fear associated with contexts of hunger with fear in the contexts of warfare. Battell, and Samuel Purchas as his editor, surely had motivations for promoting him as a fearless Englishman in the lands of hostile foreigners, Catholic Portuguese, idolatrous Mbundu, and "savage" Imbangala. Yet explicitly accentuating the fears and anxieties of situations where food was scarce or undesirable had the effect of increasing the dramatic tension in "Strange Adventures" beyond tales of armed conflict. The correlation between Battell's most harrowing episodes of survival and his ability to recall the food he was eating at the time are surprisingly strong. In only a few instances—such as when he was near death during the bad fever that laid him up in Luanda—did Battell omit descriptions of food consumption. Instead, the "Strange Adventures" catalogs an impressive list of exotic foods that our hero used to sustain himself during conspicuously terrifying events: oranges, plantains, seal (and perhaps walrus) meat, maize, impala, roebuck, water buffalo, and lungfish. He also drank water scraped from the roots of trees.

## Imbangala Greed, Waste, and Terrorizing

Although Battell's consumption of foods that saved his life are eye-catching, the most noticeable descriptions of eating relate to the voracious, insatiable, and allegedly man-eating Imbangala. At times throughout history, people have turned to eating human flesh as a last resort for dealing with the otherwise fatal prospect of starvation. Those who have enough food are typically horrified by even the stories of such desperation. But "Strange Adventures" implies that Andrew Battell was not afraid of the Imbangalas' alleged cannibalism or of their eating his flesh. Indeed, he chose to live among them rather than survive on his own in the woods or as a prisoner. Even more curious than Battell's lack of fear of these supposed cannibals is his description of how the Imbangala did not eat human flesh out of necessity, since they lived a lifestyle that provided ample access to cattle, grains, and alcohol. The Imbangala among whom Battell lived in fact had an overabundance of comestibles that allowed for ritualized wastefulness. Battell's description of the Imbangala suggests that there might be varieties of cannibalism just as there are varieties of starving or consumption. While cannibalism is usually defined as either a rational response to the fear of starvation or an irregularly occurring ritual performance, in "Strange Adventures," cannibalism denotes a purposefully and publicly wasteful ingestion of wealth.

Battell's narrative of the Imbangala provides explicit depictions of the politics of terrorism some peoples in Angola used during the very disquieting decades of drought, war, and growing slaving before and after 1600. Battell met the Imbangala while he was trading near Old Benguela for Furtado de Mendoça. At the conclusion of their initial peaceful round of trading, the leader whose name or title was Imbe Calundula, negotiated with the Europeans for the use of their canoes to ferry his soldiers across the Cuvo River. He wanted to lay waste to the villages on the northern bank of the river. In exchange, presumably, Battell and the traders benefited from whatever booty they ransacked. After the victory Battell, noted that the severed heads of the captured village leaders were thrown at Imbe Calundula's feet. "The men, women, and children that were brought in captive alive, and the dead corpses that were brought to be eaten were strange to behold. For these [Imbangala] are the greatest cannibals and man-eaters that be in the world, for they feed chiefly upon man's flesh [despite their] having all the cattle of that country."[28] Note Battell's (or Purchas's) shock that even though the Imbangala had more cattle than anyone else they chose to eat human flesh.

The Imbangala groups like the one Battell met near Old Benguela descended from cattle-keeping pastoralists that were native to the drier regions of southern Angola. Groups of these pastoralists had begun moving north in the 1560s and by the early decades of the 1600s had completely altered the political landscape of Angola.[29] They had helped bring about the end of the Ndongo political unity of the Mbundu-speaking agriculturalists and would later replace them with more centralized polities such as Kasanje and Matamba. The Imbangala were also sometimes allies and sometimes enemies of the Portuguese colonial establishment, and the Portuguese could hire groups of them as mercenaries at times. Some groups of Imbangala engaged in violent armed conflict that resulted in the sale of captives as slaves for the transatlantic trade. It is possible that all of these activities were exacerbated by a context of increasing aridity and prolonged droughts from the 1580s through 1620s, which were punctuated by only a few years of regular or above average rainfall.[30] During the droughts, agriculture would have been less viable and some people were likely made vulnerable to capture and sale as environmental refugees when their crops failed. If agriculture was not a sustainable way to produce food during this time, pastoralists would have had incentives to maintain their herds and the warrior ethic that was required to protect them.

The Imbangala pastoralists who Battell met did not eat their cattle because pastoralists don't eat their cattle. Pastoralists use livestock products like milk or blood for food and they might from time to time make a ritual sacrifice. But in general, they derive personal and social identities from their cattle; the cattle are their wealth. In contrast, the agriculturalists the Imbangala attacked measured wealth in the quantity of people they could gather and the quality of reciprocal social bonds among them.[31] If the alleged cannibalism can be believed, the Imbangala captives' flesh could be consumed because these foreigners had no internal measure of wealth. Even if one does not believe the claims about eating human flesh in this hyperbolic claim that the Imbangala were the most bloodthirsty cannibals in the world, the symbolic consumption of human flesh is still conspicuous in this moment, as people who were murdered in armed violence or as the captives who were being enslaved and sold in the increasingly capitalistic transatlantic trade in which humans were exchanged as commodities.

Over the next five months, Battell and his group made two more trading expeditions from Luanda to Imbe Calundula's group. When they arrived for a fourth encounter, they discovered that the Imbangala had left in search of new territory to raid. Imbe Calundula's Imbangala had not been entirely satisfied in the lands near Old Benguela, even though they "lacked almost nothing," having stores of cattle, wheat, and other commodities. But in this part of the country there were no palm trees and the Imbangala voraciously consumed palm wine (*malavu*).[32] Thus, once again, Battell highlighted the gluttonous habits of the Imbangala. He contrasted the Mbundu agriculturalists' practices of extracting palm wine with that of the Imbangala. Successful agriculturalists counted the palm trees as part of the prestige and wealth of their community.[33] They would bore a small hole at the top of a palm tree and sustainably gather the liquid daily in pots as it ran out of the living tree. In contrast, the Imbangala, according to Battell, would invade a territory, chop down the trees and bleed them dry in a matter of weeks.[34] Thus, the Imbangala performed as conspicuous consumers for the purpose of intimidating, even terrorizing, the agriculturalists. They literally drank Mbundu-speakers' wealth and left their landscape devastated while refusing to spend any of their own wealth in livestock.

Battell and the others went in search of Imbe Calundula's group, which had moved inland looking for palm groves. Along the way, a powerful local African lord named Mafrigosat captured them. He eventually agreed to let the company go after they promised that they would return and trade with him. To enforce their return he required that someone remain as a hostage. Battell was left. After two months, his companions had not returned. Fearing for his life because the Portuguese had broken their promise to return, Battell happened upon some Imbangala that he knew. He slipped away with them and was reunited with Imbe Calundula. "Among the cannibal people, I determined to live, hoping in God, that they would travel so far to the westeward, 'til we should see the sea again."[35] Once again he accentuated their frivolous eating practices. During the four months he stayed with them, they had "plenty of cattle, corn, wine, and oil." Battell also witnessed military victories, dancing, drinking and feasting "with man's flesh, which was a heavy sight to behold."[36] The alleged flesh eating is, of course, remarkable but so is the food that was also available. Just as Europeans might find it inconceivable that anyone would prefer to eat human flesh when beef was prevalent, Battell claimed that the Imbangala ate people even when supplied with desirable foods such as corn, oil, and wine.

Battell explicitly and repeatedly remarked that the Imbangalas' conspicuous consumption was part of the fabric of their society. For example, Imbe Calundula maintained strict laws about warfare. He executed and cannibalized any of his soldiers who became "fainthearted" and tried to flee during a battle.[37] Battell does not claim that he saw this happen, which suggests that the specter that they could be eaten maintained bravery among the warriors. Also, Imbe Calundula purposely fostered an aura of fear created by eye-catching eating behavior in order to reduce the risks associated with raiding. Before attacking any well-defended village, the Imbangala would camp within sight of it for up to two months. The besieged agriculturalists had to watch the Imbangala eat their crops and steal their livestock, dreading the impending attack. Imbe Calundula told Battell that the visibility of this devouring was as psychologically damaging to the locals as if he fought with them every day.[38] And the most climactic description of cannibalism, and one of the few with any real details at all, involved a ceremony of human flesh-eating that was attended by the Devil himself. The night before an assault, Imbe Calundula conducted a series of rituals and gave valiant speeches to embolden his soldiers. Part of the ceremony included Calundula ritually killing a boy and two men inside the camp. Battell claimed that at this point, he was sent out of the enclosure, "as I was a Christian, for then the Devil doth appear to them, as they say." After he left, the Imbangala made animal sacrifices both inside and outside the camp walls. They sprinkled blood from the sacrifices on the fire and they ate the bodies of the slaughtered animals with "great feasting and triumph." The text is unclear about whether the Imbangala ate the bodies of the boy and the men along with the animals; instead, it mentions the presence of the cadavers in the ceremony to imply that they were.[39]

Although the text of "Strange Adventures" alleges literal cannibalism, other Imbangala activities also wasted and devoured human flesh. Imbe Calundula's warrior corps was composed almost entirely of child soldiers. Battell claimed that among Imbe Calundula's group, any child born to an Imbangala woman was birthed directly into a hole in the ground and buried alive.[40] The warriors were the young boys of conquered villages who had been forcibly incorporated into the Imbangala war camp. All reproduction of Imbangala society was predicated on the seemingly tenuous strategies of mobility, violence, and slavery. As outsiders and victims of violence, these unfree children might have needed the threat and specter of cannibalism to keep them in the camp. Although the Imbangala killed many of the adults in the villages they attacked, they enslaved others and sold them into the transatlantic trade. That the Imbangala voraciously and visibly gobbled palm trees, agriculturalists' crops and children, and the bodies of victims as slaves or (again, allegedly) as food is evidence that they, like Andrew Battell, understood the power of conspicuous consumption for creating an aura about themselves. Battell wanted to be the hero and they wanted to be terrorists, but the strategy was the same.

## Conspicuous Consumption, Capitalism, and Cannibalism

I have considered "Strange Adventures" through the analytical lens of varying types of conspicuous consumptions. Andrew Battell and the Imbangala were at the frontier of the increasingly capitalistic world of transatlantic trading practices that commodified everything, even people, and displayed the devouring of those commodities as publicly as possible so that others could remark upon them. Their displays of consumption might help them gain prestige and infamy as either a brave hero (Battell) or a terrifying cannibal (the Imbangala).

An analysis of consumptions that compares and contrasts the noticeable eating episodes in "Strange Adventures" also suggests that descriptions of the food the characters ingested helped Europeans map the knowable world. Sandra Young has demonstrated how mapmakers constructed a "knowable Africa" by designing editorial paradigms that subjected geographical reckoning and graphing to new evidentiary procedures.[41] Samuel Purchas was working toward a very similar project on a global scale that questioned what it meant to be human.[42] In doing so, he sought out eyewitnesses such as Andrew Battell who helped create an Africa that was more cognoscible for Europeans, in part by contrasting the foods various groups of people ate. Battell was distinguishable from his readers as a traveler and a hero because he ate oranges and plantains and seal and water buffalo. These exotic foods contrasted with the wine, grains, and beef consumed in Europe, but they also contrasted with the palm wine the Imbangala drank and the human flesh they allegedly ingested. Specifying the food available in a given locale and the inhabitants' eating habits helped Battell's readers demarcate familiar and civilized peoples and environments from the savage and inhospitable lands like Seal Island and from peoples like the greedy Imbangala.

Finally, consideration of the conspicuous consumptions of alleged African cannibals also sheds light on a cruel circularity between actions and ideas in the context of transatlantic slaving. The Imbangala cannibals might have marked the boundary that divided knowable Africa from savage Africa for Europeans interested in slaving adventures, but the presence of alleged cannibals justified those same ventures.

For centuries, Westerners would claim that American slavery saved Africans from cannibals like the Imbangala (a claim they would revive as justification for nineteenth-century colonial and missionary activities under the guise of humanitarianism). Thus, the alleged cannibals' ravenous ingestion of human flesh during the increasingly commodified economy of the early seventeenth century was met with even more consumptions of African bodies as Europeans purchased West Central Africans over the next two centuries. I am reminded of Marcus Rediker's analysis of sharks that trailed slave ships on the Middle Passage.[43] Slave-ship captains used the dramatic threat of throwing the enslaved overboard to be eaten by sharks to keep their human cargo docile. Sharks do, from time to time, kill people, but their swimming in the wake of a slave ship and eating those who were cast overboard was a learned behavior that was made possible because of the presence of those ships and the bodies cast out of them. Perhaps it is useful to question whether the alleged cannibals Europeans found throughout the Atlantic also learned behaviors that were possible only in the context of commodity slaving. As groups like the Imbangala followed the new profit opportunities the transatlantic slave purchasers, the capitalistic dealers of death, created, they devised terrorizing methods for professional slaving and developed greedy social ethics of conspicuous consumption. Maybe chasing the slave ships incentivized behavioral changes that propelled them from being bellicose groups of warriors who might occasionally be violent (the sort that may exist in any time or place) to the historically specific "cannibals" that sixteenth- and seventeenth-century Europeans seemed to find throughout the Atlantic.

CHAPTER 10

# "The Black People Were Not Good to Eat"

## Cannibalism, Cooperation, and Hunger at Sea

RACHEL B. HERRMANN

Slavery consumed enslaved bodies. Former bondpeople who wrote accounts of their capture and enslavement filled their pages with contrasting images of eating, hunger, and, sometimes, cannibalism. These references to cannibalism symbolized the corruption of Africans who participated in the slave trade by enslaving other Africans and the exploitative nature of white slavers, who figuratively and sometimes literally allowed sailors on their ships to eat the bodies of the enslaved.[1] Although these passages are significant because they contributed to abolitionists' efforts to end the slave trade, they are instructive for two additional reasons. First, formerly enslaved authors, by linking discussions of cannibalism to portrayals of hunger, revealed power struggles over food that add another dimension to the fraught shipboard relationships between sailors and enslaved Africans in the Atlantic world. Second, these narratives also expose moments of cooperation between slaves and sailors. In slave narratives and abolitionist texts, writers recorded enslaved peoples supplementing the terrible provisions white sailors received by offering food to their captors. This chapter's exploration of food-related interactions during peoples' overland and oceanic travels offers a broader understanding of how people who crossed water—both by choice and involuntarily—experienced hunger during the late eighteenth and early nineteenth centuries.

Current work on slave narratives focuses on questions about genre and the ways black authors subverted the genres of autobiography and captivity and religious conversion narratives. Studies of writers such as Olaudah Equiano have analyzed the topics of identity, memory, and race in these publications.[2] W. Jeffrey Bolster, who has undertaken a comprehensive study of black seafarers, demonstrates that by 1803, the proportion of black sailors in the Atlantic world had grown to 18 percent, whereas in 1740 the maritime population was mostly white. Several of the former slaves whose writings I discuss in this essay would have lived through this transition, one that enabled black men to find common ground with white sailors but did not eliminate the racism they experienced.[3]

Scholars have examined the ways authors wrote about the destructive, even cannibalistic, nature of the slave trade.[4] Amy Mitchell-Cook, who has assessed the importance of race in incidents of shipboard cannibalism, has argued that in the wake of a number of shipwrecks in the period 1660 to 1840, people maintained social, religious, and gender boundaries by adhering to a hunger topos when they cannibalized others.[5] They ate voyagers of different races first and considered consuming family members only when no other passengers were left alive.[6] The infamous case of cannibalism on the whaling ship *Essex* in 1820 involved the murder and consumption of four black men. Shipwrecked sailors ate these fellow crewmembers after the ship, which had sailed from Nantucket, Massachusetts, was attacked by a whale and sank in the middle of the Pacific Ocean.[7] Vincent Woodard emphasized the connection between cannibalism, the Middle Passage, and homoeroticism.[8] Woodard's work underscores how white sailors literally and figuratively cannibalized enslaved bodies when they interacted with male slaves. Lynn R. Johnson is interested in cannibalism metaphors and in how food and water deprivation negatively affected the African children who voyaged across the ocean.[9] Her essay is unusual in its attention to cannibalism and hunger in the same piece. In the late eighteenth century, the case of the slave ship *Zong* came to court when people learned that the commander had ordered 133 Africans thrown overboard while falsely claiming that the ship lacked potable water.[10] He facilitated these murders to claim insurance benefits on his "cargo," suggesting that slave ship captains were familiar enough with the situation of diminishing food and water supplies to use it as an excuse for violence. The 1839 slave insurrection on the *Amistad* supposedly took place because the Mende leader, Sengbe Pieh, worried that Spanish slavers wanted to cannibalize him and his fellow captive voyagers.[11]

Enslaved people may have feared being eaten first when food stores ran low or when shipwrecks occurred. These relationships between cannibalism and slavery and cannibalism and hunger merit further investigation of the power relations that centered on hunger.[12] In focusing on cannibalism before the Middle Passage, on cannibalism during the Middle Passage, and on the ties between cannibalism, hunger, food sharing, and power in eighteenth- and nineteenth-century narratives, this chapter uncovers both moments of cooperation and moments of conflict. It shows that uncertainty about provisions and hunger shaped relations between blacks and whites and between enslaved people and free persons on sea voyages. Hunger had multiple meanings for the enslaved peoples who crossed oceans, for those who transported them, and for those who wrote about the journeys of slaves and sailors. Hunger could foster violence on slave ships, but it could also create moments of unexpected generosity and thus of unpredictable power relations. In linking these related but often distinct nodes of scholarship, this essay urges readers to pay closer attention to the specific contexts of hunger in time and space.

■ ■ ■

This chapter considers several different slave narratives in its exploration of early modern enslaved peoples' hunger, eating, and fears of cannibalization, including the anonymously authored work *The Royal African* in 1750 (supposedly a biography of Prince William Ansah Sessarakoo) and works by Briton Hammon in 1760, Quobna Ottobah Cugoano in 1787, Olaudah Equiano in 1789, Venture Smith in 1798, Boyrereau Brinch (alias Jeffrey Brace) in 1810, and Omar Ibn Said in 1831.[13] It also examines an abolitionist tract by Thomas Clarkson and a longer work by Alexander Falconbridge, both written in the late eighteenth century.[14] Although some of these slave narratives do not feature in this chapter to the same extent as others because they do not mention hunger, cannibalism, or the Middle Passage, I draw upon them for information about enslaved peoples' overland journey to the African coast. When considered alongside publications by leading abolitionists who wrote about provisions for both sailors and slaves, these texts offer helpful commentary about notions of cannibalism in Africa and about provisioning and hunger in slave narratives.[15] Most antislavery material served one of three purposes: to illustrate the horrors of slavery and the slave trade, to argue for the abolition of slavery, and to allow writers to create a mythic African unity and claim a place as God's chosen people.[16] Although some scholars have classified some of these works, such as Equiano's, as travel narratives and autobiographies, at the time they were written they also functioned as pieces of writing that bolstered the abolitionist cause.[17]

As one of the most literate and prominent writers, Olaudah Equiano looms large in this essay, necessitating an explanatory gloss on his words. Recent work on Equiano's birthplace and identity requires writers to take extra care when analyzing the meanings of the cannibalism he mentions in his text.[18] Vincent Carretta has argued that although Equiano claimed to be of Igbo birth and traced his passage on the *Ogden* from the Bight of Biafra, he was in all likelihood born in South Carolina.[19] Carretta's solution to the problem of Equiano's background is to treat his description of the Middle Passage "as if it were true, expecting readers to keep in mind that this part of his account of his life may be historical fiction rather than autobiography."[20] This strategy works for Carretta, a literary scholar; historians of cannibalism must also ask questions about our abilities to recover the truth. Cannibalism scholars have been wrangling with similar questions about accuracy for nearly half a century, since the publication of William Arens's *The Man-Eating Myth.*[21] Peter Hulme built on Arens's work in his study of cannibalism discourse. He avoided claiming that he had uncovered the definitive, "true" story of what had happened in the several instances of colonial contact he analyzed in his book. Instead, he suggested that scholars could uncover an "explanatory superiority" for any given event by considering conflicting evidence, choosing the best option, and admitting that full recovery was never possible.[22] Given the evidence, it does not seem feasible to treat Equiano's narrative of the Middle Passage as an accurate one. What historians *can* do is read this section of *The Interesting Narrative* as a composite set of stories that resemble the rival claims Hulme discusses. Using this approach, Equiano's experiences become representative of the unfree Africans who were taken to the Americas and, more meaningfully, they also provide evidence of what Equiano wanted his audience to think about the Middle Passage. Whether readers believe Equiano hailed from the Bight of Biafra or South Carolina, the truthfulness of his narrative is less important than the message it sent to readers at the time. Formerly enslaved writers, wherever they were born, played a crucial role in crafting an interconnected discourse of cannibalism, hunger, and slavery in the early modern Atlantic world.

These writers' ideas about cannibalism influenced the way they experienced—or claimed to experience—their interactions with their captors in Africa. Cannibalism had specific meanings for Africans. In 1770, when he was thirteen, Quobna Ottobah Cugoano was forced from Ghana to Grenada. He first feared being eaten after three unidentified African "villains" seized him and his companions.[23] Cugoano worried that they "meant to feast on us as their prey."[24] As early as the sixteenth century, cannibalism served as "an idiom for exploitation" in myriad parts of West Central African life.[25] People used the language of eating in metaphors that connoted power and accumulation.[26] In Sierra Leone by the eighteenth and nineteenth centuries, powerful rulers who went beyond acceptable moral behavior could expect to be called cannibals.[27] In portraying his abductors as man-eating villains, Cugoano was arguing that the slave trade corrupted Africans. Although Africans associated Europeans with cannibalism because they exploited enslaved bodies, enslaved Africans also tied the Africans who captured them and sold them into slavery to cannibalism.[28]

Cugoano belonged to the Fante group, a people who eventually associated whiteness (and by inference European people) with ideas about cannibalism. Igbo, Bakongo, and Guinea peoples made similar connections.[29] When Cugoano saw "several white people" at a town on his forced journey to the coast, he was "afraid that they would eat me." He explained that he and other children "in the inland parts of the country" thought of Europeans as cannibals.[30] Cugoano and others like him grew up fearing European cannibals even though they had never seen any Europeans and such fears influenced the way they interacted with non-Africans upon capture.

It is also clear that once on board, the enslaved were afraid that white sailors would eat them. Of the writers considered here, Equiano is the only one who explicitly claimed that he worried about being eaten while at sea. Equiano "remembered" a swift series of events on his way to Barbados: he first arrived on the Biafran coast; then glimpsed the *Ogden,* his floating prison; was next "carried on board . . . immediately handled and tossed up to see if [he was] sound by some of the crew"; then he glimpsed "a large furnace or copper boiling, and a multitude of black people of every description chained together"; and then "no longer doubted" that he would be consumed. His narrative states that he subsequently fainted, revived, and asked his fellow captives "if we were not to be eaten by those white men with horrible looks, red faces, and loose hair."[31] Although cannibalism retained African-specific meanings throughout the early modern period, Equiano's narrative makes clear that he, like Cugoano, associated Europeans with man-eating. The men in Equiano's narrative were clearly white, as evidenced by their sunburned "red faces," a detail that might also have connoted drunkenness. Equiano claimed that his apprehensions dissipated during the voyage but then reappeared when the ship reached Bridge Town, Barbados. There, "merchants and planters" boarded the ship, divided the enslaved passengers, examined them, and gestured toward the land. He said that their behavior made him think "we should be eaten by these ugly men."[32] Once again, Equiano suggested that fears of cannibalization stemmed more from contact with unknown Europeans than from interactions with enslaved Africans. Africans, he asserted, were initially the ones responsible for allaying his fears of being consumed.[33]

Carretta observes that although Equiano's famous description of the Middle Passage may have been constructed, the remainder of the account maps quite consistently onto the historical record.[34] It is therefore instructive that Equiano claimed that he worried about being eaten not only on his "first" (likely fictionalized) voyage but also on the subsequent maritime journeys that followed while he was still enslaved. Equiano related that on a passage from North America to England, the captain made cannibal jokes at Equiano's expense. When the crew was short of food, he wrote, "the captain and people told me in jest they would kill and eat me; but I thought them in earnest, and was depressed beyond measure."[35] It was on this voyage that Equiano developed a complicated friendship with a young white American slave owner named Richard Baker, nicknamed Dick, with whom the captain was also friends.[36] Equiano described how the captain would tell Dick "jocularly that he would kill me to eat."

> Sometimes he would say to me—the black people were not good to eat, and would ask me if we did not eat people in my country. I said, No: then he said he would kill Dick (as he always called him) first, and afterwards me. Though this hearing relieved my mind a little as to myself, I was alarmed for Dick and whenever he was called I used to be very much afraid he was to be killed.[37]

The captain's jests left Equiano feeling quite uneasy. If the captain meant what he said, then Equiano had one of several bad choices to make. He could succumb to being eaten, resist with violence, or witness his friend killed and consumed before suffering the same fate. Woodard has suggested that the captain's jokes "belied a real, acquired taste for the enslaved African person."[38] The captain could tell Dick that he planned to eat Equiano—and laugh about it—because he already participated in an economy that consumed enslaved men and women.

Boyrereau Brinch, who was taken from Bow-Woo (Mali) on the Niger River in the mid-1750s, made similar points about a slave captain's innate destructiveness by emphasizing the monstrosity of the captain's mouth. It "had destroyed about one third of his face, and each wing was about attacking his ears, with ammunition within, called teeth." His lips were as thick as "the blade of a case knife."[39] Lynn Johnson's analysis of this portrayal suggests that although Brinch made no specific references to cannibalism, he described the captain's mouth as being capable of demolishing not only its owner's face but also, metaphorically, the bodies imprisoned below deck.[40] The captain's features symbolized his all-consuming appetite.

Three additional points emerge from former slaves' characterizations of ship captains, and from Equiano's description of the captain's continued threats. The first is these writers' insistence that the cannibals were not Africans. Equiano denied that Africans ate each other in his conversation with the captain, implying that Africans therefore did not deserve to be cannibalized.[41] On Brinch's voyage it was the white captain who had a voracious mouth. As Carl Plasa has observed, Equiano's reversal of the trope of the African cannibal undermined pro-slavery writings about Africa and the Caribbean during the late eighteenth century.[42] These writings asserted that a state of slavery was more civilized than the fate of being cannibalized. Equiano rejected the claim that Europeans who participated in the slave trade were "saving" Africans. Africans did not need to be rescued from African cannibals because African cannibals did not exist.

The second point to underscore is the inverted hunger topos that emerges from Equiano's portrayal of the appetites of the slave ship captain. Instead of beginning by cannibalizing a black person—who in other shipboard incidents and depictions of shipwrecks would have been eaten first—the captain planned to start by eating Dick. Perhaps Equiano was aware of accounts of cannibalism in contemporary shipwreck narratives; even if he was not, he reversed the hunger topos that was common to them. Because the captain also threatened to cannibalize Dick, a white slaveowner, perhaps Equiano wanted to alert readers to the fact that slave ship captains were willing to cannibalize white sailors as well as slaves; the point was that slavery resulted in unnatural hunger. The final reason why such depictions matter is that although Equiano continued to fear being cannibalized, his relationships with Europeans had evolved to such an extent that by the end of the voyage, he recognized that they had not followed through on their threats to eat him.

While Equiano was worried about actual cannibalism, episodes in other abolitionist texts can be read as a fear of what we might call proxy cannibalism. In the fall of 1788, abolitionist Thomas Clarkson interviewed twenty-two people associated with the slave trade, more than half of whom were captains, masters, or gunners; men, in other words, in positions of authority. Alexander Falconbridge based his work on his experience as a surgeon on board slave ships.[43] During the moments they described, sharks and, to a lesser extent, hogs became crucial representations of the consuming nature of slavery. On some slave ships, hogs performed the work of eating the dead and dying. Clarkson reproduced testimony from a mate who had served on a ship traveling from Scotland to Grenada. This man had witnessed the removal of "apparently dead" slaves from the hold. Hogs "were suffered to tear their carcasses . . . their legs and sinews, and all this before they were quite dead." The mate saw "the slaves draw up their legs, and move their arms, while the said hogs were tearing at them."[44] All along the Windward, Gold, and Slave Coasts, bull and tiger sharks followed slave ships until their captains had acquired enough human cargo to justify undertaking the transatlantic voyage. Once these ships were at sea, blue, silky, shortfin mako, and oceanic whitefin sharks floated just below the waterline, awaiting fresh corpses.[45] Captains used the presence of ravenous sharks to instill terror in their crew: they deterred white seamen from deserting as slave ships bobbed along the coast, filling their holds with enslaved bodies, and they discouraged enslaved individuals from attempting suicide—although, as Marcus Rediker notes, some crewmen still deserted and some slaves jumped to their deaths anyway.[46]

Thomas Clarkson and Alexander Falconbridge both described sharks eating enslaved bodies. Some English voyagers refused to eat sharks because sharks ate men.[47] Clarkson reported on the case of a black cook who was "suspected of having encouraged the slaves to rise." He was placed in the maintop and slowly starved on water and one plantain a day over a five-week period spanning two voyages until he was "relieved by death," thrown into the water, and "devoured by the sharks."[48] Other enslaved people became shark meat after denying themselves food. Falconbridge recounted the case of a woman who was struck with dysentery and refused food and medical aid. When she died, she was thrown overboard, where "her body was instantly torn to pieces by the sharks."[49] He also related an incident where fifteen people attempted suicide by jumping into the Bonny River in Nigeria. "Very few were saved," Falconbridge remarked, "and the residue fell a sacrifice to the sharks."[50] As it was animals that feasted on enslaved peoples, authors did not quite call this cannibalism, but their grammar did not blame the animals either. These authors' use of the passive voice suggested that humans facilitated animals' consumption of enslaved peoples' bodies. Humans set hogs loose on enslaved people and corpses and used sharks to cultivate fear; animals became symbolic proxies for white destruction, even cannibalization, of black flesh. Although Clarkson and Falconbridge wrote with the aim of creating sympathy for enslaved peoples and may have embellished such testimonies, the preponderance of shark-related imagery in the historical record makes such evidence difficult to discount.

Black writers treated the animals with more ambivalence. Equiano's encounter with a shark aptly illustrates that black peoples' attitudes toward these animals differed from those of white people. During a time of hunger on the voyage when the captain jokingly promised to eat Equiano, the crew caught "a large shark, and got it on board." Equiano described his happiness, because he "thought it would serve the people to eat instead of their eating me." He was wrong: to his "astonishment, they cut off a small part of the tail, and tossed the rest over the side," which "renewed" his "consternation."[51] Carretta observes that this action would have made sense to the Englishmen: sharks ate people and were consequently taboo fish and by maiming the animal they doomed it to a slow, punishing death.[52] But some Africans ate sharks. Although the people of New Calabar apparently avoided eating sharks because they were sacred to them, Fante people ate them.[53] Equiano expected to eat them, and had anyone on Cugoano's voyage speared a shark, he, too, would likely have anticipated eating it rather than wasting it. To Equiano, the decision to waste the catch seemed an illogical response to hunger. Equiano's words are instructive to historians because they reveal an additional trope in slave narratives: misunderstandings about and power struggles over foodstuffs.

▪ ▪ ▪

In the texts I have considered so far, mentions of cannibalism frequently appear in close proximity to discussions of hunger. The slave narratives and Clarkson's and Falconbridge's works about the slave trade show how the enslaved and their enslavers fought over food and in so doing worked out a state of uneven power relations. Enslavers exercised power by alternately withholding food and force-feeding slaves. The enslaved retained power by stealing food and refusing to eat. These power struggles reveal clashes and cooperation between the two groups, but just as significantly, they shed light on the many shifting notions of early modern hunger.

Thomas Clarkson and Alexander Falconbridge collected evidence about the paucity of the provisions made available to slaves on ships. Although their works are by no means comprehensive (and the lack of uniformity in their observations on provisions makes quantification challenging), they offer some idea of the sort of food that slaves ate (see Table 1).[54]

Although some diets offered variety, others were monotonous. Someone who sailed on a ship destined for an unidentified location in Africa in 1768 and 1769 recorded a diet consisting solely of horse beans and rice.[55] Although *Vicia faba*, or the fava bean, is synonymous with the horse bean, early modern meanings of the term indicate that the beans were usually grown as food for cattle. That they were fed to slaves reinforces the idea that slave ship captains considered their captives subhuman.[56] Clarkson observed that a varied and unrestricted diet prevented mortality. On a 1771 voyage from Bonny to St. Lucia, people received brandy, biscuits, rice, beans, and palm oil. The account stated that "only three" people died on this Middle Passage.[57] Enslavers weighed the costs of providing a ship with a varied range of provisions to keep their human cargo alive against the chances of increased mortality as a result of monotonous victualling. Falconbridge reminded readers of the humanity of enslaved peoples by noting that food preferences varied by location: Igbo people from the Bight of Benin preferred yams and captives from the Gold and Windward Coasts preferred rice or corn.[58] By detailing the lack of food choices on ships, Falconbridge provided further evidence that slaves were deprived of their personhood.

Geography also influenced how formerly enslaved peoples remembered their hunger while they were enslaved at sea. Lynn Johnson argues that Boyrereau Brinch's silence about certain aspects of eating on the Middle Passage allowed him to craft an "alimentary grammar," a set of observations about the Middle Passage that he could apply to the experiences of African children as they coped with hunger and water deprivation. Brinch shifted the meanings of food throughout his narrative from sustenance to "tropological or metonymic expressions of cannibalism, erotic desire, authoritarianism, and intellectual reckoning."[59] When Brinch's ship neared Barbados, he used his and fellow captives' hunger to critique the system of slavery. The ship made port with the approximately 300 enslaved men, women, and children "who had not either died with disease, mourned themselves to death or starved." Brinch asserted that "many of the children actually died with hunger, pent up in the same ship where midnight and beastly intoxication, bloated the miserable owner." He decried the hypocrisy

**Table 1.** Weekly provisions per person on eighteenth-century slave ships

| | | Provisions | | |
|---|---|---|---|---|
| Year | Route | Water | Meat | Fish |
| 1760, 1761; 1768, 1769 | Sierra Leone to Fredericksburg, VA | Half a pint at a time | — | — |
| 1767 | Old Calabar to Puerto Rico | Not mentioned | .02–.03 lbs. beef or pork | 3 stock fish[1] |
| 1767–72 | Various travels from London, Bordeaux, Brest, the River Gambia, Angola, and the River Cameroon | 7 qts. | — | Yes; quantity not stated |
| 1768, 1769 | Liverpool to Africa | 7 pints | — | — |
| 1771 | Bonny to St. Lucia | Not mentioned | — | — |
| Unknown | River Bonny to the West Indies | Not mentioned | "Sometimes . . . a small quantity of beef or pork" | — |

*Source*: Information compiled from Thomas Clarkson, *The Substance of the Evidence of Sundry Persons on the Slave-Trade, Collected in the Course of a Tour Made in the Autumn of the Year 1788* (London: James Phillips, 1789), 3 (1767 voyage), 27 (1768, 1769, unknown voyages), 31 (1771 voyage), 58 (1760, 1761, 1768, 1769 voyages), 65 (1767–1772 voyages).

of the Christian captain who refused "to bestow a morcel of bread upon his infant captive, even enough to save his life."[60]

Similarly, the meanings of hunger changed throughout Equiano's narrative. Equiano's depictions of hunger were determined by his location. After leaving Barbados and sailing to Virginia, he observed, "we were better treated than when we were coming from Africa, and we had plenty of rice and fat pork."[61] He connected his experiences

| Yams | Plantains | Horse Beans | Rice | Palm oil | Biscuits | Brandy |
|---|---|---|---|---|---|---|
| — | — | Either, quantity not stated, twice a day | | — | — | — |
| —[2] | — | — | — | — | — | — |
| Yes; quantity not stated | Yes; quantity not stated | Yes; quantity not stated | Yes; quantity not stated | Yes; quantity not stated | — | — |
| — | — | 3.5 qts. | 3.5 qts. | — | — | — |
| Yes (for the sick); quantity not stated | — | Either, unlimited quantity, twice a day | | Yes; quantity not stated | 3.5 | 7 glasses |
| Yes; quantity not stated | — | Yes; quantity not stated | Yes; quantity not stated | — | — | — |

Notes

1. Stock fish were cod, haddock, hake, or other fish of the gadoid order, cured and air-dried without salt. Stock fish required beating before cooking to make them palatable, but it is unclear whether slave ship cooks did so.

2. The ship had yams on board but the captain did not distribute them.

directly to geography; the route to Virginia from Barbados was freer from hunger than the voyage from the Bight of Biafra to Barbados. His situation improved even more on a ship bound for England: "I now thought my condition much mended," he wrote. "I had sails to lie on, and plenty of good victuals to eat; and every body on board used me very kindly, quite contrary to what I had seen of any white people before." He "began to think that they were not all of the same disposition."[62] Equiano tied the quantity and variety of provisions to proximity to England, to his treatment, and to his realization that race was not always an indicator of a person's capacity for ill treatment. Although Equiano remained enslaved at this point in the narrative, Equiano's reader might have guessed that England represented freedom from hunger and, given developments such as the 1772 Somerset decision, broader initiatives to abolish slavery.[63] When the ship reached England, the captain disembarked to obtain fresh provisions, and when he sent them on board, Equiano and the crew's "famine was soon turned into feasting, almost without ending."[64]

If some, like Equiano, experienced freedom from hunger, other enslaved peoples continued to experience want, controlled access to food, and, sometimes, starvation. In noting the undistributed yams on one slave ship, Thomas Clarkson was commenting on a deliberate decision to withhold food from captives.[65] His observations about a well-provisioned slave ship going from Bonny to the West Indies suggested that some captains assumed that well-fed slaves were likelier to rebel.[66] Equiano's description of white sailors throwing away excess fish they had caught instead of feeding them to slaves tallies with this view.[67] Clarkson's gruesome depiction of Jamaican slaves who, having been convicted of murdering a white shopkeeper, were slowly starved to death in a pillory for so long that one man gnawed and ate "part of his own shoulder" added further commentary on the all-consuming nature of slavery.[68] In maritime communities, forced starvation could result in autocannibalism (the consumption of one's own body).[69] Vincent Woodard has argued that masters used starvation as a form of control that limited disobedience and resistance.[70]

Slaves who rejected food during their trans-Atlantic journey were compelled to eat through a number of means. Clarkson mentioned gagging and flogging as a form of punishment for not eating.[71] Falconbridge described the application of hot coals to lips so "as to scorch and burn them" when the enslaved refused to eat.[72] Equiano claimed that he was gagged, which prevented him from eating, but he also said that his captors force-fed him. When his kidnappers separated him from his sister, he wrote, he "cried and grieved continually," eating only "what they forced into my mouth."[73] Some people took the step of pouring liquefied food down captives' throats with the aid of a funnel or horn.[74] As Kyla Wazana Tompkins suggests, the meaning of the mouth in the nineteenth-century United States was by no means uniform.[75] The mouth could be a site of vulnerability, aggression, laughter, consumption, and pleasure, to name only a few options. Enslavers consistently attempted to control the mouths of the enslaved. In many respects, the moments when slaves hungered were moments of powerlessness.

Enslaved people sometimes welcomed hunger. Although some bondpeople stopped eating because the shock of the Middle Passage prompted apathy, despair, and depression, others made a conscious choice to stop eating because it allowed them to retain some semblance of control over their bodies. Earlier works attributed captives' loss of appetite to depression that often resulted in suicide, but recent scholarship has located power in slave suicides.[76] During some moments, hunger was a positive force that represented one's will to live *or* die. Food refusal in slave narratives served multiple purposes. Not eating could be interpreted as a display of resistance.[77]

There are myriad instances of enslaved people ignoring hunger. Significantly, several episodes of food refusal occurred after authors experienced fear of cannibalism. Equiano wrote that in their grief after being captured, he and his sister privileged sleep over eating, refusing the "victuals" given to them. Because they did so after their captors gagged them, their voluntary fast could also be read as a critique of people who tried to regulate captive mouths.[78] The most memorable moment of food refusal in Equiano's narrative occurred just after he worried about being cannibalized. In his account of his first voyage, he wrote that after asking whether sailors intended to eat him, he was taken below deck where, "sick and low," he was "not able" to eat and refused to do so.[79] Similarly, after feeling fear that the men who originally seized him meant to take him somewhere where they would cannibalize him, Cugoano "refused to eat or drink, for whole days together."[80] In these two instances, it becomes apparent that these writers' portrayals (whether real or imagined) of the power to not eat could serve multiple purposes: an attempt to foil would-be cannibals by providing them with less meat from self-starved bodies, a commentary on whites' efforts to force enslaved peoples to consume, a critique of the all-consuming nature of slavery, and a reminder to the reader that physical sustenance was sometimes less important than emotional or religious support. Authors who had been enslaved, in other words, figured hunger as a trope that changed, from the interior to the African coast to the ocean crossing. Just as there were good and bad things to eat, so too were there good and bad *times* to eat.

Enslaved people also tried to prevent hunger by fighting for food. Slaves seized the opportunity to steal provisions, often at great risk. After several white sailors on the ship that carried Equiano from Africa caught a number of fish and tossed what they could not eat into the sea, several slaves "took an opportunity, when they thought no one saw them, of trying to get a little privately." They were caught and subjected to "some very severe floggings."[81] On the one hand, perhaps it is odd to think of sailors preventing enslaved peoples from eating, given the desire of slave ship captains to keep their human cargo alive to maximize their profit. On the other hand, it is also clear that at times food deprivation was a form of power. Clarkson's collection of evidence exposed the efforts of bondpeople to obtain food by any means, even stealing. He explained that slave "boys, who are loose about the ship, very often steal a portion of . . . provisions" from the

Table 2. Weekly provisions per person for sailors on eighteenth-century slave ships

| | | Provisions | | | |
|---|---|---|---|---|---|
| Year | Route | Water | Meat | Bread | Fish |
| Unknown | Unknown | Yes | Yes; quantity not stated[1] | 5 lbs. | — |
| Unknown | Unknown | Not specified | Yes; quantity not stated[2] | 4 lbs. | — |
| Unknown | Unknown | Not specified | 3.5 lbs. | 3.5 lbs. | — |
| Unknown | Unknown | Not specified | 7 lbs. salt pork | 4 lbs. | — |

*Source*: Information compiled Thomas Clarkson, *The Substance of the Evidence of Sundry Persons on the Slave-Trade, Collected in the Course of a Tour Made in the Autumn of the Year 1788* (London: James Phillips, 1789), 16, 20, 24, 27.

sailors.[82] Younger children who were not subjected to the same physical restraints as older men and women may have been able to pilfer food to take to those chained below deck.

Although the majority of interactions between sailors and slaves were fraught with violence, several episodes in the writings discussed in this chapter suggest that hunger also led to ephemeral moments of cooperation. Some of these moments move beyond the trope of cannibalism, but cannibalism continues to matter in several. The provisions for sailors were terrible, just as they were for the enslaved people. Falconbridge and Clarkson both had a tendency to segue from descriptions of enslaved foodstuffs to sailors' rations, though they each had far less to say about the routes of these voyages. Captains were notorious for depriving sailors of food.[83] Compared to the slave diets Falconbridge and Clarkson described, the rations given to white sailors had both less variety and smaller quantities. Although other factors such as disease likely played a role in killing sailors, historians cannot discount the influence of poor diets. Vincent Carretta has even pointed to data that confirm abolitionists' claims that slave ship crews had higher mortality rates than slaves.[84]

| Yams | Plantains | Horse Beans | Rice | Palm oil | Biscuits | Brandy |
|---|---|---|---|---|---|---|
| — | — | — | — | — | — | — |
| — | — | — | — | — | — | — |
| — | — | — | — | — | — | — |
| — | — | — | — | — | — | — |

Notes

1. "The little beef that was given them, was either excessively bad in itself or damaged" (16).

2. "A small portion of damaged beef" (20).

Given the fact that sailors ate poorly, historians need to consider the possibility that enslaved peoples' fears of cannibalism, however exaggerated, are evidence of white sailors' hunger on slave ships. Falconbridge explained that some slaves' provisions were "frequently taken from the provisions laid in for the sailors," meaning that those sailors would receive less food than they anticipated.[85] Clarkson wrote that seamen who were reduced to damaged beef and half a pound of bread a day were "obliged to beg victuals of the slaves."[86] Slaves received provisions originally intended for sailors without asking for them, whereas sailors had to beg enslaved peoples for food to satisfy their hunger. These brief mentions of slaves giving food to sailors hint that cooperation between slaves and sailors may have existed on some voyages. Such cooperation does not, of course, negate the violent measures that other sailors may have taken to procure food from slaves or ignore the possibility that captains fed slaves more food than sailors because they wanted to foster animosity between crews and bondpeople. There were myriad types of hunger on these voyages, but writers most vocally critiqued the kind captains deliberately created, regardless of whether voyagers were free or enslaved.

■ ■ ■

In eighteenth- and nineteenth-century slave narratives and abolitionist literature, the linked themes of hunger, eating, and cannibalism are important because they reveal the spectrum of power struggles enslaved people experienced. These themes are also significant because they show both conflict and cooperation between sailors and people of African descent. As kidnapped African captives journeyed to the coast, their fears of cannibalism symbolized how slavery corrupted Europeans. Writers' records of these fears also suggested that Africans involved in the slave trade were corrupt. Once enslaved peoples boarded a ship, captains represented the destructiveness of slavery with behaviors such as making jokes about cannibalism and using animals as proxy cannibals of African bodies. Once removed from the African continent, enslaved peoples were not perceived as good to eat; they did not eat each other, nor, as Equiano's captain observed, would they make good meals.

Although it is tempting to read hunger as similar for everyone who experienced it, these texts reveal several ideas about hunger in maritime contexts. Some captains on slave ships paid only cursory attention to slaves' hunger, choosing to let people die rather than providing a varied diet for them. Other captains made efforts to feed people based on regional preferences. Some formerly enslaved writers, such as Boyrereau Brinch, described how their hunger as slaves changed over time, whereas for others, for example Equiano, hunger was tied more to geography: the Caribbean seas were places of hunger, proximity to coastal Virginia provided freedom from want, and the English coast offered nearly limitless bounty. Hunger could be horrifying, as when it forced imprisoned slaves to cannibalize their own bodies. But self-cannibalization, or allowing one's body to consume itself as it battled the pressing needs of hunger, could also be a good thing, a signifier of resistance through choosing when and how to starve.

# Conclusion
## Beyond Jamestown

RACHEL B. HERRMANN

After reading these chapters as a whole, it is worth thinking about how they build upon and echo each other. Several themes run throughout the essays in this volume, including contemporaries' questions about whether cannibalism took place; theorizing about eating, hunger, and savagery; thinking about epistemology; and the Atlantic world paradigm. If, as I suggested in this book's introduction, cannibalism must be studied in close connection with something else, then it is necessary to ask how those other subjects alter what we know about cannibalism and the early modern Atlantic and about the Atlantic world as a whole.

To an extent, works about cannibalism do still have to wrangle with William Arens—to decide whether cannibalism occurred—and thus with Jamestown, too. But the writers in this volume are more interested in how people in the fifteenth through nineteenth centuries debated this question rather than going back in time to definitively authenticate specific instances. Contributors have homed in on historical representations of and denials about cannibalism: Gregory Smithers on Europeans' accusations that Native Americans ate each other or ate Europeans (and by contrast, Native Americans' uses of cannibalism stories to delimit social behavior); Elena Daniele in urging caution when generalizing about cannibal tropes in early Italian mercantile reports of the New World; Julie Gammon, Jessica Hower, and Matt Williamson on assessing how representations of English cannibals reflected imperial projects; Rebecca Earle on how attitudes toward wheat bread and alcohol consumption related to attitudes toward cannibals; Jared Staller on Europeans' beliefs that Africans consumed each other; and my chapter on Africans' counterarguments—articulated by white slave traders—that black people were bad to eat. As Kelly

Watson and Gregory Smithers remind us, accusations of cannibalism bolstered settler colonialism and imperial expansion, although as Julie Gammon and Matt Williamson observe, cannibal tropes sometimes encouraged deeper introspection about emerging colonial capitalism.

Debates about cannibalism changed throughout the early modern period. Kelly Watson finds that Spanish colonizers in the Caribbean and Latin America mostly stopped deploying cannibal accusations to justify imperial expansion after the seventeenth century. Gregory Smithers and I suggest that, in contrast, Anglo-American invaders continued to levy charges of cannibalism against North American Indians and Africans in the eighteenth and nineteenth centuries. Denials of man-eating during these periods sometimes helped foster reform efforts, as when Olaudah Equiano reminded his readers that Africans were not cannibals so he could garner support for the abolitionist cause. In other instances, cannibalism returned to haunt the English at home. Julie Gammon argues that the familiarity of the Sawney Bean story and authors' tendencies to rewrite the tale about a Scottish cannibal to include English cannibals forced people to reckon with the incivility of English crime in certain regions of the country, such as Devon. These stories could then be circulated in myriad coastal regions in and outside of Great Britain. By the late eighteenth century, discussions of cannibalism could be used both to push back against imperialism and to ask questions about domestic lawlessness.

In analyzing how early modern people used accusations of cannibalism, some of the scholars in this volume have provided helpful background on early modern writers that help us place cannibalism stories into fuller context. Elena Daniele's chapter provides details about the literary education of Italians, such as Peter Martyr D'Anghiera and Nicolò Scillacio, helping us to think more precisely about how humanists altered New World reports. Europeans learned about a New World inhabited by cannibals through Columbus's letter (which was written in the classical and medieval travel traditions); but the inner circle of the court and the Italian merchants (who were direct observers of the Columbian enterprise) were at first skeptical about stories of cannibalism in their communication via circular newsletters. Kelly Watson's chapter does similar work by making such writers more palpably, violently human—such as when she wonders whether Michele da Cuneo described an indigenous woman as a cannibal to explain why he raped her. Even if there is no straight connection between this assumption and his actions, it is clear that Spanish conquerors assumed that peoples in the New World wanted to be subjugated. In doing this contextual work, this book's contributors offer new ways of thinking about cannibalism, including theories about honor eating (as in the case of Robert Appelbaum's chapter) and proxy cannibalism (as in my essay).

By trying to pin down the specifics of reports of cannibalism, contributors have also worked through concepts of eating and hunger. Gregory Smithers's work urges further study of the connection between cannibalism and eating taboos. Robert Appelbaum's chapter offers the concept of honor eating to explain how cycles of cannibalism supposedly flourished among the Tupinamba in sixteenth-century Brazil. In his theoretical framework, cannibalism was necessary. Jared Staller's analysis of conspicuous consumptions builds on Appelbaum's analysis by suggesting that there is often a connection between food choices, hunger, and taste and that the quantity of food consumed must be examined alongside these other factors. Relatedly, it becomes clear that throughout the early modern Atlantic world, hunger retained meanings that were specific to time and place. Some people, like Andrew Battell in sixteenth-century South America, Angola, and Loango, feared hunger especially when they faced the prospect of having to eat unfamiliar foods. As Rebecca Earle observes, Spaniards voiced similar worries about New World crops and about the Amerindians who consumed Old World wheat and wine. Other people, like Equiano and Boyrereau Brinch, as they recalled the times when enslaved people ignored or embraced hunger, used those incidents to make points about the barbarity of slave owners. These various meanings of hunger should alert scholars to the danger of overstating the role of hunger in prompting peoples' actions.

Hunger could be a tie that bound people together, but it could also drive people apart. Earle's study of the relationship between cannibalism and the use of wheat bread and wine in the Eucharist suggests how inconsistently Spaniards used food practices to separate themselves from indigenous peoples. It is true that the Eucharist prompted confusion between Natives and non-Natives. At the same time, debates and misunderstandings about the consumption of the Host revealed moments of unity between Europeans and Amerindians and divisions between Protestants and Catholics. My chapter also finds evidence of momentary cooperation between people, in the case of enslaved Africans and white sailors on slave ships. Given the poor state of sailors' rations, it seems likely that some slaves shared food with their enslavers. To an extent, this focus on bonds between people has also encouraged writers' interest in intragroup divisions. Matt Williamson, for example, locates discord within the European community. Players on stage, in contemplating the cannibalization of another English character, acted out their uneasiness with colonial expansion abroad. Such anxiety existed alongside European approval of non-Natives attacks against Indigenous peoples.

Engaging with violence in the early modern Atlantic has enabled scholars to pursue two additional ideas in this volume: savagery and Europeans' definitions of it and European knowledge-making more broadly. Kelly Watson finds that the way that Europeans conceived of civilized and uncivilized Native Americans had much to do with cannibalism. Such conceptions also, however, depended on European ideas about sexuality and a whole suite of additional behaviors. Europeans said that Native Americans were "uncivilized" not only because they supposedly ate human flesh but also because Spaniards believed they went naked, were promiscuous, and lacked centralized government. Julie Gammon echoes many of these themes as she teases out the gendered meanings of non-English cannibalism in the eighteenth and nineteenth centuries. Robert Appelbaum's delineation of the rationale behind Tupinamba cannibalism does away with the notion of cannibalism as an unthinking practice. His chapter provides further evidence of the uncritical way early modern actors levied charges of savagery at indigenous peoples. Europeans' understandings of eating in the early modern Atlantic also contributed to the broader task of knowledge formation. In Daniele's chapter, knowledge about the New World, based mainly on the Columbus letter, but with additions originating in the inner circle of the Spanish court, spread initially via the Italian mercantile and diplomatic network, and from there to the public at large. Jared Staller explains that a century later, Battell's descriptions of food and eating enabled Europeans to map a knowable world. Fear of hunger made Battell denigrate some regions in Latin America, whereas the reported existence of cannibals did not necessarily inhibit his travels in Africa; in some cases, in fact, it encouraged them.

Finally, these authors demonstrate their investment in testing the geography and chronology of the Atlantic world. Robert Appelbaum would have us recall that the Tupinamba had their own history and were not stuck in the golden age in which Montaigne depicted them. Some of the earliest studies of cannibalism focused on Brazil and the Caribbean, and such geographies can and should continue to feature in current works on man-eating. Elena Daniele's work reminds us that Italians merchants shaped the early discourse about cannibalism through their direct interrogation of participants in the Columbian expeditions. Jessica Hower's focus on Ireland toward the end of her chapter disrupts a familiar chronology in which colonialism in Ireland created a staging ground for later periods of British imperialism. From the 1560s to the 1580s—in other words, before Ireland and long before Jamestown—British tales of cannibalism reflected domestic politics. Julie Gammon reminds us that the same might be said of Scotland's relationship to England after the 1707 Act of Union. Chapters by Rebecca Earle, Kelly Watson, Gregory Smithers, Jared Staller, and myself call for attention to the Spanish, Native, and African Atlantic contexts in further studies of man-eating. And so perhaps this volume ends where it began: with the significance of Jamestown to studies of cannibalism but also with the importance of moving beyond Jamestown in our study of cannibals and cannibal stories.

# NOTES

## Introduction

1. John Almon, *The Allies—Par Nobile Fratrum!*, London, February 3, 1780, Prints and Photographs Division, Library of Congress, accessed October 30, 2017, https://tinyurl.com/ychku38l.

2. For other analyses of this image, see Troy Bickham, *Making Headlines: The American Revolution as Seen through the British Press* (DeKalb: Northern Illinois University Press, 2009), 221; Holger Hoock, *Scars of Independence: America's Violent Birth* (New York: Crown, 2017), 279–281. For the figure as Lord North, see Peter Silver, *Our Savage Neighbors: How Indian War Transformed Early America* (New York: W. W. Norton, 2008), 247–249.

3. On American accusations to this effect, see Silver, *Our Savage Neighbors*, 227–260, esp. 239–243. For British writers who made similar charges, see Alan Taylor, *The Divided Ground: Indians, Settlers, and the Northern Borderland of the American Revolution* (New York: Vintage, 2006), 98.

4. On types of cannibalism, see William Arens, *The Man-Eating Myth: Anthropology & Anthropophagy* (New York: Oxford University Press, 1979), 17–18; Aparecida Vilaça, "Relations between Funerary Cannibalism and Warfare Cannibalism: The Question of Predation," *Ethnos* 65, no. 1 (2000): 83–106; and Beth A. Conklin, *Consuming Grief: Compassionate Cannibalism in an Amazonian Society* (Austin: University of Texas Press, 2001).

5. Rachel B. Herrmann, "'No useless Mouth': Iroquoian Food Diplomacy in the American Revolution," *Diplomatic History* 47, no. 1 (2017): 29–31, 44–45.

6. Wellcome Trust Grant number 105351/Z/14/Z. The conference program is available at http://tinyurl.com/zlz2mqw, accessed September 14, 2016.

7. On cannibalism versus anthropophagy, see Kelly L. Watson, *Insatiable Appetites: Imperial Encounters with Cannibals in the North Atlantic World* (New York: New York University Press, 2015), 18. On how Caribbean peoples became associated with cannibalism, see Peter Hulme, *Colonial Encounters: Europe and the Native Caribbean, 1492–1797* (London: Methuen, 1986), 15, 17, 86. See also Gananath Obeyesekere, *Cannibal Talk: The Man-Eating Myth and Human Sacrifice in the South Seas* (Berkeley: University of California Press, 2005), 14; Louis Allaire, "Visions of Cannibals: Distant Islands and Distant Lands," in *The Lesser Antilles in the Age of European Expansion*, edited by Robert L. Paquette and Stanley L. Engerman (Gainesville: University Press of Florida, 1996), 33–49.

8. Reay Tannahill, *Flesh and Blood: A History of the Cannibal Complex* (New York: Stein and Day, 1975), 9; Marvin Harris, *Cannibals and Kings: The Origins of Cultures* (New York: Random House, 1977), 102, 109; Marvin Harris, *Good to Eat: Riddles of Food and Culture* (Long Grove, Illinois: Waveland Press, Inc., 1998), 203.

9. Claude Lévi-Strauss, "The Culinary Triangle," in *Food and Culture: A Reader*,

2nd ed., edited by Carole Counihan and Penny Van Esterik (New York: Routledge, 2008), 36–37; Arens, *The Man-Eating Myth,* 17.

10. Harris, *Good to Eat,* 220.

11. One could classify early modern writers—such as Michel de Montaigne, Hans Staden, and Jean de Léry—with these anthropologists if one thinks of them as early (albeit biased) ethnographers. See Bart Moore-Gilbert, "'New worlds, new selves': Montaigne, 'the Atlantic' and the Emergence of Modern Autobiography," *Atlantic Studies* 2, no. 1 (2005): 1–14; Neil L. Whitehead, "Hans Staden and the Cultural Politics of Cannibalism," *Hispanic American Historical Review* 80, no. 4 (2000): 721–751; Adam Asher Duker, "The Protestant Israelites of Sancerre: Jean de Léry and the Confessional Demarcation of Cannibalism," *Journal of Early Modern History* 18, no. 3 (2014): 255–286, esp. 284.

12. Harris, *Good to Eat,* 207–208.

13. Peggy Reeves Sanday, *Divine Hunger: Cannibalism as a Cultural Symbol* (Cambridge: Cambridge University Press, 1986).

14. Frank Lestringant, *Cannibals: The Discovery and Representation of the Cannibal from Columbus to Jules Verne,* translated by Rosemary Morris (Berkeley: University of California Press, 1997).

15. George Franklin Feldman, *Cannibalism, Headhunting and Human Sacrifice in North America: A History Forgotten* (Chambersburg, PA.: Alan C. Hood & Company, 2008).

16. Thomas S. Abler, "Iroquois Cannibalism: Fact Not Fiction," *Ethnohistory* 27, no. 4 (1980): 309–316.

17. Obeyesekere, *Cannibal Talk.*

18. Joseph Stromberg, "Starving Settlers in Jamestown Colony Resorted to Cannibalism," *Smithsonian.com,* April 30, 2013, accessed August 8, 2016, http://tinyurl.com/nkrlaq3; Jane O'Brien, "'Proof' Jamestown Settlers Turned to Cannibalism," *BBC News,* May 1, 2013, accessed August 8, 2016, http://tinyurl.com/j4uotbu; Nicholas Wade, "Girl's Bones Bear Signs of Cannibalism by Starving Virginia Colonists," *New York Times,* May 1, 2013, accessed August 8, 2016, http://tinyurl.com/jgwxz60; Liat Clark, "Meet Jane, Eaten by Her 17th Century Jamestown Co-Settlers," *Wired,* May 2, 2013, accessed August 8, 2016, http://tinyurl.com/znm4qly; Maev Kennedy, "Excavated Skull Suggests Jamestown Colonists Resorted to Cannibalism," *The Guardian,* May 2, 2013, accessed August 8, 2016, http://tinyurl.com/zv3wnau; Paula Neely, "Jamestown Colonists Resorted to Cannibalism," *National Geographic News,* May 3, 2013, accessed August 8, 2016, http://tinyurl.com/d26ztz9.

19. James Horn, William Kelso, Douglas Owsley, and Beverly Straube, *Jane: Starvation, Cannibalism, and Endurance at Jamestown* (Richmond, VA: Carter Printing, 2013).

20. William M. Kelso, *Jamestown: The Truth Revealed* (Charlottesville, VA: University of Virginia Press, 2017).

21. For the region's Native inhabitants, which included Algonquian-, Iroquoian-, and Siouan-speaking Chickahominy; Doeg; Mangoag; Mannahoac; Massawomeck; Monacan; Pamunkey; Patawomeck; Powhatan; Susquehannock; and Tuscarora Indians, see Karen Ordahl Kupperman, ed., *Captain John Smith: A Select Edition of His Writings* (Chapel Hill: University of North Carolina Press, 1988), 8–10; and James Horn, *A Land as God Made It: Jamestown and the Birth of America* (New York: Basic Books, 2005), 11–14.

22. This literature is vast. For representative examples, see Edmund S. Morgan, *American Slavery, American Freedom: The Ordeal of Colonial Virginia* (New York: W. W. Norton & Company, 1975), 73; Richard J. Hooker, *Food and Drink in America: A History* (New York: Bobbs-Merrill, 1981), 18; Kathleen M. Brown, *Good Wives, Nasty Wenches, and Anxious Patriarchs: Gender, Race, and Power in Colonial Virginia* (Chapel Hill: University of North Carolina Press, 1996), 62; Karen Ordahl Kupperman, *The Jamestown Project* (Cambridge, MA: The Belknap Press of Harvard University Press, 2007), 253; Horn, *A Land as God Made It*, 176; James E. McWilliams, *A Revolution in Eating: How the Quest for Food Shaped America* (New York: Columbia University Press, 2005), 101; Rachel B. Herrmann, "The 'tragicall historie': Cannibalism and Abundance in Colonial Jamestown," *William and Mary Quarterly* 68, no. 1 (2011): 47–74.

23. Kelso, *Jamestown*, 185.

24. Herrmann, "The 'tragicall historie.'"

25. The following discussion is based on a blog post I wrote when news of the findings first broke. See Rachel Herrmann, "Digging Out My Cannibal Girl Hat," *The Junto: A Group Blog on Early American History*, May 2, 2013, accessed August 26, 2016, http://tinyurl.com/jzwkaqe.

26. On the trash pit, see Horn et al., *Jane*, 3, 6; O'Brien, "'Proof' Jamestown Settlers Turned to Cannibalism"; and Kelso, *Jamestown*, 185. For snakes and horses, see Kupperman, *Captain John Smith*, 130; George Percy, *A Trewe Relacyon*, in *Captain John Smith: Writings with Other Narratives of Roanoke, Jamestown, and the First English Settlement of America*, edited by James Horn (New York: Library of America, 2007), 1099.

27. Horn et al., *Jane*, 25.

28. Kelso, *Jamestown*, 189–190, 263n1.

29. Kupperman, *Captain John Smith*, 130; Percy, *A Trewe Relacyon*, 1100.

30. Kupperman, *Captain John Smith*, 130.

31. Daniel Walden, "America's First Coastal Community: A Cis- and Circumatlantic Reading of John Smith's *The Generall Historie of Virginia*," *Atlantic Studies* 7, no. 3 (2010): 329–330.

32 Virginia Council, *A Trve Declaration of the Estate of the Colonie in Virginia, with a Confutation of Such Scandalous Reports as Haue Tended to the Disgrace of So Worthy an Enterprise* (London, 1610), 38–39.

33. Horn et al., *Jane*, 20; Kelso, *Jamestown*, 195–196.

34. On their motivations, see Herrmann, "The 'tragicall historie,'" 52, 55.

35. Obeyesekere, *Cannibal Talk*.

36. Hulme, *Colonial Encounters;* Francis Barker, Peter Hulme, and Margaret Iversen, eds., *Cannibalism and the Colonial World* (Cambridge: Cambridge University Press, 1998); Laurence R. Goldman, *The Anthropology of Cannibalism* (Westport: Praeger, 1999). The term man-eating is of course not gender-neutral, and scholars do tend to use it interchangeably with cannibalism. Its continued use signifies the lasting importance of and engagement with Arens, and the fact that the people cannibalized were often (but not always) men.

37. Hulme, *Colonial Encounters*, xiii–xiv, 5.

38. In this vein, see Neil L. Whitehead, "Carib Cannibalism: The Historical Evidence," *Journal de la Société des Américanistes* 70 (1984): 69–87; Philip Levy, "Man-Eating and Menace on Richard Hore's Expedition to America," *Atlantic*

*Studies* 2, no. 2 (2005): 131; Herrmann, "The 'tragicall historie,'" 47–74; Peter C. Mancall, "The Raw and the Cold: Five English Sailors in Sixteenth-Century Nunavut," *William and Mary Quarterly* 70, no. 1 (2013): 31.

39. For monsters and sexuality, see Merrall Llewelyn Price, *Consuming Passions: The Uses of Cannibalism in Late Medieval and Early Modern Europe* (New York: Routledge, 2003). For nationalism, see Heather Blurton, *Cannibalism in High Medieval English Literature* (New York: Palgrave Macmillan, 2007).

40. Cătălin Avramescu, *An Intellectual History of Cannibalism*, translated by Alistair I. Blyth (Princeton, NJ: Princeton University Press, 2009).

41. Jennifer Brown, *Cannibalism in Literature and Film* (Basingstoke: Palgrave Macmillan, 2012).

42. Watson, *Insatiable Appetites*.

43. Richard Sugg, *Mummies, Cannibals, and Vampires: The History of Corpse Medicine from the Renaissance to the Victorians* (New York: Routledge, 2011); Christine Louise Noble, *Medicinal Cannibalism in Early Modern English Literature and Culture* (New York: Palgrave Macmillan, 2011).

44. Karen Gordon-Grube, "Evidence of Medicinal Cannibalism in Puritan New England: 'Mummy' and Related Remedies in Edward Taylor's 'Dispensatory,'" *Early American Literature* 28, no. 3 (1993): 185–186; P. Kenneth Himmelman, "The Medicinal Body: An Analysis of Medicinal Cannibalism in Europe, 1300–1700," *Dialectical Anthropology* 22, no. 2 (1997): 183–203.

45. Hans Askenasy, *Cannibalism: From Sacrifice to Survival* (Amherst, NY: Prometheus Books, 1994). Similarly, see Carole A. Travis-Henikoff, *Dinner with a Cannibal: The Complete History of Mankind's Oldest Taboo* (Santa Monica, CA: Santa Monica Press, 2008); and Cormac Ó Gráda, *Eating People Is Wrong, and Other Essays on Famine, Its Past, and Its Future* (Princeton, NJ: Princeton University Press, 2015).

46. Nathan Constantine, *A History of Cannibalism: From Ancient Cultures to Survival Stories and Modern Psychopaths* (London: Arcturus Publishing, 2006).

47. Daniel Diehl and Mark P. Donnelly, *Eat Thy Neighbour: A History of Cannibalism* (Stroud: Sutton, 2006).

48. Because contributors in this volume work in different fields of history and other disciplines, I have not standardized terminology for Native Americans, Amerindians, or Indigenous peoples, preferring instead to let contributors use the phrasing most common to their disciplines.

49. See, for example, Sidney Mintz, *Sweetness and Power: The Place of Sugar in Modern History* (New York: Viking Press, 1985); Mark Kurlansky, *Cod: A Biography of the Fish that Changed the World* (New York: Penguin, 1998); and Mark Kurlansky, *Salt: A World History* (New York: Penguin, 2003). See also the extensive series on single-commodity foodstuffs published by Reaktion Books Ltd. For in-depth histories of food and consumption, see Peter Thompson, *Rum Punch and Revolution: Taverngoing and Public Life in Eighteenth-Century Philadelphia* (Philadelphia: University of Pennsylvania Press, 1999); McWilliams, *A Revolution in Eating;* Psyche A. Williams-Forson, *Building Houses Out of Chicken Legs: Black Women, Food, & Power* (Chapel Hill: University of North Carolina Press, 2006); Marcy Norton, *Sacred Gifts, Profane Pleasures: A History of Tobacco and Chocolate in the Atlantic World* (Ithaca, NY: Cornell University Press, 2008); Sarah Hand Meacham, *Every Home a Distillery: Alcohol, Gender, and Technology in the Colonial Chesapeake*

(Baltimore, MD: Johns Hopkins University Press, 2009); David Hancock, *Oceans of Wine: Madeira and the Emergence of American Trade and Taste* (New Haven, CT: Yale University Press, 2009); Michael A. LaCombe, *Political Gastronomy: Food and Authority in the English Atlantic World* (Philadelphia: University of Pennsylvania Press, 2012); Kyla Wazana Tompkins, *Racial Indigestion: Eating Bodies in the 19th Century* (New York: New York University Press, 2012).

50. James Vernon, *Hunger: A Modern History* (Cambridge, MA: Harvard University Press, 2007); Nick Cullather, *The Hungry World: America's Cold War Battle Against Poverty in Asia* (Cambridge, MA: Harvard University Press, 2010).

## Chapter 1

1. John R. Swanton, *Myths and Tales of the Southeastern Indians* (1929; repr., Norman: University of Oklahoma Press, 1995), 222.

2. The following analysis of the Natchez narrative of "Lodge Boy and Thrown-Away" is derived from Swanton, *Myths and Tales of the Southeastern Indians,* 222–228. For analysis of other versions of this story, see William Nelson Fenton, *The Great Law and the Longhouse: A Political History of the Iroquois Confederacy* (Norman: University of Oklahoma Press, 1988), 35, 38; and Anthony W. Wonderley, *At the Font of the Marvelous: Exploring Oral Narrative and Mythic Imagery of the Iroquois and Their Neighbors* (Syracuse, NY: Syracuse University Press, 2009), 84, 93, 105.

3. Robert H. Lowie, *Myths and Traditions of the Crow Indians* (Lincoln: University of Nebraska Press, 1993), 74–85; Wonderley, *At the Font of the Marvelous,* 108; George E. Lankford, *Native American Legends of the Southeast: Tales from the Natchez, Caddo Biloxi, Chickasaw, and Other Nations* (Tuscaloosa: University of Alabama Press, 2011), 160–161; Michelle Smith, *Legends, Lore, and True Tales of the Chattahoochee* (Charleston: History Press, 2013), 17–18.

4. William Arens, *The Man-Eating Myth: Anthropology and Anthropophagy* (New York: Oxford University Press, 1979), 49; Jeff Berglund, *Cannibal Fictions: American Explorations of Colonialism, Race, Gender, and Sexuality* (Madison: University of Wisconsin Press, 2006), 3; Cătălin Avramescu, *An Intellectual History of Cannibalism,* translated by Alistair I. Blyth (Princeton, NJ: Princeton University Press, 2009), 106. To underscore the savagery of the Native peoples he encountered, Columbus described castration practices in the same context as cannibalism. See Jose Piedra, "Loving Columbus," in *Amerindian Images and the Legacy of Columbus,* edited by Rene Jara and Nicholas Spadaccini (Minneapolis: University of Minnesota Press, 1992), 260. See also Frank Lestringant, *Cannibals: The Discovery and Representation of the Cannibal from Columbus to Jules Verne,* translated by Rosemary Morris (Berkeley: University of California Press, 1997).

5. John Nicholl, *An Houre Glass of Indian Newes* (London: Nathaniell Butter, 1607); John Speed, *A Prospect of the Most Famous Parts of the World, viz. Asia, Africa, Europe, America, in his The Theatre of the Empire of Great-Britain* (London: Thomas Basset, 1676), 43.

6. Maggie Kilgour, "The Function of Cannibalism at the Present Time," in *Cannibalism and the Colonial World,* edited by Peter Hulme and Margaret Iverson (New York: Cambridge University Press, 1998), 239.

7. Gananath Obeyesekere, *Cannibal Talk: The Man-Eating Myth and Human Sacrifice in the South Seas* (Berkeley: University of California Press, 2005), 8–9. See also Neil L. Whitehead, *Of Cannibals and Kings: Primal Anthropology in the Americas* (University Park: Pennsylvania State University Press, 1992), 16; Eric Cheyfitz, *The Poetics of Imperialism: Translation and Colonization from The Tempest to Tarzan* (Philadelphia: University of Pennsylvania Press, 1991), 42; George F. Feldman, *Cannibalism, Headhunting and Human Sacrifice in North America: A History Forgotten* (Chambersburg, PA: Alan C. Hood and Co., 2008), 85. See also Ellen B. Basso, *The Last Cannibals: A South American Oral History* (Austin: University of Texas Press, 1995); Berglund, *Cannibal Fictions,* 71; Vincent Woodward, *The Delectable Negro: Human Consumption and Homoeroticism within US Slave Culture* (New York: New York University Press, 2014), 69; Carl Hoffman, *Savage Harvest: A Tale of Cannibals, Colonialism, and Michael Rockefeller's Tragic Quest* (New York: William Morrow, 2014); and Nancy Shoemaker, *Native American Whalemen and the World: Indigenous Encounters and the Contingency of Race* (Chapel Hill: University of North Carolina Press, 2015), 112, 115.

8. Peter Burke, "Frontiers of the Monstrous: Perceiving National Characters in Early Modern Europe," in *Monstrous Bodies/Political Monstrosities in Early Modern Europe,* edited by Laura L. Knoppers and Joan B. Landes (Ithaca, NY: Cornell University Press, 2004), 28. Such narratives extend across time and space and can be found in ancient Greek culture and in the stories of Hindu holy men. See Heike Behrend, *Resurrecting Cannibals: The Catholic Church, Witch-Hunts, and the Production of Pagans in Western Uganda* (Rochester, NY: James Currey, 2011), 48–49; and Paul Raffaele, *Among the Cannibals: Adventures on the Trail of Man's Darkest Ritual* (New York: HarperCollins, 2008), 2–3.

9. The bulk of the scholarship that addresses Indigenous history and cannibalism focuses on Latin America. See for example, Eduardo Viveiros, *From the Enemy's Point of View: Humanity and Divinity in an Amazonian Society* (Chicago: University of Chicago Press, 1992); Neil Whitehead, "Hans Staden and the Cultural Politics of Cannibalism," *Hispanic American Historical Review,* 80, no. 4 (2000): 741–772; Lewis Petrinovich, *The Cannibal Within* (New York: Aldine de Gruyter, 2000); and Andre Resendez, *A Land So Strange: The Epic Journey of Cabeza de Vaca* (New York: Basic Books, 2007), 144.

10. Jack D. Forbes, *Columbus and Other Cannibals: The Wetiko Disease of Exploitation, Imperialism, and Terrorism,* rev. ed. (New York: Seven Stories Press, 2008), 49.

11. Robert W. Small, interview with T. C. Carriger, January 10, 1938, 7, https://digital.libraries.ou.edu/cdm/ref/collection/indianpp/id/6875, Indian-Pioneer History Project (hereafter IPHP), Works Project Administration, Western History Collections, University of Oklahoma Library, Norman.

12. See for example, Tara Houska, "14-Year-Old Girl Testifying against Native American Mascots Says Crowd Shouted 'Get Off the Stage Squaw,'" *Huffington Post,* January 13, 2016, accessed July 20, 2016, https://tinyurl.com/zhbhjr8; Noreen G. Lape, *West of the Border: The Multicultural Literature of the Western American Frontiers* (Athens: Ohio University Press, 2000), 50.

13. Max Greenwood, "Ben Shapiro Apologizes for Columbus Day Video Slammed as Racist," *The Hill,* October 10, 2017, accessed 23 October 2017, https://tinyurl.com/ya4nskbf.

14. Philip P. Boucher, *Cannibal Encounters: Europeans and Island Caribs, 1492–1763* (Baltimore, MD: Johns Hopkins University Press, 2009), 50; Obeyesekere, *Cannibal Talk,* 127–128; Feldman, *Cannibalism, Headhunting and Human Sacrifice,* 105; Gregory D. Smithers, "Rethinking Genocide in North America," in *The Oxford Handbook of Genocide Studies,* edited by Donald Bloxham and A. Dirk Moses (Oxford: Oxford University Press, 2010), 322–341; Santiago Colas, "From Caliban to Cronus: A Critique of Cannibalism as Metaphor for Cuban Revolutionary Culture," in *Eating Their Words: Cannibalism and the Boundaries of Cultural Identity,* edited by Kristen Guest (Albany: State University of New York Press, 2001), 129–130.

15. Robert V. O'Brien, "Cannibalism in Edmund Spenser's *Faerie Queene,* Ireland, and the Americas," in *Eating Their Words: Cannibalism and the Boundaries of Cultural Identity,* edited by Kristen Guest (Albany: State University of New York Press, 2001), 51–52.

16. Deborah L. Nichols and Patricia L. Crown, "Dismembering the Trope: Imagining Cannibalism in the Ancient Pueblo World," in *Social Violence in the Prehispanic American Southwest,* edited by Deborah L. Nichols and Patricia L. Crown (Tucson: University of Arizona Press, 2008), 40.

17. Jacques le Moyne de Morgues, *Narrative of le Moyne: An Artist Who Accompanied the French Expedition to Florida* (Boston: James R. Osgood and Company, 1875), 10. See also Richard Slotkin, *Regeneration through Violence: The Mythology of the American Frontier, 1600–1860* (Norman: University of Oklahoma Press, 1973), 35.

18. Le Moyne de Morgues, *Narrative of le Moyne,* 15.

19. Le Moyne de Morgues, *Narrative of le Moyne,* 6.

20. Bernard Bailyn, *The Barbarous Years: The Peopling of British North America: The Conflict of Civilizations, 1600–1675* (New York: Vintage Books, 2012), 6, 19, 38, 184; Carville V. Earle, "Environment, Disease, and Mortality in Early Virginia," in *The Chesapeake in the Seventeenth Century: Essays on Anglo-American Society,* edited by Thad W. Tate and David Ammerman (New York: W. W. Norton and Company, 1979), 108.

21. Bailyn, *The Barbarous Years,* 6, 19, 38, 184; Rachel B. Herrmann, "The 'tragicall historie': Cannibalism and Abundance in Colonial Jamestown," *William and Mary Quarterly* 68, no. 1 (2011): 47–74.

22. David J. Weber, *The Spanish Frontier in North America* (New Haven, CT: Yale University Press, 1992), 36.

23. Robin Beck, *Chiefdoms, Collapse, and Coalescence in the Early American South* (New York: Cambridge University Press, 2013), 131. See also Justin Winsor, *Narrative and Critical History of America,* 8 vols. (Boston: Houghton, Mifflin, and Company, 1886), vol. II, 597; Benjamin Schmidt, *Innocence Abroad: The Dutch Imagination and the New World, 1570–1670* (Cambridge: Cambridge University Press, 2001), 37; Ronald Wright, *Stolen Continents: Five Hundred Years of Conquest and Resistance in the Americas,* rev. ed. (Boston: Houghton Mifflin Company, 2005), 13.

24. Edmond Atkin, *The Appalachian Indian Frontier: Edmond Atkin Report and Plan of 1755* (Lincoln: University of Nebraska Press, 1967), xv.

25. Kenneth M. Morrison, "Towards a History of Intimate Encounters: Algonkian Folklore, Jesuit Missionaries, and Kiwakwe, the Cannibal Giant," *American Indian Culture and Research Journal* 3, no. 4 (1979): 51–80.

26. Kenneth M. Morrison, *The Embattled Northeast: The Elusive Ideal of Alliance in Abenaki* (Berkeley: University of California Press, 1984), 99–100.

27. Edwin C. McReynolds, *The Seminoles* (Norman: University of Oklahoma Press, 1957), 6.

28. Virginia Van der Veer Hamilton, *Alabama: A History* (New York: W. W. Norton, 1977), 152. See also S. W. Woodhouse, *A Naturalist in Indian Territory: The Journals of S. W. Woodhouse, 1849–1850* (Norman: University of Oklahoma Press, 1992), 164.

29. Robbie Ethridge, *Creek Country: The Creek Indians and Their World* (Chapel Hill: University of North Carolina Press, 2003), 147, 150, 159, 179.

30. Angie Debo, *The Rise and Fall of the Choctaw Republic* (1934; repr., Norman: University of Oklahoma Press, 1961), 10–13; Margaret Z. Searcy, "Choctaw Subsistence, 1540–1830: Hunting, Fishing, Farming, and Gathering," in *The Choctaw before Removal,* edited by Carolyn Keller Reeves (Jackson: University Press of Mississippi, 1985), 50–51; Patricia Galloway, *Choctaw Genesis, 1500–1700* (Lincoln: University of Nebraska Press, 1995), 46, 348; Michelene E. Pesantubbee, *Choctaw Women in a Chaotic World: The Clash of Cultures in the Colonial Southeast* (Albuquerque: University of New Mexico Press, 2005), 28.

31. William A. Read, *Louisiana Place Names of Indian Origin: A Collection of Words* (Tuscaloosa: University of Alabama Press, 2008), 6; Donald E. Chipman and Harriett Denise Joseph, *Spanish Texas, 1519–1821,* rev. ed. (Austin: University of Texas Press, 2010), 15; Randolph B. Campbell, *Gone to Texas: A History of the Lone Star State* (New York: Oxford University Press, 2012), 16, 28.

32. Edward J. Cashin, *Guardians of the Valley: Chickasaws in Colonial South Carolina and Georgia* (Columbia: University of South Carolina Press, 2009), 8.

33. Alan Gallay, *The Indian Slave Trade: The Rise of the English Empire in the American South, 1670–1717* (New Haven, CT: Yale University Press, 2002), 299

34. John T. Juricek, "The Westo Indians," *Ethnohistory* 11, no. 2 (1964): 134–173; Daniel K. Richter, *The Ordeal of the Longhouse: The Peoples of the Iroquois League in the Era of European Colonization* (Chapel Hill: University of North Carolina Press, 1992), 35–6; Eric E. Browne, *The Westo Indians: Slave Traders of the Early Colonial South* (Tuscaloosa: University of Alabama Press, 2005), 104; Christina Snyder, *Slavery in Indian Country: The Changing Face of Captivity in Early America* (Cambridge, MA: Harvard University Press, 2010), 76; Larry E. Ivers, *This Torrent of Indians: War on the Southern Frontier, 1715–28* (Columbia: University of South Carolina Press, 2016).

35. Gallay, *The Indian Slave Trade,* 51.

36. John R. Swanton, *Early History of the Creek Indians and Their Neighbors* (Washington, DC: U.S. Government Printing Office, 1922), 305.

37. W. Noel Sainsbury, ed., *Calendar of State Papers, Colonial Series, America and the West Indies, 1669–1674,* vol. 7 (London: Her Majesty's Stationary Office, 1889), 90.

38. Report of James Taylor and James Brannon, two illiterate traders, June 4, 1746, CO 5/455, South Carolina, Journal of Minutes of Council: Jan. 1745/46–May 1747; Report May 25, 1752, CO 5/467, South Carolina, Journal of Council: Feb. 1752–Nov. 1752, both in National Archives of Great Britain, Kew, England.

39. Donna L. Akers, *Culture and Customs of the Choctaw Indians* (Santa Barbara, CA: Greenwood, 2013), 65.

40. Cushman, *History of the Choctaw, Chickasaw and Natchez Indians,* 213.

41. Valerie Lambert, *Choctaw Nation: A Story of American Indian Resurgence* (Lincoln: University of Nebraska Press, 2007), 24.

42. Fred B. Kniffen, Hiram F. Gregory, and George A. Stokes, *The Historic Indian Tribes of Louisiana: From 1542 to the Present* (Baton Rouge: Louisiana State University Press, 1987), 207.

43. Lisa T. Brooks, *The Common Pot: The Recovery of Native Space in the Northeast* (Minneapolis: University of Minnesota Press, 2008), 2–4.

44. Zaidee B. Bland, interview with Matthew Maytubbie, July 22, 1937, 5, https://digital.libraries.ou.edu/cdm/ref/collection/indianpp/id/456, IPHP. For "iron pots," see E. F. Dodson, interview with Mrs. E. H. Whitmire, April 16, 1937, 2, https://digital.libraries.ou.edu/cdm/ref/collection/indianpp/id/5782, IPHP.

45. James F. Barnett Jr., *Mississippi's American Indians* (Jackson: University Press of Mississippi, 2012), 155.

46. James Adair, *The History of the American Indians* (London: Edward and Charles Dilly, 1775), 113. See also Sarah Tuttle, *Letters on the Chickasaw and Osage Missions,* 2nd ed. (Boston: Massachusetts Sabbath School Society, 1833), 129, 135; John R. Swanton, *Chickasaw Society and Religion* (1928; repr., Lincoln: University of Nebraska Press, 2006), 50–51; Ethridge, *From Chicaza to Chickasaw,* 37–38, 142, 177.

47. Horatio Bardwell Cushman, *History of the Choctaw, Chickasaw and Natchez Indians* (Greenville, TX: Headlight Printing House, 1899), 139.

48. William Waits, *The Modern Christmas in America: A Cultural History of Gift Giving* (New York: New York University Press, 1994); Penne L. Restad, *Christmas in America: A History* (New York: Oxford University Press, 1995).

49. Ina Baghdiantz McCabe, *A History of Global Consumption: 1500–1800* (London: Routledge, 2015), 69.

50. Armstrong Starkey, *European and Native American Warfare, 1675–1815* (London: UCL Press, 1998), 30.

51. Hartley B. Alexander, *Native American Mythology* (1916; repr., Mineola, NY: Dover Publications. Inc., 2015), 145; Teresa Pijoan, *Native American Creation Stories of Family and Friendship* (Santa Fe, NM: Sunstone Press, 2011), 170; Amelia M. Trevelyan, *Miskwabik, Metal of Ritual: Metallurgy in Precontact Eastern North America* (Lexington: University of Kentucky Press, 2004), 102; Cameron B. Strang, "Indian Storytelling, Scientific Knowledge, and Power in the Florida Borderlands," *William and Mary Quarterly* 70, no. 4 (2013): 671–700.

52. Frank G. Speck, *Ethnology of the Yuchi Indians* (Philadelphia: University Museum of the University of Pennsylvania, 1909), 140.

53. Stith Thompson, *Tales of the North American Indians* (1929; repr., Mineola, NY: Dover Publications, Inc., 2000), 207, 219–222, 262, 364.

54. Thomas A. Green, *Native American Folktales* (Westport, CT: Greenwood Press, 2009), 34.

55. W. Stitt Robinson, *James Glen: From Scottish Provost to Royal Governor of South Carolina* (Westport, CT: Greenwood Press, 1996), 41.

56. James Oglethorpe to the Trustees of Georgia, December 29, 1739, CO 5/654, Georgia, Original Correspondence, Sec. of State: 1735–1741, Part-1, The National Archives, Kew.

57. William L. Anderson, Jane L. Brown, and Anne F. Rogers, eds., *The*

*Payne-Butrick Papers: Volumes One, Two, Three* (Lincoln: University of Nebraska Press, 2010), 12, 208.

58. William L. Anderson, Jane L. Brown, and Anne F. Rogers, eds., *The Payne-Butrick Papers: Volumes Four, Five, Six* (Lincoln: University of Nebraska Press, 2010), 210.

59. For the use of "flesh" to intimidate Indian warriors, see Theodore Roosevelt, *Anthony Wayne's Expedition into the Northwest* (Fort Wayne, IN.: Fort Wayne Convention Bureau, 1964), 11. For "hengre for white mans flesh," see Anthony Wayne to Thomas Hughes, Head Quarters, Pittsburgh, November 12, 1792, f. 83, vol. XXIII, Anthony Wayne Papers, Historical Society of Pennsylvania. I'd like to thank Rachel Herrmann for bringing this source to my attention and so generously sharing it with me.

60. Henry T. Malone, *Cherokees of the Old South: A People in Transition* (1956; repr., Athens: University of Georgia Press, 2010), 44–45.

61. Cecil L. Sumners, Chief Tishomingo: *A History of the Chickasaw Indians, and Some Historical Events of Their Era, 1737–1839* (Iuka, MS: American Revolution Bicentennial Edition), 10; Robbie Ethridge, *From Chicaza to Chickasaw: The European Invasion and the Transformation of the Mississippian World, 1540–1715* (Chapel Hill: University of North Carolina Press, 2010), 138.

62. James Adair, *History of the American Indians, 1775*, edited by Kathryn E. Holland Braund (Tuscaloosa: University of Alabama Press, 2005), 173; Bernard W. Sheehan, *Seeds of Extinction: Jeffersonian Philanthropy and the American Indian* (Chapel Hill: University of North Carolina Press, 1973), 200.

63. William W. Osborn, "American Indian Cannibalism," in *Cannibals: Shocking True Tales of the Last Taboo on the Land and at Sea*, edited by Joseph Cummins (Guilford, CT: The Lyons Press, 2001), 159–164, esp. 162, 164. See also W. H. Holmes, *An Ancient Quarry in Indian Territory* (Washington, DC: U.S. Government Printing Office, 1894), 16; William M. Osborn, *The Wild Frontier: Atrocities during the American-Indian War from Jamestown Colony to Wounded Knee* (New York: Random House, 2009), 6.

## Chapter 2

1. Geoffrey Symcox, "Introduction," in *Italian Reports on America, 1493–1522: Letters, Dispatches, and Papal Bulls*, edited by Geoffrey Symcox and Giovanna Rabitti, translated by Peter D. Diehl (Turnhout, Belgium: Brepols, 2001), 3–24.

2. Nicolás Wey-Gómez, "A Poetics of Dismemberment: The Book of Job and the Cannibals of Cariay in Columbus's Account of the Fourth Voyage," *Colonial Latin American Review* 16, no. 1, (2007): 120.

3. Margarita Zamora, *Reading Columbus* (Berkeley: University of California Press, 1993), 11.

4. See Valerie Flint, "Travel Fact and Travel Fiction in the Voyages of Columbus," in *Travel Fact and Travel Fiction*, edited by Zweder von Martels (Leiden: Brill, 1994), 94–110.

5. Cecil H. Clough, "The New World and the Italian Renaissance," in *The European Outthrust and Encounter: The First Phase c. 1400–c. 1700: Essays in*

*Tribute to David Beers Quinn on His 85th Birthday,* edited by Cecil H. Clough and P. E. H. Hair (Liverpool: Liverpool University Press, 1994), 304–305.

6. Valerie I. J. Flint, *The Imaginative Landscape of Christopher Columbus* (Princeton, NJ: Princeton University Press, 1992), 131–132.

7. Flint, *The Imaginative Landscape of Christopher Columbus,* 145.

8. Columbus's letter, the first information on the new lands to reach a wide European public, enjoyed immediate and lasting notoriety. Its declared purpose was to describe from firsthand experience territories that had previously been described on the basis of conjecture. The letter was promptly published in Barcelona at the beginning of April 1493, and within just a few months of Columbus's return it was already circulating in various editions and in three different languages throughout Europe. By 1500, it had been published in sixteen editions in several European languages. These editions were put together without careful preparation and sophistication. Their target was a broad public; they were intended to be inexpensive, informative, and to circulate in great numbers.

9. Christopher Columbus, *The Journal: Account of the First Voyage and Discovery of the Indies,* edited by Paolo Emilio Taviani and Consuelo Varela, translated by Marc A. Beckwith and Luciano F. Farina, vol. 1 (Roma: Istituto Poligrafico e Zecca dello Stato, 1990), part I, 43.

10. Columbus, *The Journal,* 93.

11. Bartolomé de Las Casas used the third-person pronoun and the term "the Admiral" here and elsewhere in his rendition of Columbus's original diary. Columbus, *The Journal,* 125–127.

12. Columbus, *The Journal,* 159.

13. Columbus, *The Journal,* 173.

14. Columbus, *The Journal,* 243.

15. Columbus, *The Journal,* 119.

16. Columbus, *The Journal,* 249.

17. For the Spanish letter, see Juan Gil and Consuelo Varela, eds., *Cartas de particulares a Colón y Relaciones coetáneas* (Madrid: Alianza Editorial, 1984), 144–146.

18. Symcox, "Introduction," 4–8.

19. Symcox, "Introduction."

20. Symcox, "Introduction," 8–9.

21. Symcox, "Introduction," 8.

22. Symcox, "Introduction," 9.

23. Giacomo Trotti, Milan, 21 April 1493, in Symcox, *Italian Reports on America: Letters, Dispatches, and Papal Bulls,* 27–28.

24. Luca Fancelli, Florence, 22 April 1493, in Symcox, *Italian Reports on America: Letters, Dispatches, and Papal Bulls,* 28 (for Eden); Taddeo Vimercati, Venice, 27 April 1493, in Symcox, *Italian Reports on America: Letters, Dispatches, and Papal Bulls,* 29 (for economic pursuits); Giovanni Andrea Bocciaccio, Rome, 21 June 1493, in Symcox, *Italian Reports on America: Letters, Dispatches, and Papal Bulls,* 39 (for the civilizing and evangelical mission).

25. Alexander VI, Rome, 3 May 1493, "Inter cetera" 1, in Symcox, *Italian Reports on America: Letters, Dispatches, and Papal Bulls,* 31–34.

26. Marco Polo's and Sir John Mandeville's accounts of journeys to the East, which were repeatedly copied, abridged, and translated during the Middle Ages in

manuscript form, retained their popularity with the advent of print. See Anthony Grafton, *New World, Ancient Texts: The Power of Tradition and the Shock of Discovery* (Cambridge, MA: Harvard University Press, 1992), 72–73.

27. Dr. Chanca had served as royal physician at the Spanish court and had joined Columbus's second expedition to serve as a doctor in the new settlement. Nothing is known of Guillermo Coma. He might have belonged to the same medical milieu as Chanca and Scillacio. See Gil and Varela, *Cartas de particulares a Colón y Relaciones coetáneas,* 177.

28. Nicolò Scillacio was originally from Messina. After spending some years in Spain, he joined the University of Pavia in 1486. He lectured there in metaphysics, natural philosophy, and medicine, before returning to Spain in 1495. See Gil and Varela, *Cartas de particulares a Colón y Relaciones coetáneas,* 179.

29. Da Cuneo's letter was a personal communication to a fellow merchant from Liguria and was meant to inform his colleague on the outcome of the expedition. Da Cuneo devoted much attention to a description of the land and an assessment of the goods and their marketability.

30. Michele da Cuneo, Letter to Gerolamo Annari, 15 October 1495, in *Italian Reports on America, 1493–1522: Accounts by Contemporary Observers,* edited by Geoffrey Symcox and Luciano Formisano, translated by Theodore J. Cachey Jr. and John C. McLucas (Turnhout, Belgium: Brepols, 2002), 51.

31. Diego Alvarez Chanca, "Letter" to the Mayor of Seville, in *Christopher Columbus's Discoveries in the Testimonials of Diego Alvarez Chanca and Andrés Bernáldez.* Introduction and notes by Anna Unali. Translated into English by Gioacchino Triolo and Luciano F. Farina (Rome: Istituto Poligrafico e Zecca dello Stato, 1992), 12–59.

32. Chanca, "Letter" to the mayor of Seville, 21.

33. Chanca, "Letter" to the mayor of Seville, 23.

34. Michele da Cuneo, Letter to Gerolamo Annari, 15 October 1495, in *Italian Reports on America, 1493–1522: Accounts by Contemporary Observers,* 57.

35. Peter Hulme, "Introduction: The Cannibal Scene," in *Cannibalism and the Colonial World,* edited by Francis Barker, Peter Hulme, and Margaret Iversen (Cambridge: Cambridge University Press, 1998), 17.

36. Hulme, "Introduction," 17–18. Anna Unali notes that the first-person narrator in Chanca's and Da Cuneo's texts emerges in connection with topics of interest to them, primarily concerning their professional involvement, their personal impressions, or tales of their individual actions. In the rest of their texts, they report events, thoughts, and even feelings using a collective "we," thus implying a general uniformity of thought and action among the members of the expedition. See Unali, *Christopher Columbus's Discoveries,* 227.

37. Hulme, "Introduction," 17–18.

38. Gabriella Airaldi, "Michele De Cuneo," in *Dizionario Biografico degli Italiani,* vol. 74 (Roma: Treccani, 2010), 157–161.

39. Antonello Gerbi, *Nature in the New World: From Christopher Columbus to Gonzalo Fernández de Oviedo,* translated by Jeremy Moyle (Pittsburgh: University of Pittsburgh Press, 1985), 31.

40. William Arens, *The Man-Eating Myth: Anthropology and Anthropophagy* (New York: Oxford University Press, 1979), 28.

41. Nicolò Scillacio, The Islands Recently Discovered in the Southern and

Indian Seas, in *Italian Reports on America, 1493–1522: Accounts by Contemporary Observers,* 35.

42. Maria Grazia Scelfo Micci, "Introduzione," in Nicolò Scillacio, *Sulle isole meridionali e del mare Indico nuovamente trovate,* edited by Maria Grazia Scelfo Micci (Roma: Bulzoni, 1990), 11–49.

43. Anthony Pagden, *The Fall of the Natural Man: The American Indian and the Origins of Comparative Ethnology* (Cambridge: Cambridge University Press, 1982), 7.

44. Gil and Varela, *Cartas de particulares a Colón y Relaciones coetáneas,* 177.

45. Scelfo Micci, "Introduzione."

46. Nicolò Scillacio, in *Italian Reports on America, 1493–1522: Accounts by Contemporary Observers,* 38.

47. Scillacio, in *Italian Reports on America, 1493–1522: Accounts by Contemporary Observers,* 40.

48. Pietro Martire D'Anghiera, *The Discovery of the New World in the Writings of Peter Martyr of Anghiera,* edited by Ernesto Lunardi, Elisa Magioncalda, and Rosanna Mazzacane, Nuova Raccolta Colombiana, vol. 2 (Roma: Istituto Poligrafico e Zecca dello Stato, 1992), 57.

49. Simone dal Verde, Valladolid, 20 March–10 May 1494, in *Italian Reports on America, 1493–1522: Accounts by Contemporary Observers,* 31–32.

50. Verde, Valladolid, 20 March–10 May 1494, 32.

51. Hulme, "Introduction," 17.

52. Joan-Pau Rubiés, *Travel and Ethnology in the Renaissance: South India through European Eyes, 1250–1625* (Cambridge: Cambridge University Press, 2000), 145.

## Chapter 3

1. For more on Columbus's rationale for sailing west and south and his understanding of the relationship between land and water, see Nicolás Wey-Gómez, *The Tropics of Empire: Why Columbus Sailed South to the Indies* (Cambridge, MA: MIT Press, 2008). Wey-Gómez's book is particularly useful for illuminating both why Columbus's voyage was controversial and why he expected to arrive in Asia.

2. Wey-Gómez, *The Tropics of Empire,* 339.

3. Christopher Columbus, *The* Diario *of Christopher Columbus's First Voyage to America, 1492–1493,* abstracted by Fray Bartolomé de las Casas, transcribed and translated by Oliver Dunn and James E. Kelley Jr. (Norman: University of Oklahoma Press, 1989), 321.

4. R. H. Major, ed., *Select Letters of Christopher Columbus with Other Original Documents Relating to His Four Voyages to the New World,* 2nd ed., translated by R. H. Major (London: Hakluyt Society, 1870), 109–110, 131–146; Wey-Gómez, *The Tropics of Empire,* 398.

5. Major, *Select Letters of Christopher Columbus,* 136.

6. Anne McClintock, *Imperial Leather: Race, Gender, and Sexuality in a Colonial Context* (New York: Routledge, 1995), 21–30; Wey-Gómez, *The Tropics of Empire,* 116.

7. The distinction between these two intersections is obviously less rigid than

is presented here, but for the sake of clarity and brevity, I am limiting my discussion to the two most prominent discursive connections. For further examples of the overlap between cannibalistic appetites and sex, see Merrall Llewelyn Price, *Consuming Passions: The Uses of Cannibalism in Late Medieval and Early Modern Europe* (New York: Routledge, 2003); Peter Sigal "The *Cuiloni,* the *Patlache,* and the Abominable Sin: Homosexualities in Early Colonial Nahua Society," *Hispanic American Historical Review* 85, no. 4 (2005): 555–593; Richard Trexler, *Sex and Conquest: Gendered Violence, Political Order, and European Conquest of the Americas* (Ithaca, NY: Cornell University Press, 1995).

8. Gustav Jahoda, *Images of Savages: Ancient Roots of Modern Prejudice in Western Culture* (New York: Routledge, 1999), 97.

9. For example, early seventeenth-century writer Pierre D'Avity argued that there were five indicators of brutishness: a lack of reason, a lack of clothing, a lack of government, improper housing, and an inappropriate diet. Olive P. Dickason, *The Myth of the Savage and the Beginnings of French Colonialism in the Americas* (Edmonton: University of Alberta Press, 1984), 66–67.

10. Michele da Cuneo, in *Italian Reports on America, 1493–1522: Accounts by Contemporary Observers,* edited by G. Symcox and L. Formasiano (Turnhout, Belgium: Brepols, 2002), 51.

11. Phillip P. Boucher, *Cannibal Encounters: Europeans and Island Caribs, 1492–1763* (Baltimore: Johns Hopkins University Press, 1992); Dave D. Davis and R. Christopher Goodwin, "Island Carib Origins: Evidence and Nonevidence," *American Antiquity* 55, no. 1 (1990): 37–48; Peter Hulme and Neil Whitehead, eds., *Wild Majesty: Encounters with Caribs from Columbus to the Present Day* (New York: Oxford University Press, 1992); Irving Rouse, *The Tainos: Rise and Decline of the People Who Greeted Columbus* (New Haven, CT: Yale University Press, 1992).

12. Several other first- and second-hand accounts mention the Carib practice of castrating captives. See Peter Martyr, *De Orbe Novo: The Eight Decades of Peter Matryr D'Anghera,* vol. 1, translated by Francis August MacNutt (New York: G. P. Putnam's Sons, 1912), 63; Marcantonio Coccio, "Book One ... of the Account of Happenings in the Unknown Regions," in *Italian Reports on America, 1493–1522: Accounts by Contemporary Observers,* edited by G. Symcox and L. Formasiano (Turnhout, Belgium: Brepols, 2002); Marcantonio Coccio, "Book One . . . of the Account of Happenings in the Unknown Regions," in *Italian Reports on America, 1493–1522: Accounts by Contemporary Observers,* edited by G. Symcox and L. Formasiano (Turnhout, Belgium: Brepols, 2002); Angelo Trevisan, "Libretto" in *Italian Reports on America, 1493–1522: Accounts by Contemporary Observers,* edited by G. Symcox and L. Formasiano (Turnhout, Belgium: Brepols, 2002), 83.

13. Cuneo, *Italian Reports on America,* 57.

14. Cuneo, *Italian Reports on America,* 51.

15. Cuneo, *Italian Reports on America,* 56.

16. Cuneo, *Italian Reports on America,* 57–58.

17. On page 58 of his account, Cuneo wrote: "[The Cannibals and Indians] have sexual intercourse openly whenever the desire arises, and except for brothers and sisters, all others are shared. . . . From what we have observed on all islands we visited, the Indians as well as the Cannibals are sodomites, a practice that I believe they follow without knowing whether it is right or wrong. We concluded that the damnable vice had been communicated to the Indians from the Cannibals, because, as I said

above, they may also have perpetrated that excess upon them in order to scorn them, and subsequently it passed from one group to the other."

18. Luciano Formisano, ed., *Letters from a New World: Amerigo Vespucci's Discovery of America,* translated by David Jacobson (New York: Marsilio Publishers, 1992), xx–xxi; Seymour Schwartz, "The Greatest Misnomer on Planet Earth," *Proceedings of the American Philosophical Society* 146, no. 3 (2002): 264–281.

19. Amerigo Vespucci, "Mundus Novus," in *Letters from a New World: Amerigo Vespucci's Discovery of America,* edited by Luciano Formisano, translated by David Jacobson (New York: Marsilio Publishers, 1992), 50.

20. Vespucci, "Mundus Novus," 50–51; Amerigo Vespucci, "Letter to Soderini," in *Letters from a New World,* 63.

21. Vespucci, "Letter to Soderini," 65.

22. Vespucci, "Letter to Soderini," 66.

23. Similar laws were signed in 1511 and 1533. Michael Palencia-Roth, "Cannibal Law of 1503," in *Early Images of the Americas: Transfer and Invention,* edited by Jerry M. Williams and Robert Earl Lewis (Tucson: University of Arizona Press, 1993), 22.

24. Palencia-Roth, "Cannibal Law of 1503," 24. The subjects of many of the sentences in the original Spanish are implied rather than explicit. Thus, for ease of the reader and clarity, Roth indicates with brackets where "the cannibals" can be inferred. The original reads: "*Por ende por la presente doy licencia é facultad á todas é cualesquier personas que con mi mandado fueren, así á las Islas é Tierra-firme del dicho mar Océano que fasta agora estan descubiertas, como á los que fueren á descobrir otras cualesquier Islas é Tierra-firme, para que si todavia los dichos Caníbales resistieren, é non quisieren rescibir é acogar en sus tierras á los Capitanes é gentes que por mi mandado fueren á facer los dichos viages, é oirlos para ser dotrinados en las cosas de nuestra Santa Fe Católica, é estar en mi servicio é so mi obediencia, los puedan cautivar é cautiven para los llevar á las tierras é Islas donde fueren . . . pagándonos la parte que dellos nos pertensca, é para que puedan vender é aprovecharse dellos, sin que por ello cayan nin incurran en pena alguna, porque trayéndose á estas partes é serviéndose dellos Cristianos, podrán ser mas ligeramente convertidos é atraidos á nuestra Santa Fe Católica.*"

25. Neil Whitehead, "Carib Cannibalism: The Historical Evidence," *Journal de la Société des Américanistes* 70, no.1 (1984): 71.

26. For example, Francisco López de Gómara wrote that "they [the Tlaxcalans] provided them [the Spaniards] with everything for their means, and many offered their daughters as a token of true friendship, so they might bear children by such valorous men and bring into the world a new warrior caste." Francisco López de Gómara, *Cortés: The Life of the Conqueror by His Secretary,* translated by Lesley Byrd Simpson (Berkeley: University of California Press, 1966), 116.

27. López de Gómara, *Cortés,* 118; Camilla Townsend, *Malintzin's Choices: An Indian Woman in the Conquest of Mexico* (Albuquerque: University of New Mexico Press, 2006), 72.

28. For other examples of women given as gifts to the Spaniards, see Bernal Díaz del Castillo, *The Discovery and Conquest of Mexico, 1517–1521,* translated by A. P. Maudsley (New York: Farrar, Strauss, and Cudahy, 1956), 62–63, 102, 122, 136, 153–154.

29. Díaz del Castillo, *The Discovery and Conquest of Mexico,* 102.

30. Díaz del Castillo, *The Discovery and Conquest of Mexico,* 106.

31. Díaz del Castillo, *The Discovery and Conquest of Mexico*, 153–154.

32. Díaz del Castillo, *The Discovery and Conquest of Mexico*, 236.

33. For example, see William Arens, *The Man-Eating Myth: Anthropology and Anthropophagy* (New York: Oxford University Press, 1980); Herodotus, *The Histories*, translated by Robin Waterfield (New York: Oxford University Press, 2008); Pliny the Elder, *Natural History*, translated by W. H. S. Jones, vol. 7 (Cambridge, MA: Harvard University Press, 1956); Tom Sharp, "The Acts of Matthew and Andrew in the City of Cannibals," *Medieval Forum* 2 (2003), accessed July 23, 2016, http://tinyurl.com/zu37gva; Stephen A. Barney, W. J. Lewis, J. A. Beach, and Oliver Berghof, eds., *The Etymologies of Isidore of Seville* (Cambridge: Cambridge University Press, 2006); Marco Polo, *The Travels of Marco Polo*, translated by Ronald Latham (New York: Penguin Books, 1958); John Mandeville, *The Travels of Sir John Mandeville: The 14th-Century Account of a Journey to the East* (Mineola, NY: Dover Publications, 2006).

34. See William F. Keegan, "Columbus Was a Cannibal: Myth and First Encounters," in *The Lesser Antilles in the Age of European Expansion*, edited by Robert L. Paquette and Stanley L. Engerman (Gainesville: University of Florida Press, 1996), 18–19.

35. Columbus, *The* Diario *of Christopher Columbus's First Voyage to America*, 133.

36. John Mandeville, *The Travels of Sir John Mandeville: The Version from the Cotton Manuscript in Modern Spelling with Three Narratives, in Illustration of It from Hakluyt's Navigations, Voyages, and Discoveries* (London: Macmillan and Co., 1915), 130; Polo, *The Travels of Marco Polo*, 258.

37. The definition of sodomy in the early modern world encompassed more than anal intercourse; it included a wider array of nonprocreative sex acts such as oral sex.

38. Columbus didn't actually meet any of these so-called cannibals or Caribs on the first journey, but he undertook his second journey to find them. Alessandro Zorzi, "Various Information about the Voyages," in *Italian Reports on America, 1493–1522: Accounts by Contemporary Observers*, edited by G. Symcox and L. Formasiano (Turnhout, Belgium: Brepols, 2002), 107.

39. Columbus, "Letter to Santángel," in Columbus, *The* Diario *of Christopher Columbus's First Voyage to America*, 269–270; Samuel Eliot Morison, *Admiral of the Ocean Sea: A Life of Christopher Columbus* (Boston: Northeastern University Press, 1983), 315.

40. Columbus, *The* Diario *of Christopher Columbus's First Voyage*, 339–343.

41. Martyr, *De Orbe Novo*, 63.

42. Ferdinand Columbus, for example, remarked that "the Caribs do not eat or kill women, but keep them alive as slaves." Ferdinand Columbus, *The Life of the Admiral Christopher Columbus by His Son Ferdinand*, translated by Benjamin Keen (New Brunswick, NJ: Rutgers University Press, 1992), 113.

43. Dr. Diego Alvarez Chanca, "Letter of Dr. Chanca on the Second Voyage of Columbus," *American Journeys: Eyewitness of Early Exploration and Settlement*, doc. AJ-065, accessed April 22, 2018, http://www.americanjourneys.org/aj-065/index.asp.

44. Chanca, "Letter of Dr. Chanca on the Second Voyage of Columbus."

45. Vespucci, "Mundus Novus," 48.

46. Vespucci, "Mundus Novus," 49.

47. Vespucci, "Letter to Soderini," 63.

48. Amerigo Vespucci, "Letter to Soderini," 37–38.

49. Vespucci, "Letter to Soderini," 38.

50. Price, *Consuming Passions,* 98.

51. My translation. Original text: "Estas gentes tienan la tria peccatela que decia el Italiano: no creen en Dios; son casi todos sodomitas: comen carne humana." Alonso Zuazo, "Carta Del Licenciado Alonso Zuazo," in *Colección de documentos para la historia de México,* edited by Joaquin Garcia Icazbalceta (Mexico: Liberia de J.M Andrade, 1858), 565.

52. Hernan Cortés, *Letters from Mexico,* edited and translated by Anthony Pagden (New Haven, CT: Yale University Press, 1986), 146.

53. López de Gómara, *Cortés,* 114.

54. For example, the Anonymous Conqueror accused Indians of treating their women inappropriately and having little regard for their purity, arguing that "there are no people in the world who hold women in less esteem, for they never tell them what to do, even though they should know that by doing so they would be benefited." Patricia de Fuentes, ed., *The Conquistadors: First-Person Accounts of the Conquest of Mexico* (New York: The Orion Press, 1963), 75.

55. Fuentes, *The Conquistadors,* 79–80.

56. For more on the definition of sodomy in early modern Spain and Mexico, see Sigal, "The *Cuiloni,* the *Patlache,* and the Abominable Sin"; Trexler, *Sex and Conquest.*

57. Bartolomé de las Casas, *In Defense of the Indians: A Defense of the Most Reverend Lord, Don Fray Bartolomé de las Casas, Order of the Preachers, Late Bishop of Chiapa, against the Persecutors and Slanderers of the Peoples of the New World Discovered across the Seas,* translated by Stafford Poole (DeKalb: Northern Illinois University Press, 1992), 42–43.

58. He described the Turks as civilized in terms of government and social organization, but nonetheless saw them as "an effeminate and luxury-loving people, given to every sort of sexual immorality." Las Casas, *In Defense of the Indians,* 51.

59. Las Casas, *In Defense of the Indians,* 191.

60. Allan Greer, *Mohawk Saint: Catherine Tekakwitha and the Jesuits* (New York: Oxford University Press, 2005), 183.

61. For example, see Thomas Brown, *A Plain Narrative of the Uncommon Sufferings, and Remarkable Deliverance of Thomas Brown, of Charlestown, in New-England* (1760), Garland Library of Narratives of North American Indian Captivities, vol. 8,.edited by Wilcomb Washburn (New York: Garland Publishing, 1977), 20–21.

62. Greer, *Mohawk Saint,* 186.

63. Greer, *Mohawk Saint,* 173.

## Chapter 4

1. Juan Ginés de Sepúlveda, *Demócrates segundo o De las justas causas de la guerra contra los indios,* edited and translated by Marcelino Menéndez y Pelayo, *Boletín de la Real Academia de la Historia* 21 (1892): 309.

2. Alonso de la Peña Montenegro, *Itinerario para parochos de indios en que se*

*tratan las materias mas particulares, tocantes a ellos, para su buena administración* (Madrid, 1668), 202.

3. Gonzalo Fernández de Oviedo, *Historia general y natural de las Indias,* vol. 2, edited by Juan Pérez de Tudela Bueso (Madrid: Biblioteca de Autores Españoles, 1959), 198.

4. "Consulta del consejo de las indias sobre los servicios personales de los indios," 1596, in *Colección de documentos para la historia de la formación social de Hispanoamérica, 1493–1810,* vol. 2, edited by Richard Konetzke (Madrid: Consejo Superior de Investigaciones Científicas, 1953), 45.

5. For an overview, see Rebecca Earle, "Indians and Drunkenness in Spanish America," in *Cultures of Intoxication,* edited by Phil Withington and Angela McShane, *Past & Present Supplement 9* (Oxford: Oxford University Press, 2014).

6. Amerigo Vespucci, "Letter on His Third Voyage to Lorenzo Pietro Francesco di Medici," 1503, in *The Letters of Amerigo Vespucci and Other Documents Illustrative of His Career,* edited by Clements R. Markham (London, 1894), 6 (quote); Christopher Columbus, Diary of the First Voyage, entries for December 17, 1492, and January 13, 1493, and "Carta del Almirante a los reyes católicos," all in *Los cuatro viajes del almirante y su testamento,* edited by Ignacio Anzoátegui (Madrid: Espasa, 1971), 92, 127, 173, respectively; Peter Martyr D'Anghera, *De Orbe Novo: The Eight Decades of Peter Martyr D'Anghera,* vol. 1, translated by Francis Augustus MacNutt (New York: G. Putnam's Sons, 1912), decade 2, book 1, and decade 3, book 5; Bernal Díaz del Castillo, *The True History of the Conquest of New Spain,* ca. 1568, translated by Alfred Percival Maudslay, 5 vols. (Cambridge: Cambridge University Press, 2010), 1:186, 196, 4:189, 5:15, 263; Sebastián de Covarrubias, *Parte primera del tesoro de la lengua castellana, or española* (Madrid, 1674), 51.

7. Fernández de Oviedo, *Historia general y natural de las Indias,* 2:246 (quote), 254. See also Martin Fernández de Enciso, *Suma de geographía que trata de todas las partes y provincias del mundo: en especial de las Indias* (Seville, 1530), li–liii; Nicolás Federman, *Historia indiana,* 1557, translated by Juan Friede (Madrid: Aro-Artes Gráficas, 1958), 63; Francisco López de Gómara, *Historia general de las Indias* (1552) (Barcelona: Linkgua, 2006), 99, 135, 138, 140, 166, 222; Kelly Watson, *Insatiable Appetites: Imperial Encounters with Cannibals in the North Atlantic World* (New York: New York University Press, 2015), 61.

8. The Dominican priest Bartolomé de las Casas thus complained that despite the abundant evidence to the contrary, "some believe that eating human flesh had its origin in these lands." Bartolomé de las Casas, *Apologética histórica sumaria* (ca. 1550), in *Obras escogidas,* vol. 4 (Madrid: Biblioteca de Autores Españoles, 1958), 152; Carlos Jáuregui, "'El plato más sabroso': Eucaristía, plagio diabólico, y la traducción criolla del caníbal," *Colonial Latin American Review,* 12, no. 2 (2003): 207. For an excellent analysis of visual representations, see Yobenj Aucardo Chicangana-Bayona, *Imágenes de caníbales y salvajes del Nuevo Mundo: De lo maravilloso medieval a lo exótico colonial, siglos XV–XVII* (Bogotá: Editorial Universidad del Rosario, 2013).

9. Carlos Jáuregui, *Canibalia: Canibalismo, calibanismo, antropofagía cultural y consumo en América Latina* (Madrid: Vervuert, 2008), 14.

10. William Arens, *The Man-Eating Myth* (New York: Oxford University Press, 1979); Peter Hulme, *Colonial Encounters: Europe and the Native Caribbean, 1492–1797* (London: Methuen, 1986); Philip Boucher, *Cannibal Encounters: Europeans and Island Caribs, 1492–1763* (Baltimore, MD: Johns Hopkins Press, 1992); Michael

Palencia-Roth, "The Cannibal Law of 1503," in *Early Images of the Americas*, edited by J. Williams and R. Lewis (Tucson: University of Arizona Press, 1993); Frank Lestringant, *Cannibals: The Discovery and Representation of the Cannibal from Columbus to Jules Verne*, translated by Rosemary Morris (Berkeley: University of California Press, 1997); Francis Barker, Peter Hulme, and Margaret Iversen, eds., *Cannibalism and the Colonial World* (Cambridge: Cambridge University Press, 1998).

11. Gareth Griffiths, "The Myth of Authenticity," in *De-Scribing Empire: Postcolonialism and Textuality*, edited by Chris Tiffin and Alan Lawson (London and New York: Routledge, 1994), 72.

12. See, in addition to the sources in note 10, Anthony Pagden, "Identity Formation in Spanish America," in *Colonial Identity in the Atlantic World, 1500–1800*, edited by Nicholas Canny and Anthony Pagden (Princeton, NJ: Princeton University Press, 1987), 75; Jonathan Goldberg, *Sodometries: Renaissance Texts, Modern Sexualities* (Stanford, CA: Stanford University Press, 1992); Federico Garza Carvajal, *Vir: Perceptions of Manliness in Andalucía and Mexico, 1561–1699* (Amsterdam: Amsterdamse Historische Reeks, 2000), 166.

13. Stephen Greenblatt, *Marvelous Possessions: The Wonder of the New World* (Oxford: Clarendon Press, 1991). See also William Taylor, *Drinking, Homicide, and Rebellion in Colonial Mexican Villages* (Stanford, CA: Stanford University Press, 1979).

14. Neil Whitehead, "Hans Staden and the Cultural Politics of Cannibalism," *Hispanic American Historical Review* 80, no. 4 (2000); Hans Staden, *Hans Staden's True History: An Account of Cannibal Captivity in Brazil*, edited and translated by Neil Whitehead and Michael Harbsmeier (Durham, NC: Duke University Press, 2008). Whitehead attracted sharp criticism for his use of this colonial source. For the debate between Whitehead and Michaela Schmölz-Häberlein and Mark Häberlein, see Neil Whitehead, "The Häberleins and the Political Culture of Scholarship," *Hispanic American Historical Review*, 81, nos. 3–4 (2001): 753–756; and Michaela Schmölz-Häberlein and Mark Häberlein, Hans Staden, Neil L. Whitehead, and the Cultural Politics of Scholarly Publishing," *Hispanic American Historical Review*, 81, nos. 3–4 (2001): 745–751. See also Fernando Santos-Granero, *Vital Enemies: Slavery, Predation and the Amerindian Political Economy of Life* (Austin: University of Texas Press, 2009).

15. Charles Gibson, *The Aztecs under Spanish Rule: A History of the Indians of the Valley of Mexico, 1519–1810* (Stanford, CA: Stanford University Press, 1964), 7, 150, 409; William Madsen and Claudia Madsen, "The Cultural Structure of Mexican Drinking Behaviour," in *Contemporary Cultures and Societies of Latin America*, edited by Dwight Heath (New York: Waveland Press, 1974), 439; Taylor, *Drinking, Homicide, and Rebellion;* Serge Gruzinski, *The Conquest of Mexico: The Incorporation of Indian Societies into the Western World, 16th–18th Centuries* (Cambridge: Polity Press, 1993), 203; Peter Mancall, *Deadly Medicine: Indians and Alcohol in Early America* (Ithaca, NY: Cornell University Press, 1995); Christine Eber, *Women and Alcohol in a Highland Maya Town* (Austin: University of Texas Press, 2001).

16. See in particular Sabine MacCormack, *Religion in the Andes: Vision and Imagination in Early Colonial Peru* (Princeton, NJ: Princeton University Press, 1991); Carolyn Dean, *Inka Bodies and the Body of Christ: Corpus Christi in Colonial Cuzco, Peru* (Durham, NC: Duke University Press, 1999), 1 (quote); Jáuregui, "'El plato más sabroso'"; Osvaldo Pardo, *The Origins of Mexican Catholicism: Nahua Rituals and Christian Sacraments in Sixteenth-Century Mexico* (Ann Arbor: University of Michigan Press, 2004); Jaime Lara, *Christian Texts for*

*Aztecs: Art and Liturgy in Colonial Mexico* (Notre Dame: University of Notre Dame Press, 2008). See also Miri Rubin, *Corpus Christi: The Eucharist in Late Medieval Culture* (Cambridge: Cambridge University Press, 1991); and Christopher Elwood, *The Body Broken: The Calvinist Doctrine of the Eucharist and the Symbolization of Power in Sixteenth-Century France* (Oxford: Oxford University Press, 1999).

17. Kate Teltscher, *India Inscribed: European and British Writing on India 1600–1800* (Oxford: Oxford University Press, 1995), 151.

18. Pedro Sánchez de Aguilar, "Informe contra los idólatras de Yucatán" (1613), in *Hechicerías e idolatrías del México antiguo*, edited by Pilar Máynez (Mexico City: Cien de México, 2008), 185.

19. Rebecca Earle, *The Body of the Conquistador: Food, Race and the Colonial Experience in Spanish America, 1492–1700* (Cambridge: Cambridge University Press, 2012), 54–83.

20. Francisco Hernández, *The Mexican Treasury: The Writings of Dr. Francisco Hernández*, edited and translated by Simon Varey, Rafael Chabrán, and Cynthia Chamberlain (Stanford, CA: Stanford University Press, 2000), 111.

21. Bernabé Cobo, *Historia del Nuevo Mundo*, 1653, in *Obras*, vol. 1, edited by Francisco Mateos (Madrid: Biblioteca de Autores Españoles, 1956), 391.

22. Viceroy Marqués de Villmanrique to King Philip II, Mexico, July 20, 1587, Audiencia de México 21, N. 19, fol. 10, Archivo General de Indias, Seville (hereafter AGI).

23. Luis Lobera de Avila, *Vergel de sanidad que por otro nombre se llamaba banquete de caballeros y orden de vivir* (Alcalá de Henares, 1542), xx recto; Francisco Nuñez de Oria, *Regimiento y aviso de sanidad, que trata de todos los generos de alimentos y del regimiento della* (Medina del Campo, 1586), 61r–73v; Carmen Peña and Fernando Girón, *La prevención de la enfermedad en la España bajo medieval* (Granada: Universidad de Granada, 2006), 196; Ken Albala, *Eating Right in the Renaissance* (Berkeley: University of California Press, 2002), 67.

24. Cristóbal de Villalón, *El scholástico*, 1538–1541, edited by José Miguel Martínez Torrejón (Barcelona: Crítica, 1997), 161–164; Pedro Mexía, *Silva de varia lección* (1540), vol. 2, edited by Antonio Castro (Madrid: Cátedra, 1989), 101–110; Pedro de Mercado, *Diálogos de philosophia natural y moral* (Granada, 1574), dialogue 4; José de Acosta, *De procuranda indorum salute* (1588), vol. 1, translated by L. Pereña, V. Abril, C. Baciero, A. García, D. Ramos, J. Barrientos, and F. Maseda (Madrid: Consejo Superior de Investigaciones Científicas, 1984), 569; Juan de Torres, *Philosophía moral de príncipes para su buena criança y govierno: y para personas de todo estado* (Burgos, 1596), 459–501; Benito de Peñaloza y Mondragón, *Libro de las cinco excelencias del español que despueblan a España para su mayor potencia y dilatición* (Pamplona, 1629), 141–144; Fernando de Avendaño, *Sermones de los misterios de nuestra santa fe católica, en lengua castellana y la general del inca, impugnandose los errores particulares que los indios han tenido* (Lima, 1648), 49.

25. Esteban de Salazar, *Veinte discursos sobre el credo, en declaración de nuestra sancta fe catholica, y doctrina chrisitina muy necessarios a todos los fieles en este tiempo* (Seville, 1586), 200; Miguel Herrero García, *Ideas de los españoles del siglo XVII* (Madrid: Gredos, 1966), 59–61; Taylor, *Drinking, Homicide, and Rebellion*, 41; Earle, "Indians and Drunkenness."

26. Letter of Tomás López Medel, March 25, 1551, Audiencia de Guatemala 9A, R. 18, N. 77, fol. 1, AGI.

27. Thomas Aquinas, *Summa Theologica,* third part, question 74; Rubin, *Corpus Christi,* 37–49.

28. Lee Palmer Wandel, *The Eucharist in the Reformation: Incarnation and History* (Cambridge: Cambridge University Press, 2006), 216, 222–223; Jerónimo de Ripalda, *Doctrina cristiana del P. Jerónimo de Ripalda e intento bibliográfico de la misma, años 1591–1900,* edited by Juan Sánchez (Madrid: Imprenta Alemana, 1909), 28.

29. Conquistador Anónimo, "Relación de algunas cosas de la Nueva España," in *Colección de documentos para la historia de México,* vol. 1, edited by Joaquín García Icazbalceta (Mexico City: J. M. Andrade, 1858), 398.

30. Viceroy Marqués de Villmanrique to King Philip II, fols. 4, 6, 18, AGI.

31. Viceroy Conde de Monterrey to King Philip II, Mexico, April 25, 1598, Audiencia de Mexico 24, no. 8, fol. 14, AGI.

32. Juan de la Cruz, *Doctrina christiana en la lengua guasteca con la lengua castellana . . . compuesta por yndustria de un frayle de la orden del glorioso Sanct Augustin* (Mexico City, 1571), 19; Acosta, *De procuranda,* 1:555; Alonso de Ovalle, *Histórica relación del Reyno de Chile* (1646) (Santiago: Instituto de Literatura Chilena, 1969), 24; Juan de Solórzano Pereira, *Política indiana* (1647), vol. 1 (Madrid, 1736), 190; Avendaño, *Sermones,* 49–51; Hernando Ruiz de Alarcón, *Tratado de las supersticiones y costumbres gentílicas que hoy viven entre los indios naturales de esta Nueva España,* trat. 3, ch. 1, accessed May 19, 2018, https://tinyurl.com/yaqwtt32; Earle, *The Body of the Conquistador,* 167–174.

33. Earle, *The Body of the Conquistador.*

34. Juan Rodríguez Freyle, *Conquista y descubrimiento del Nuevo Reino de Granada* (1636) (Bogotá: Samper Matiz, 1890), 10.

35. Acosta, *De procuranda,* 1:551 (quote), 563, 573. It is impossible to generalize about the diverse roles alcohol and intoxication played in indigenous religious practices. For studies examining both the distant and more recent past, see John Kennedy, "Tesguino Complex: The Role of Beer in Tarahumara Culture," *American Anthropologist* 65, no. 3 (1963): 620–640; Taylor, *Drinking, Homicide, and Rebellion;* Catherine Allen, *The Hold Life Has: Coca and Cultural Identity in an Andean Community* (Washington: Smithsonian Books, 1988); M. J. Weismantel, "Maize Beer and Andean Social Transformations: Drunken Indians, Bread Babies and Chosen Women," *MLN* 106, no. 4 (1991): 861<n>879; Thomas Cummins, *Toasts with the Inca: Andean Abstraction and Colonial Images on Quero Vessels* (Ann Arbor: University of Michigan Press, 2002); Eber, *Women and Alcohol in a Highland Maya Town.*

36. Pedro José de Arriaga, *Extirpación de la idolatría del Piru,* 1621, in *Crónicas peruanas del interés indígena,* edited by Francisco Esteve Barba (Madrid: Biblioteca de Autores Españoles, 1968), 239 (quote), 258; "Relación de las costumbres antiguas de los naturales del Pirú," ca. 1550, in *Crónicas peruanas del interés indígena,* 174, 177; Auto of Marquez de Mancera, Lima, July 28, 1646, in Francisco de Avila, *Tratado de los evangelios que nuestra madre propone en todo el año* ([Lima], [1648]); Solórzano Pereira, *Política indiana,* 1:191.

37. Miguel de Olabarrieta Medrano, *Recuerdo de las obligaciones del ministerio apostólico en la cura de las almas* (Lima, 1717), 106.

38. Mónica Patricia Martini, *El indio y los sacramentos en Hispanoamérica: Circunstancias adversas y malas interpretaciones* (Buenos Aires: CONICET, 1993), 175–199; Pardo, *The Origins of Mexican Catholicism,* 131–158. See also Diego Durán, *Historia de las Indias de Nueva España e islas de la Tierra Firme* (1570), vol. 1, edited

by Angel Garibay (Mexico City: Porrúa, 1967) 202, 272; Diego Valadés, *Retórica cristiana,* 1579, edited by Esteban Palomera, Alfonso Castro Pallares, and Tarsicio Herrera Zapién (Mexico City: Fondo de Cultura Económica, 1989), 423–447; José de Acosta, *De procuranda indorum salute* (1588), vol. 2, translated by L. Pereña, V. Abril, C. Baciero, A. García, D. Ramos, J. Barrientos, and F. Maseda (Madrid: Consejo Superior de Investigaciones Científicas, 1984), 401, 413; Juan Baptista, *Advertencias para los confessores de los naturales* (Sanctiago Tlatilulco, 1600), 56–59; Sánchez de Aguilar, "Informe contra los idólatras de Yucatán," 186; Juan de Torquemada, *Monarchia yndiana,* vol. 3 (Seville, 1615), 213–214; Peña Montenegro, *Itinerario para parochos,* 277–278, 440, 446; Olabarrieta Medrano, *Recuerdo de los obligaciones del ministerio apostólico,* 46–55.

39. Pedro de Feria, *Doctrina christiana en lengua castellana y çapoteca* (Mexico City, 1567), 86 (quote); Bartolomé de Alva, *A Guide to Confession Large and Small in the Mexican Language, 1634,* edited by Barry Sell and John F. Schwaller (Norman: University of Nebraska Press, 1999), 92–93, 96–97, 120, 123, 128–129.

40. Torquemada, *Monarchia yndiana,* 212; Peña Montenegro, *Itinerario para parochos,* 277.

41. Acosta, *De procuranda,* 2:391–399; Torquemada, *Monarchia yndiana,* 213; Peña Montenegro, *Itinerario para parochos,* 441.

42. Jáuregui, "'El plato más sabroso'"; Jorge Cañizares-Esguerra, *Puritan Conquistadors: Iberianizing the Atlantic, 1550–1700* (Stanford, CA: Stanford University Press, 2006), 100–104.

43. Jáuregui, "'El plato más sabroso,'" 205. For the place of cannibalism in Mexica cosmology, see David Carrasco, "Cosmic Jaws: We Eat the Gods and the Gods Eat Us," *Journal of the American Academy of Religion,* 63, no. 3 (1995): 429–463; Inga Clendinnen, *Aztecs: An Interpretation* (Cambridge: Cambridge University Press, 1995).

44. Cañizares-Esguerra, *Puritan Conquistadors,* 88–95.

45. Solórzano Pereira, *Política indiana,* 1:189–190. For sodomy, see also Kelly Watson's chapter in this volume.

46. Acosta, *De procuranda,* 2:403.

47. Homi Bhabha, "Of Mimicry and Man: The Ambivalence of Colonial Discourse," *October* 28 (Spring 1984): 125–133; Ann Laura Stoler, *Race and the Education of Desire: Foucault's History of Sexuality and the Colonial Order of Things* (Durham, MC: Duke University Press, 1995); Earle, *The Body of the Conquistador.*

48. Marcy Norton, *Sacred Gifts, Profane Pleasures: A History of Tobacco and Chocolate in the Atlantic World* (Ithaca, NY: Cornell University Press, 2008), 131.

49. The centrality of evangelization to the colonial endeavor is stressed in *Recopilación de leyes de los reynos de las Indias,* vol. 1 (1791) (Madrid: Ediciones Cultura Hispánica, 1943), 1–10.

50. Michael Palencia-Roth, "Cannibalism and the New Man of Latin America in the 15th- and 16th-Century European Imagination," *Comparative Civilizations Review,* 12, no. 12 (1985): 1–27, esp. 20 ("in any culturally significant way"); Frank Lestringant, "Le cannibale et ses paradoxes," *Mentalités/Mentalities,* 1, nos. 1–2 (1983), 6 ("it was constantly discussed and represented"); Charles Zika, "Cannibalism and Witchcraft in Early Modern Europe: Reading the Visual Images," *History Workshop Journal* 44 (1997): 126.

51. Francisco de Vitoria, "On Self-Restraint," 1537, in *Political Writings,* edited by Anthony Pagden and Jeremy Lawrence (Cambridge: Cambridge University

Press, 1991), 207–212; Juan Focher and Diego Valadés, *Itinerario del misionero en América,* 1574, edited by Antonio Eguiluz (Madrid: Librería General Victoriano Suárez, 1960), 301–319; Peña Montenegro, *Itinerario para parochos de indios,* 461; Thomas Cummins, "To Serve Man: Pre-Columbian Art, Western Discourses of Idolatry, and Cannibalism," *RES: Anthropology and Aesthetics* 42 (Autumn 2002): 119–120. On Europe's cannibals, see Piero Camporesi, *Bread of Dreams: Food and Fantasy in Early Modern Europe,* translated by David Gentilcore (Chicago: University of Chicago Press, 1989), 40–41, 87; Maggie Kilgour, *From Communion to Cannibalism: An Anatomy of Metaphors of Incorporation* (Princeton, NJ: Princeton University Press, 1990); Lestringant, *Cannibals;* Geraldine Heng, *Empire of Magic: Medieval Romance and the Politics of Cultural Fantasy* (New York: Columbia University Press, 2003), 17–61; Merrall Llewelyn Price, *Consuming Passions: The Uses of Cannibalism in Late Medieval and Early Modern Europe* (New York: Routledge, 2003), 8–11.

52. Nuñez de Oria, *Regimiento y aviso de sanidad,* 32r (quote); Piero Camporesi, *The Incorruptible Flesh. Bodily Mutation and Mortification in Religion and Folklore,* translated by Tania Croft-Murray (Cambridge: Cambridge University Press, 1988); Camporesi, *Bread of Dreams,* 23, 44–46; Richard Sugg, *Mummies, Cannibals and Vampires: A History of Corpse Medicine from the Renaissance to the Victorians* (London: Routledge, 2011).

53. Frank Lestringant, "Catholiques et cannibales: Le Thème du cannibalisme dans les discours protestant au temps des guerres de religion," in *Pratiques et discours alimentaires à la Renaissance,* edited by Jean-Claude Margolin (Paris: Maisonneuve & Larose, 1982); Lestringant, "Le canibale et ses paradoxes." See also Jean de Léry, *History of a Voyage to the Land of Brazil,* 1580, edited and translated by Janet Whatley (Berkeley: University of California Press, 1992).

54. Margaret Greer, "Imperialism and Anthropophagy in Early Modern Spanish Tragedy: The Unthought Known," in *Reason and Its Others: Italy, Spain and the New World,* edited by David Castillo and Massimo Lollini (Nashville: Vanderbilt University Press, 2006), 291.

55. Greer, "Imperialism and Anthropophagy," 290 (quote); Heng, *Empire of Magic,* 17–61.

56. Cummins, "To Serve Man," 116.

57. Bartolomé de las Casas, *Breve relación de la destrucción de las Indias Occidentales* (1542) (Philadelphia: J. F. Hurtel, 1821), 109; Theodore de Bry, illustrations for Bartolomé de Las Casas, *Narratio Regionum indicarum per Hispanos Quosdam devastatarum verissima* (Frankfurt, 1598); Tom Conley, "De Bry's Las Casas" and Georges Baudot, "Amerindian Image and Utopian Project: Motolinía and Millenarian Discourse," both in *Amerindian Images and the Legacy of Columbus,* edited by René Jara and Nicholas Spadaccini (Minneapolis: University of Minnesota Press, 1992), 103–131, 383.

58. Pedro Simón, *Noticias historiales de las conquistas de Tierra Firme en las Indias Occidentales* (1627), vol. 1, edited by Juan Friede (Bogotá: Biblioteca Banco Popular, 1981), 196–197 (quote), 199–202.

59. Felipe de Hutten, "Diario," *Descubrimiento y conquista de Venezuela,* vol. 2, edited by Joaquín Gabaldón Márquez (Caracas: Academia Nacional de la Historia, 1962), 368 (quote); Fernando Pizarro y Orellana, *Varones ilustres del nuevo mundo* (Madrid, 1639), 353.

60. D'Anghera, *De Orbe Novo,* vol. 1, decade 2, book 10.

61. López de Gómara, *Historia general,* 104–105, 109, 251, 361. See also Álvar Núñez Cabeza de Vaca, "Naufragios y relación de la jornada que hizo a la Florida," 1555, in *Historiadores primitivos de Indias,* vol. 1, edited by Enrique de Vedia (Madrid, 1852), 531.

62. Price, *Consuming Passions,* 32, 80 (quote); Elwood, *The Body Broken,* 34–41; Wandel, *The Eucharist in the Reformation,* 8, 225–227.

63. Price, *Consuming Passions.*

64. Cruz, *Doctrina christiana en la lengua guasteca,* 19; James Clifton with David Nirenberg and Linda Elaine Neagley, *The Body of Christ in the Art of Europe and New Spain, 1150–1800* (Munich: Presel, 1997), 114–115, 120–123.

65. Roberto Belarminio, *Declaración copiosa de las quatro partes mas essenciales, y necessarias de la doctrina christiana,* translated by Bartolomé Jurado Palomino (Lima, 1649), 113–122; Elwood, *The Body Broken; Wandel, The Eucharist in the Reformation,* 21.

66. Wandel, *The Eucharist in the Reformation,* 217–221, 239 (quote). For a poetic example, see Benito Arias Montano, *Humanae Salutis Monumenta,* 1571, edited by Benito Feliú de San Pedro (Madrid: Editorial Swan, 1984), 282.

67. Anonymous, *Doctrina christiana en lengua española y mexicana* (Mexico City, 1550), 102; Feria, *Doctrina christiana en lengua castellana y çapoteca,* 85 (first quote); Belarminio, *Declaración copiosa,* prologue; Peña Montenegro, *Itinerario para parochos de indios,* 278–279 (second quote).

68. Alonso de Sandoval, *De Instauranda aethiopum salute: El mundo de la esclavitud negra en América* (1627), edited by Angel Valtierra (Bogotá: Biblioteca de la Presidencia de Colombia, 1956), 67–68.

69. Goldberg, *Sodometries,* 208.

70. Acosta, *De procuranda,* 1:239.

71. Antonio Ruiz de Montoya, *Conquista hecha por los religiosos de la compañía de Jesús en las provincias del Paraguay, Paraná, Uruguay y Tape* (1639) (Bilbao: Imprenta del Corazón de Jesús, 1892), 129.

72. Jan Szeminski, "'Why Kill the Spaniard?' New Perspectives on Andean Insurrectionary Ideology in the Eighteenth Century," in *Resistance, Rebellion and Consciousness in the Andean Peasant World, 18th to 20th Centuries,* edited by Steve Stern (Madison: University of Wisconsin Press, 1987); Mary Weismantel, *Cholas and Pishtacos: Stories of Race and Sex in the Andes* (Chicago: University of Chicago Press, 2001).

73. Richard Adams, "A Nutritional Research Program in Guatemala," in *Health, Community and Culture: Case Studies of Public Reactions to Health Programs,* edited by Benjamin Paul (New York City: Russell Sage Foundation, 1955). I am grateful to Josh Moulding for this reference.

74. Luise White, *Speaking with Vampires: Rumor and History in Colonial Africa* (Berkeley: University of California Press, 2000).

75. Acosta, *De procuranda,* 1:239.

76. Alonso de Molina, *Confessionario mayor en la lengua mexicana y castellana,* 1569, edited by Roberto Moreno (Mexico City: Universidad Nacional Autónoma de México, 1984), 82.

77. Visita al repartimiento de las batatas de doña Francisca Malaver, 1623, Visitas de Santander, tomo 6, doc. 7, fol. 599r, Archivo General de la Nación, Bogotá,

Colonia; Gregorio Saldarriaga, *Alimentación e identidades en el Nuevo Reino de Granada, siglos XVI y XVII* (Bogotá: Biblioteca Básica de Cocinas Tradicionales de Colombia, 2012), 322. I am grateful to Gregorio Saldarriaga Escobar for the material in the Colombian national archive.

78. Focher and Valadés, *Itinerario del misionero en América,* 315; Cummins, "To Serve Man," 120–121.

## Chapter 5

1. Eustace Chapuys to the Emperor Charles V, January 21, 1536, in *Calendar of State Papers, Spain,* vol. 5, part 2, edited by Pascual de Gayangos (London: 1888), no. 9.

2. For "abomination of religious persons," see "Remembrances," February 4[?], 1536, in *Letters and Papers, Foreign and Domestic, Henry VIII* (hereafter *LP*), vol. 10, edited by James Gairdner (London: 1887), no. 254. For religious changes, see *The Statutes of the Realm* (London: 1810–1828), 3:663; and Christopher Haigh, *English Reformations: Religion, Politics, and Society under the Tudors* (Oxford: Oxford University Press, 1993), 128–130.

3. "The voyage of M. Hore and diuers other gentlemen, to Newfoundland, and Cape Briton, in the yere 1536 and in the 28 yere of king Henry the 8.," in Richard Hakluyt, *The Principal Nauigations, Voyages, Traffiques, and Discoueries of the English Nation* (hereafter *PN*), vol. 3 (London, 1599–1600), 129.

4. "Voyage of Hore" in Hakluyt, *PN,* 3:129.

5. 24 Hen. VIII c. 12, in *The Statutes of the Realm,* 3:427. Throughout much of this essay, I use the term "British" rather than "English," in keeping with both contemporary and more modern usage. From Henry VII's accession onward, contemporaries perceived of and explicitly styled the dynasty and its activities as British. This conscious self-fashioning reflected the multiple identities (English, Welsh, Scottish, and Irish) of those involved in Tudor ventures at home and overseas, the geographical space the Tudor crown claimed, and the ideological bases for those claims. This is not to say that adoption of the term "British" was broad or complete, that appeals to Englishness abated, or that Tudor rule actually encompassed all of Britain. Rather, it signals a budding British theory and project.

6. Indeed, the word's origin is probably Welsh (a merger of the words *pen,* meaning head, and *gwyn,* meaning white) and the Tudors were of Welsh descent, though at times they were ambivalent about embracing that identity. See *Oxford English Dictionary Online,* s.v. "penguin"; C. S. L. Davies, "Tudor: What's in a Name?" *History* 97, no. 325 (2012): 24–42. To contemporaries, then, native use of the word penguin was a significant sign of Welsh presence in the New World. It fit with Tudor imperial mythology, which claimed that the Welsh Prince Madoc had colonized the American continent in the twelfth century, well ahead of any competitors. See John Dee, *The Limits of the British Empire* (1578), edited by Ken MacMillan with Jennifer Abeles (Westport, CT: Praeger, 2004); David Powell, *The historie of Cambria, now called Wales* ([London], 1584), 229. For further analysis, see Ken MacMillan, "Discourse on History, Geography, and Law: John Dee and the Limits of the British Empire, 1576–80," *Canadian Journal of History* 36, no. 1 (2001): 1–25.

7. "Voyage of Hore," in Hakluyt, *PN,* 3:130.

8. "Voyage of Hore," in Hakluyt, *PN,* 3:130.

9. Retha M. Warnicke, *The Rise and Fall of Anne Boleyn: Family Politics at the Court of Henry VIII* (Cambridge: Cambridge University Press, 1989); Eric Ives, *The Life and Death of Anne Boleyn* (Oxford: Blackwell, 2004); G. W. Bernard, *Anne Boleyn: Fatal Attractions* (New Haven, CT: Yale University Press, 2010).

10. The term comes from Robert Appelbaum, *Aguecheek's Beef, Belch's Hiccup, and Other Gastronomic Interjections: Literature, Culture, and Food among the Early Moderns* (Chicago: University of Chicago Press, 2006), 263. On the hunger topos in Virginia, see Rachel B. Herrmann, "The 'tragicall historie': Cannibalism and Abundance in Colonial Jamestown," *William and Mary Quarterly* 68, no. 1 (2011): 47–74.

11. "Voyage of Hore," in Hakluyt, *PN*, 3:130.

12. "Voyage of Hore," in Hakluyt, *PN*, 3:130.

13. "Voyage of Hore," in Hakluyt, *PN*, 3:130.

14. "Voyage of Hore," in Hakluyt, *PN*, 3:131. The first edition leaves out this development, moving directly from the captain's oration to the arrival of the French ship, see Richard Hakluyt, *The Principall Navigations, Voiages and Discoveries of the English Nation* (London, 1589), 517–519.

15. For useful summaries of the historiographical debate on Anne's demise, see Greg Walker, "Rethinking the Fall of Anne Boleyn," *The Historical Journal* 45, no. 1 (2002): 1–29; and Retha Warnicke, *Wicked Women of Tudor England: Queens, Aristocrats, Commoners* (New York: Palgrave Macmillan, 2012), 15–43.

16. For a cogent, synthetic summary of these developments in 1536 and 1537, see John Guy, *Tudor England* (Oxford: Oxford University Press, 1988), esp. 116–177; Susan Brigden, *New Worlds, Lost Worlds: The Rule of the Tudors, 1485–1603* (New York: Penguin, 2000), esp. 101–139.

17. "Voyage of Hore," in Hakluyt, *PN*, 3:131.

18. "Voyage of Hore," in Hakluyt, *PN*, 3:131. For further analysis, see E. G. R. Taylor, "Master Hore's Voyage of 1536," *Geographical Journal* 77, no. 5 (1531): 469–470; Philip Levy, "Man-Eating and Menace on Richard Hore's Expedition to America," *Atlantic Studies* 2, no. 2 (2005): 129–151.

19. This essay employs a twofold definition of empire. The first, which stems from the Latin *imperium* to convey national sovereignty and omnicompetent supremacy, has figured prominently in work on the English Renaissance and Reformation by Walter Ullmann, John Guy, and others. The second, which denotes territorial expansion and rule overseas, is central to specialists who look beyond England, including David Armitage, Nicholas Canny, and Anthony Pagden. See Walter Ullmann, "'This Realm of England Is an Empire,'" *Journal of Ecclesiastical History* 30, no. 2 (1979): 175–203; John Guy, "Thomas Cromwell and the Intellectual Origins of the Henrician Revolution," in *Reassessing the Henrician Age: Humanism, Politics and Reform 1500–1550*, edited by Alistair Fox and John Guy (Oxford: Basil Blackwell, 1986), 151–178; Dale Hoak, ed., *Tudor Political Culture* (New York: Cambridge University Press, 1995); David Armitage, *The Ideological Origins of the British Empire* (Cambridge: Cambridge University Press, 2000); Nicholas Canny, *The Oxford History of the British Empire: The Origins of Empire: British Overseas Enterprise to the Close of the Seventeenth Century* (Oxford: Oxford University Press, 1998); and Anthony Pagden, *Lords of All the World: Ideologies of Empire in Spain, Britain, and France, c. 1500–c. 1800* (New Haven, CT: Yale University Press, 1995).

20. For further discussion, see Jessica Hower, "An Experiment in British Empire:

Henry VIII in Tournai, 1513–1519," *Memoires de la Societé Royale d'Histoire et d'Archéologie de Tournai* 14 (2014): 81–145.

21. Hakluyt's role attests to the significance of the voyage and its cannibal element for later imperial promoters. As Peter Mancall notes, "His willingness to become the intermediary allowed him to retell a notorious story of an English expedition to Newfoundland in 1536—an expedition made infamous by allegations of cannibalism among the English themselves." See Peter C. Mancall, *Hakluyt's Promise: An Elizabethan's Obsession for an English America* (New Haven, CT: Yale University Press, 2007), 187.

22. See Kathleen Wilson, ed., *A New Imperial History: Culture, Identity, and Modernity in Britain and the Empire, 1660–1840* (Cambridge: Cambridge University Press, 2004); James Thompson, "Modern Britain and the New Imperial History," *History Compass* 5, no. 2 (2007): 455–462; and Stephen Howe, ed., *The New Imperial Histories Reader* (London: Routledge, 2010).

23. See "AHR Forum: Entangled Empires," *American Historical Review* 112, no. 3 (2007): 710–799; Bernard Bailyn, *Atlantic History: Concepts and Contours* (Cambridge, MA: Harvard University Press, 2005); and David Armitage and Michael J. Braddick, eds., *The British Atlantic World, 1500–1800* (New York: Palgrave, 2002).

24. British Atlantic histories typically begin in the seventeenth century, with England's permanent colonization of the present-day United States. For further critiques of the Atlantic world concept, see "Forum: Beyond the Atlantic," *William and Mary Quarterly* 63, no. 4 (2006): 675–742; Alison Games, "Atlantic History: Definitions, Challenges, and Opportunities," *American Historical Review* 111, no. 3 (2006): 741–757; and Jack P. Greene and Philip D. Morgan, eds., *Atlantic History: A Critical Appraisal* (Oxford: Oxford University Press, 2009).

25. There is no doubt that the Spanish and Portuguese dominated the sixteenth-century Atlantic. British crossings were rarer, their presence diffuse and hard to measure. Thus, scholars frequently treat the 1500s as a century of Iberian activity only. The idea of delayed British interest is summarized and reasserted in Trevor Burnard, "The British Atlantic," in *Atlantic History: A Critical Appraisal,* edited by Jack P. Greene and Philip D. Morgan (Oxford: Oxford University Press, 2009), 111–136.

26. J. G. A. Pocock, "British History: A Plea for a New Subject," *Journal of Modern History* 47, no. 4 (1975): 601–621; Alexander Grant and Keith Stringer, eds., *Uniting the Kingdom? The Making of British History* (New York: Routledge, 1995); Glenn Burgess, ed., *The New British History: Founding a Modern State, 1603–1715* (London: I. B. Tauris, 1999).

27. See G. R. Elton, *England under the Tudors* (London: Methuen, 1974); and Guy, *Tudor England.*

28. Influenced by the New British History, which is defined in part by its efforts to enrich a long-standing Anglocentrism and draw closer to a "four nations" history of the interactions between England, Scotland, Ireland, and Wales, some have situated the Tudors within a Renaissance milieu and have noted the limits of English hegemony. Ireland, which has received the most attention, has generated three chief paradigms. See Brendan Bradshaw, *"And so began the Irish Nation": Nationality, National Consciousness, and Nationalism in Pre-Modern Ireland* (Aldershot: Ashgate, 2015); Steven G. Ellis, *Ireland in the Age of the Tudors, 1447–1603: English Expansion and the End of Gaelic Rule* (London: Longman, 1998); Nicholas P. Canny, *The Elizabethan Conquest of Ireland: A Pattern Established, 1565–76* (New York: Barnes and Noble, 1976).

29. William Arens, *The Man-Eating Myth: Anthropology and Anthropophagy* (New York: Oxford University Press, 1979); Donald W. Forsyth, "Three Cheers for Hans Staden: The Case for Brazilian Cannibalism," *Ethnohistory* 32, no. 1 (1985): 17–36; Peter Hulme, *Colonial Encounters: Europe and the Native Caribbean, 1492–1797* (London: Routledge, 1986); Maggie Kilgour, *From Communion to Cannibalism: An Anatomy of Metaphors of Incorporation* (Princeton, NJ: Princeton University Press, 1990); Stephen Greenblatt, *Marvelous Possessions: The Wonder of the New World* (Chicago: University of Chicago Press, 1991); Philip P. Boucher, *Cannibal Encounters* (Baltimore, MD: Johns Hopkins University Press, 1992); Frank Lestringant, *Cannibals: The Discovery and Representation of the Cannibal from Columbus to Jules Verne,* translated by Rosemary Morris (Berkeley: University of California Press, 1997); Francis Barker, Peter Hulme, and Margaret Iversen, eds., *Cannibalism and the Colonial World* (Cambridge: Cambridge University Press, 1998); Laurence R. Goldman, *The Anthropology of Cannibalism* (Westport: Praeger, 1999); Neil L. Whitehead, "Hans Staden and the Cultural Politics of Cannibalism," *Hispanic American Historical Review* 80, no. 4 (2000): 721–751; Kristen Guest, ed., *Eating Their Words: Cannibalism and the Boundaries of Cultural Identity* (Albany: State University of New York Press, 2001); John Thornton, "Cannibals, Witches, and Slave Traders in the Atlantic World," *William and Mary Quarterly* 60, no. 2 (2003): 273–294; Gananath Obeyesekere, *Cannibal Talk: The Man-Eating Myth and Human Sacrifice in the South Seas* (Berkeley: University of California Press, 2005); Jeff Berglund, *Cannibal Fictions: American Explorations of Colonialism, Race, Gender and Sexuality* (Madison: University of Wisconsin Press, 2006); Luciana Villas Bôas, "The Anatomy of Cannibalism: Religious Vocabulary and Ethnographic Writing in the Sixteenth Century," *Studies in Travel Writing* 12, no. 1 (2008): 7–29; Coll Thrush, "Vancouver the Cannibal: Cuisine, Encounter, and the Dilemma of Difference on the Northwest Coast, 1774–1808," *Ethnohistory* 58, no. 1 (2011): 1–35; Kelly L. Watson, *Insatiable Appetites: Imperial Encounters with Cannibals in the North Atlantic World* (New York: New York University Press, 2015). For Columbus, see Bartolomé de las Casas, ed., *The Journal of Christopher Columbus,* translated by Lionel Cecil Jane (London: Blond, 1968), 68–69; Nicolás Wey-Gómez, "A Poetics of Dismemberment: The Book of Job and the Cannibals of the Cariay in Columbus's Account of the Fourth Voyage," *Colonial Latin American Review* 16, no. 1 (2007): 109–123; Ted Motohashi, "The Discourse of Cannibalism in Early Modern Travel Writing," in *Travel Writing and Empire: Postcolonial Theory in Transit,* edited by Stephen Clark (New York: St. Martin's Press, 1999), 83–99.

30. Claude Rawson, "Unspeakable Rites: Cultural Reticence and the Cannibal Question," *Social Research* 66, no. 1 (1999): 167–193; H. E. Martel, "Hans Staden's Captive Soul: Identity, Imperialism, and Rumors of Cannibalism in Sixteenth-Century Brazil," *Journal of World History* 17, no. 1 (2006): 51–69.

31. Herrmann, "The 'tragicall historie,'" 73.

32. Karen Ordahl Kupperman, *The Jamestown Project* (Cambridge, MA: Harvard University Press, 2007).

33. I do not intend to suggest that these were the only occasions of British engagement with cannibalism (as discourse or practice). Moreover, it bears explicit mention that Roger Barlow's "Brief Summe of Geographie," presented to Henry VIII in 1541, is among the earliest English eyewitness descriptions of America and contains an account of "guaranies" fattening, slaughtering, and eating their captives. The

Tudor court and those in Barlow's circle thus possessed a depiction of New World (specifically Tupí-Guaraní) cannibalism before the much more well-studied Hans Staden was even taken captive and an Englishman had offered an early contribution to the evolving cannibal narrative. See *A Briefe Summe of Geographie* by Roger Barlow edited by E. G. R. Taylor (London: Hakluyt Society, 1932), 157; Heather Dalton, "'Making Feast of the Prisoner': Roger Barlow, Hans Staden, and Ideas of New World Cannibalism," in *Religion, Visual Culture and the Supernatural in Early Modern Europe,* edited by Jennifer Spinks and Dagmar Eichberger (Leiden: Brill, 2015), 187–211.

34. R. G. Marsden, "Voyage of the 'Barbara,' of London, to Brazil in 1540," *English Historical Review* 24, no. 93 (1909): 96–100, esp. 97.

35. Elton, *England under the Tudors;* J. J. Scarisbrick, *Henry VIII* (New Haven, CT: Yale University Press, 1968); Guy, *Tudor England;* G. W. Bernard, *The King's Reformation: Henry VIII and the Remaking of the English Church* (New Haven, CT: Yale University Press, 2005); David Loades, *Thomas Cromwell: Servant to Henry VIII* (Gloucestershire: Amberley, 2013); Ellis, *Ireland in the Age of the Tudors.*

36. Marsden, "Voyage of the 'Barbara,'" 100, 98.

37. The map is still extant; see British Library Add. MS 5413. Marsden suggested this potential similarity. See "Voyage of the 'Barbara,'" 100.

38. Marsden, "Voyage of the 'Barbara,'" 97; Patricia Seed, *Ceremonies of Possession: Europe's Conquest of the New World, 1492–1640* (Cambridge: Cambridge University Press, 1995).

39. Marsden, "Voyage of the 'Barbara,'" 97–99.

40. R. G. Marsden, ed., "Voyage of the Barbara to Brazil, Anno 1540," in *The Naval Miscellany,* vol. 2, edited by John Knox Laughton (London, 1912), 3–66, esp. 56.

41. Marsden, "Voyage of the Barbara to Brazil," 56 ("the perelles"), 59 ("Kennyballes"). One crewman named Richard Everton claimed to have seen "Podde slain, cut up into pieces, cooked, and eaten by the savages." This quotation is Marsden's translation from the Latin original; see "Voyage of the Barbara to Brazil," *Naval Miscellany,* 9.

42. Marsden, "Voyage of the 'Barbara,'" 99.

43. Council of Spain to Charles V, September 23, 1540, *LP,* vol. 16, no. 73.

44. Chapuys to Charles V, January 2 [or 4?], 1541, *LP,* vol. 16, no. 421.

45. Marsden, "Voyage of the 'Barbara,'" 99–100.

46. Mary C. Fuller, "Ralegh's Fugitive Gold: Reference and Deferral in *The Discoverie of Guiana,*" *Representations* 33 (Winter 1991): 42–64; Mary C. Fuller, *Voyages in Print: English Travel to America, 1576–1624* (Cambridge: Cambridge University Press, 1995); Joyce Lorimer, ed., *Sir Walter Ralegh's Discoverie of Guiana* (Burlington, VT: Hakluyt Society, 2006). Hakluyt's works from the same late Elizabethan period are full of these juxtapositions.

47. Anonymous, "Of the newe la[n]des of ye people founde by the messengers of the kynge of porty[n]gale named Emanuel Of the x dyuers nacyons crystened. Of pope Iohn and his landes, and of the costely keyes and wonders molodyes that in that lande is" ([Antwerp]: [1520?]), sigs. A ii r and A ii v. Edward Arber dated the work to 1511, however I have chosen to follow the *Short Title Catalogue* dating. See Edward Arber, ed., *The First Three English Books on America* (Birmingham: n.p., 1885).

48. Whitney R. Jones, *The Mid-Tudor Crisis, 1539–1563* (London: MacMillan, 1973). Appeals to and criticism of the theory followed. See David M. Loades, *The*

*Mid-Tudor Crisis: 1545–1565* (London: Palgrave MacMillan, 1992); Jennifer Loach, *Edward VI,* edited by George W. Bernard and Penry Williams (New Haven, CT: Yale University Press, 1999); Stephen Alford, *Kingship and Politics in the Reign of Edward VI* (Cambridge: Cambridge University Press, 2002); Charles Beem, *The Lioness Roared: The Problems of Female Rule in English History* (London: Palgrave, 2006); Stephen J. Lee, *The Mid-Tudors* (London: Routledge, 2007); Susan Doran and Thomas Freeman, eds., *Mary Tudor: Old and New Perspectives* (London: Palgrave MacMillan, 2011). Even though these scholars strove to find continuity, some vital connections between all three monarchs remain unmade.

49. Nicholas Bodrugan, *An Epitome of the title that the Kynges Maiestie of Englande, hath to the souereigntie of Scotlande continued vpon the auncient writers of both nacions, from the beginnyng* (1548), STC 3196, sig. a.v.v.

50. Cecil (later Lord Burghley) would become a major player under Elizabeth I, as would his son, Robert Cecil.

51. Richard Eden, *A treatyse of the newe India* (London, 1553), sigs. aa.iii.r and v. On Eden, see Andrew Hadfield, "Eden, Richard (c. 1520–1576), translator," in *Oxford Dictionary of National Biography* (2004–2017); and the illuminating exchange among Hadfield, William Hamlin, Claire Jowitt, Anthony Pagden, and Michael Brennan in *Connotations,* 6, nos. 1–3 (1996/1997): 1–22, 46–66, 227–245, and 310–315.

52. D. B. Quinn, "Renaissance Influences in English Colonization," *Transactions of the Royal Historical Society* 26 (1976): 73–93; Kenneth R. Andrews, *Trade, Plunder, and Settlement: Maritime Enterprise and the Genesis of the British Empire, 1480–1630* (Cambridge: Cambridge University Press, 1984); D. M. Loades, *John Dudley, Duke of Northumberland, 1504–1553* (Oxford: Oxford University Press, 1996); Diarmaid MacCulloch, *The Boy King: Edward VI and the Protestant Reformation* (Berkeley: University of California Press, 2002); Andy Wood, *The 1549 Rebellions and the Making of Early Modern England* (Cambridge: Cambridge University Press, 2010).

53. Eden, *A treatyse of the newe India,* sig. G.vi.v.

54. Eden, *A treatyse of the newe India,* sigs. H.i.v–H.ii.r.

55. Eden, *A treatyse of the newe India,* sig. H.ii.v.

56. For "true Relygion in perpetual combatte agaynste learned heretykes," see Eden, *A treatyse of the newe India,* sig. A.v.v. For "great aboundaunce of golde," see sigs. aa.iiii.v–aa.v.r. For spices, see sig. aa.iiii.v.

57. Judith Richards, "Mary Tudor as 'Sole Quene'? Gendering Tudor Monarchy," *The Historical Journal* 40, no. 4 (1997): 895–924; Glyn Redworth, "'Matters Impertinent to Women': Male and Female Monarchy under Philip and Mary," *The English Historical Review* 112, no. 447 (1997): 597–613; Alexander Samson, "The Marriage of Philip of Habsburg and Mary Tudor and Anti-Spanish Sentiment in England" (DPhil thesis, University of London, 1999); Beem, *The Lioness Roared,* 63–99. This is not to claim widespread Hispanophobia but rather to note the existence of these sentiments and their utility for polemicists, who manipulated domestic and continental drama to suit their own ends. Discomfort with Mary as England's first queen regnant was also abundantly evident. Significantly, Philip was never crowned king of England; he remained king consort until Mary's death.

58. Richard Eden, *The decades of the newe worlde* (London, 1555), 138v ("wylde and wanderynge"), 31r, 39r, 67v, 187v, and 198v (for native archery practices), 142v ("lyke a pestiferous contagion"), 38v ("to hunte for mannes fleshe").

59. Eden, *The decades of the newe worlde,* 3r.

60. Eden, *The decades of the newe worlde,* 116r ("these monstrous bludsuckers"), 103v (for gold).

61. Eden, *The decades of the newe worlde,* 138v (for their intractable nature), 114v and 103v–140r (for warmongering), 138v (for defeat by force), 140r ("from theyr wylde and beastly rudenes").

62. Eden, *The decades of the newe worlde,* sig. a.ii.v.

63. Eden, *The decades of the newe worlde,* sig. b.iii.v ("decayed and impouerysshed"), sig. b.iiii.r (for Spain's richness).

64. Eden, *The decades of the newe worlde,* sig. b.ii.r.

65. Gillian Cell, *English Enterprise in Newfoundland* (Toronto: University of Toronto Press, 1969), 35.

66. Ingram claimed that "the Canibals or men eaters . . . doe most inhabite betweene *Norumbega, & Bariniah,* they haue teeth like dogsteeth, and thereby you may know them." See Hakluyt, *The Principall Navigations, Voiages and Discoveries of the English Nation,* 558. The Frobisher travel narratives similarly referenced indigenous cannibalism, see Hakluyt, *PN,* 3:38, 67–68, 93. Gilbert's "Discourse of Discoverie for a new Passage to Cataia" charged that "it seemeth very likely, that the inhabitants of the most part of those countries, by which they must haue come any other way besides by the Northwest, being for the most part Anthropophagi, or men eaters, would haue deuoured them, slaine them, or (at the least wise) kept them as wonders for the gaze." See Hakluyt, *PN,* 3:19. Written in 1566, Gilbert's tract was published in 1576; his seminal voyage followed in 1583.

67. J. A. Guy, ed., *The Reign of Elizabeth I: Court and Culture in the Last Decade* (Cambridge: Cambridge University Press, 1995); Anne N. MacLaren, *Political Culture in the Reign of Elizabeth I: Queen and Commonwealth 1558–1585* (Cambridge: Cambridge University Press, 2000); Paul E. J. Hammer, *Elizabeth's Wars: War, Government, and Society in Tudor England, 1544–1604* (Basingstoke: Palgrave Macmillan, 2003); Janet Dickinson, *Court Politics and the Earl of Essex 1589–1601* (London: Pickering and Chatto, 2011).

68. This is an important corrective to the still-dominant historiography. See David Beers Quinn, *The Elizabethans and the Irish* (Ithaca, NY: Cornell University Press, 1966); Canny, *The Elizabethan Conquest of Ireland;* Nicholas P. Canny, *Kingdom and Colony: Ireland in the Atlantic World, 1560–1800* (Baltimore, MD: Johns Hopkins University Press, 1988); K. R. Andrews, N. P. Canny, and P. E. H. Hair, eds., *The Westward Enterprise: English Activities in Ireland, the Atlantic, and America 1480–1650* (Detroit, MI: Wayne State University Press, 1979). For revisions of this thesis, see Kevin Kenny, ed., *Ireland and the British Empire* (Oxford: Oxford University Press, 2006); Audrey Horning, *Ireland in the Virginia Sea: Colonialism in the British Atlantic* (Chapel Hill: University of North Carolina Press, 2013).

69. Hiram Morgan, "Hugh O'Neill and the Nine Years War in Tudor Ireland," *The Historical Journal* 36, no. 1 (1993): 21–37.

70. John Dowdall to Lord Burghley (William Cecil), March 9, 1596, in *Calendar of State Papers, Ireland, 1592–1596,* edited by Hans Claude Hamilton (London: Her Majesty's Stationery Office, 1890), no. 19. Not attributed to Spenser until after his death, the *View* was likely written ca. 1596. See also Brian Lockey, "Spenser's Legalization of the Irish Conquest in *A View* and *Faerie Queene* VI," *English Literary Renaissance* 31, no. 3 (2001): 365–391; Robert Viking O'Brien, "Cannibalism in Edmund Spenser's *Faerie Queene,* Ireland, and the Americas," in *Eating Their Words: Cannibalism*

*and the Boundaries of Cultural Identity,* edited by Kristen Guest (Albany: State University of New York Press, 2001), 35–56; Philip Schwyzer, "Exhumation and Ethnic Conflict: From St. Erkenwald to Spenser in Ireland," *Representations* 95, no. 1 (2006): 1–26; Andrew Hadfield, *Edmund Spenser: A Life* (Oxford: Oxford University Press, 2012).

71. Edmund Spenser, *A Veue of the Present State of Ireland* (1633), in *The Complete Works in Verse and Prose of Edmund Spenser,* vol. 9, edited by Alexander B. Grosart (London: 1882–1884), 101.

72. Spenser, *A Veue of the Present State of Ireland,* 161–162 (quote on 161).

73. Fynes Moryson, *An Itinerary Containing His Ten Yeeres Travell through the Twelve Dominions of Germany, Bohmerland, Sweitzerland, Netherland, Denmarke, Poland, Italy, Turky, France, England, Scotland & Ireland,* vol. 3 (1617) (Glasgow: James MacLehose and Sons, 1908), 281–282 (quote on 281). Moryson's prose was equally colorful in the second example, describing "some old women of those parts, used to make a fier in the fields, & divers little children driving out the cattel in the cold mornings, and comming thither to warme them, were by them surprised, killed and eaten, which at last was discovered by a great girle breaking from them by strength of her body, and Captaine Trevor sending out souldiers to know the truth, they found the childrens skulles and bones, and apprehended the old women, who were executed for the fact" (282). On Moryson, see Edward H. Thompson, "Moryson, Fynes (1565/6–1630)," in *Oxford Dictionary of National Biography* (2004–2015).

74. Moryson, *An Itinerary Containing His Ten Yeeres Travell,* 3:282. Although possible, even probable, I have not yet found conclusive evidence that Moryson was reading Spenser's *View* when he wrote the *Itinerary.* John M. Breen has, however, noted similarities in style and content between the two, especially in their treatment of Irish culture and custom. See John M. Breen, "The Influence of Edmund Spenser's 'View' on Fynes Moryson's 'Itinerary,'" *Notes and Queries* 42, no. 3 (1995): 363. Andrew Hadfield has also drawn attention to both the similarities and some differences. See Andrew Hadfield, *Edmund Spenser's Irish Experience: Wilde Fruit and Salvage Soyl* (Oxford: Clarendon Press, 1997), 27–9.

75. Moryson, *An Itinerary Containing His Ten Yeeres Travell,* 3:283.

76. Barnabe Rich, *A New Description of Ireland* (London, 1610). On Rich, see Willy Maley, "Rich, Barnaby (1542–1617)," in *Oxford Dictionary of National Biography* (2004–2015); Eugene Flanagan, "The Anatomy of Jacobean Ireland: Captain Barnaby Rich, Sir John Davies, and the Failure of Reform, 1609–22," in *Political Ideology in Ireland, 1541–1641,* edited by Morgan (Dublin: Four Courts Press, 1999), 158–180.

77. As he put it, "But some will say, their cruelty doth not so much proceede from that naturall inclination that is in themselues, as from the mallice and hatred they bear to the English gouernment, which they haue alwaies spurned at, and are still desirous to shake off; but their rebellious dispositions are thereby made the more apparant, and they ought therefore to be so much the more restrained: for there is not a more daungerous thing, to relye either in the promises, or in any other assurances of those men, that are by nature ambitious, disloyall, cruell, and accustomed to shed bloud." Rich, *A New Description of Ireland,* 17–18.

78. Rich, *A New Description of Ireland,* 18.

79. Rich, *A New Description of Ireland,* 17.

80. Rich, *A New Description of Ireland,* 17.

81. John Davies, *A Discovery of the True Causes Why Ireland Was Never Entirely Subdued* (1612), in *Ireland under Elizabeth and James the First,* edited by Henry Morley (London: Routledge, 1890), 290–291 (passage begins on 290, quote on 291). Notably, on February 20, 1604, Davies wrote to Robert Cecil "touching the state of religion [in Ireland]." He asserted that there was "no more demonstration of religion [there] than amongst Tartars or cannibals"—a comparison reminiscent of the accounts of Frobisher and Gilbert, which were made readily available in Hakluyt's anthologies. C. W. Russell and John P. Prendergast, eds., *Calendar of State Papers Ireland, Relating to the Reign of James I, 1603–1606* (London: Longman, 1872), 142–8 (quote on 143). On Davies, see Hans S. Pawlisch, *Sir John Davies and the Conquest of Ireland: A Study in Legal Imperialism* (Cambridge: Cambridge University Press, 1985).

82. Davies, *A Discovery of the True Causes Why Ireland Was Never Entirely Subdued,* title page.

83. James VI also contributed to the discourse in this period. During his struggle to control the Outer Hebrides, James referred to their inhabitant as "lascivious" and "barbarous cannibals," "imagining them exactly like the inhabitants of the Americas at their most uncivilized." See Arthur H. Williamson, "Scots, Indians and Empire: The Scottish Politics of Civilization 1519–1609," *Past and Present* 150 (February 1996): 46–83 (quote on 64).

84. William Strachey, *The Historie of Travaile into Virginia,* edited by R. H. Major (London: Hakluyt Society, 1849); and William Strachey, *For the Colony in Virginea Britannia. Lawes Diuine, Morall and Martiall, &c.* (London, 1612). On Strachey, see S. G. Culliford, *William Strachey, 1572–1621* (Charlottesville: University of Virginia Press, 1965); and Kupperman, *The Jamestown Project.*

## Chapter 6

1. William M. Kelso, *Jamestown: The Truth Revealed* (Charlottesville, VA: University of Virginia Press, 2017), 86.

2. Robert Appelbaum, *Aguecheek's Beef, Belch's Hiccup, and Other Gastronomic Interjections: Literature, Culture and Food among the Early Moderns* (Chicago: University of Chicago Press, 2006), 273.

3. George Percy, *A True Relation of the Proceedings and Occurances of Moment Which Have Happened in Virginia* (London, 1625), 267.

4. Percy, *A True Relation of the Proceedings and Occurances of Moment.*

5. In 1622, the colony was almost wiped out by an alliance of local tribes, and in the months that followed the settlers faced a second Starving Time. But given that the attack occurred at the end of March and *The Sea Voyage* was licensed for performance by June of the same year, it seems unlikely that these events provided the sole direct influence on the text. See Claire Jowitt, *Voyage Drama and Gender Politics, 1589–1642: Real and Imagined Worlds* (Manchester: Manchester University Press, 2003); Teresa Walters, "'Such Stowage as These Trinkets': Trading and Tasting Women in Fletcher and Massinger's *The Sea Voyage* (1622)," in *Consuming Narratives: Gender and Monstrous Appetite in the Middle Ages and the Renaissance,* edited by Liz Herbert McAvoy and Teresa Walters (Cardiff: University of Wales Press, 2002), 67–80.

6. At the time of *The Sea Voyage*'s original performance, no printed text existed that asserted that cannibalism had happened, but the vehemence with which the Virginia Company's pamphlet denied the rumors makes evident the degree to which public knowledge of events in Jamestown preceded the publication of printed accounts.

7. Gordon McMullan, *The Politics of Unease in the Plays of John Fletcher* (Amherst: University of Massachusetts Press, 1994), 241.

8. McMullan, *The Politics of Unease in the Plays of John Fletcher,* 241.

9. Anthony Parr, "Introduction," in *Three Renaissance Travel Plays,* edited by Anthony Parr (Manchester: Manchester University Press, 1995), 1–56, quote on 22; Jowitt, *Voyage Drama and Gender Politics,* 193.

10. William Arens, *The Man-Eating Myth: Anthropology and Anthropophagy* (Oxford: Oxford University Press, 1979), 21.

11. Rachel B. Herrmann, "The 'tragicall historie': Cannibalism and Abundance in Colonial Jamestown," *William and Mary Quarterly* 68, no. 1 (2011): 47–74, quote on 68.

12. Louise Noble, "'And Make Two Pasties of Your Shameful Heads': Medicinal Cannibalism and Healing the Body Politic in *Titus Andronicus,*" *English Literary History* 70, no. 3 (2003): 677–708, quote on 679.

13. Maggie Kilgour, *From Communion to Cannibalism: An Anatomy of Metaphors of Incorporation* (Princeton, NJ: Princeton University Press, 1990).

14. David B. Goldstein, *Eating and Ethics in Shakespeare's England* (Cambridge: Cambridge University Press, 2013), 35.

15. Goldstein, *Eating and Ethics in Shakespeare's England,* 36.

16. Anthony Parr has argued that "by creating a landscape empty of natives, *The Sea Voyage* sustains the common myth that what was discovered in the New World was virgin land, and that the only question to be decided was which colonizing power held legitimate title to it." Yet by purging their play of the native population, Fletcher and Massinger also dissociated cannibal practices from that population, figuring it clearly as a European practice. Parr, "Introduction," 25.

17. Robert Brenner, *Merchants and Revolution: Commercial Change, Political Conflict and London's Overseas Traders, 1550–1653* (Cambridge: Cambridge University Press, 1993), 40.

18. I define capitalism as a system in which market relations are dominant and in which, as a consequence, the accumulation of capital is a necessary condition of economic independence. The early modern period retained numerous ideological and material features that did not accord with this model, but it is nevertheless possible to discern the emergence of specifically capitalist elements within England's socioeconomic structure. Brenner, for example, emphasizes the increasing dominance of the landlord-tenant-wage laborer triad in the agrarian relations of the period. By rooting his analysis in the self-activity of these emergent groups, he was able, as Ellen Wood has noted, to discern "an internal dynamic that did not presuppose an already existent capitalist logic," moving beyond either a reductive view of demographic pressures or the implicit assumption of capitalist tendencies inherent in the "commercialization" model, the world systems model, and traditional Marxist accounts of "bourgeois revolution." See Ellen Wood, *The Origin of Capitalism: A Longer View* (London: Verso, 2002), 52. For the demographic model, see T. H. Aston and C. H. E. Philipin, eds., *The Brenner Debate: Agrarian Class Structure and*

*Economic Development in Pre-Industrial Europe* (Cambridge: Cambridge University Press, 1985). For an example of what Wood calls the "commercialization model," see Henri Pirenne, *An Economic and Social History of Europe* (London: Routledge, 2006). For the world systems model, see Immanuel Wallerstein, *The Modern World-System* (Berkeley: University of California Press, 2011). For a defense of the Marxist term "bourgeois revolution," see Neil Davidson *How Revolutionary Were the Bourgeois Revolutions?* (Chicago: Haymarket Books, 2012).

19. Brenner, *Merchants and Revolution*, 93.

20. Early economic historians tended to follow Adam Smith in conceiving of mercantilism as a full-fledged system of economic thought, while later work disputed the utility of mercantilism as an analytic term in general, noting the diversity of views its supposed practitioners propounded. But more recent work has tended to stress its discursive dimension, with Lars Magnusson arguing that it is defined by the use of "a common terminology and traces of answers to a certain set of questions." From this perspective, it is possible to situate the varying views of the mercantilists in the context of both England's marginal position as an emergent imperial power and the changing situation Brenner has outlined with regard to its investment in a global network of trade. See Lars Magnusson, *The Political Economy of Mercantilism* (London: Routledge, 2015), 9; Adam Smith, *An Inquiry into the Nature and Causes of the Wealth of Nations*, edited by R. H. Campbell and A. S. Skinner (Oxford: Clarendon Press, 1976); Eli F. Heckscher, *Mercantilism*, 2 vols. (London: Allen & Unwin, 1962); Lars Magnusson, ed., *Mercantilist Economics* (New York: Kluwer Academic Publishers, 1993). For an analysis of how *The Sea Voyage* engages with mercantilist theory, see Gitanjali Shahani, "Of 'Barren Islands' and 'Cursèd Gold': Worth, Value, and Womanhood in *The Sea Voyage*," *Journal for Early Modern Cultural Studies* 12, no. 3 (2012): 5–27.

21. Thomas Mun, "A Discourse of Trade, From England unto the East-Indies," in *Mercantilism: Critical Concepts in the History of Economics*, vol. 1, edited by Lars Magnusson (London: Routledge, 1995), 49–80, quote on 49.

22. William Shakespeare, *Titus Andronicus*, edited by Jonathan Bate (London: Arden Shakespeare, 1995); Gary Taylor and John Lavagnino, eds., *Thomas Middleton: The Collected Works* (Oxford: Oxford University Press, 2007).

23. William Shakespeare and George Wilkins, *Pericles*, edited by Suzanne Gossett (London: Arden Shakespeare, 2014).

24. William Shakespeare, *Timon of Athens*, edited by Anthony B. Dawson and Gretchen E. Minton (London: Arden Shakespeare, 2008).

25. Goldstein, *Eating and Ethics in Shakespeare's England*, 34. In a similar manner, Frank Lestringant argues that depictions of the man-eating colonial Other are defined by a gradual shift from accounts that emphasize motives of ritual and revenge to those that highlight hunger and an inherent voracious appetite. Frank Lestringant, *Cannibals: The Discovery and Representation of the Cannibal from Columbus to Jules Verne*, translated by Rosemary Morris (Cambridge: Polity Press, 1997).

26. Thomas Cartelli, *Shakespeare, Marlowe and the Economy of Theatrical Experience* (Philadelphia: University of Pennsylvania Press, 1991), 30.

27. Shakespeare, *Titus Andronicus*, act 5, scene 3, lines 59–61.

28. See *Oxford English Dictionary Online*, s.v. "daintily, adv.," esp. def. 2.

29. The lower classes of the Midlands area rose against local landowners in May and June of 1607. The uprising was characterized by a particular emphasis on

anti-gentry violence and was fueled by hopes of uniting with rioting apprentices in London, with lower-class hunger emerging as a powerful threat to social order. See Roger Manning, *Village Revolts: Social Protest and Popular Disturbances in England, 1509–1640* (Oxford: Clarendon Press, 1988).

30. Shakespeare and Wilkins, *Pericles,* act 1, scene 4, lines 42–46.

31. Thomas Nashe, *The Works of Thomas Nashe,* vol. 2 (Oxford: Oxford University Press, 1958).

32. William Gouge, *Gods Three Arrovves Plague, Famine, Svvord, in Three Treatises* (London, 1631), 133–134.

33. Gouge, *God's Three Arrovves,* 149.

34. Shakespeare and Wilkins, *Pericles,* act 1, scene 4, line 40 ("inventions"), lines 28–29 ("stored full").

35. Church of England, *The Two Books of Homilies, Appointed to Be Read in Churches* (Oxford: Oxford University Press, 1859), 303.

36. George Hakewill, *The vanitie of the eye first beganne for the comfort of a gentlewoman bereaved of her sight, and since vpon occasion enlarged & published for the common good* (Oxford, 1615), 11.

37. Church of England, *The Two Books of Homilies,* 299.

38. Shakespeare, *Timon of Athens,* act 1, scene 2, lines 39–42.

39. Shakespeare, *Timon of Athens,* act 2, scene 2, lines 151 and 146.

40. Ben Jonson, *The Staple of News,* in *1616–1625,* vol. 5 of *The Cambridge Edition of the Works of Ben Jonson,* edited by Martin Butler and Ian Donaldson (Cambridge: Cambridge University Press, 2012), act 3, scene 2, line 157.

41. Jonson, *The Staple of News,* act 3, scene 2, lines 174–180.

42. Michel de Montaigne, *The Complete Essays,* translated and edited by M. A. Screech (London: Penguin, 1991), 234.

43. Shakespeare and Wilkins, *Pericles,* act 2, scene 1, lines 28–29.

44. Brenner, *Merchants and Revolution,* 96.

45. Jean Feerick, "'Divided in Soyle': Plantation and Degeneracy in *The Tempest* and *The Sea Voyage,*" *Renaissance Drama* 35 (2006): 27–54, quote on 29.

46. Michael Neill, *Putting History to the Question: Power, Politics, and Society in English Renaissance Drama* (New York: Columbia University Press, 2000), 314.

47. Richard Hakluyt, *The Principal Navigations, Voyages, Traffiques and Discoveries of the English Nation,* edited by Edmund Goldsmid (Edinburgh: E. and G. Goldsmid, 1885–1890), 13:183, 188.

48. John Wood Sweet, "Introduction: Sea Changes," in *Envisioning an English Empire: Jamestown and the Making of the North Atlantic World,* edited by Robert Appelbaum and John Wood Sweet (Philadelphia: University of Pennsylvania Press, 2005), 1–21, quote on 10.

49. John Fletcher and Philip Massinger, *The Sea Voyage,* in *The Double Marriage; The Elder Brother; The Little French Lawyer; The Maid in the Mill; The Prophetess; The Sea Voyage,* vol. 9 of *The Dramatic Works in the Fletcher and Beaumont Canon,* edited by Fredson Bowers (Cambridge: Cambridge University Press, 1994).

50. Fletcher and Massinger, *The Sea Voyage,* act 1, scene 4, lines 139–153.

51. Patricia Akhimie, "Travel, Drama, and Domesticity: Colonial Huswifery in John Fletcher and Philip Massinger's *The Sea Voyage,*" *Studies in Travel Writing* 13, no. 2 (2009): 153–166, quote on 154.

52. Fletcher and Massinger, *The Sea Voyage,* act 1, scene 4, line 104 ("sunk eyes"), line 105 ("are crept in").

53. Fletcher and Massinger, *The Sea Voyage,* act 1, scene 4, line 110.

54. John Smythe, *Certain discourses, vvritten by Sir Iohn Smythe, Knight: concerning the formes and effects of diuers sorts of weapons* (London, 1590), xxi.

55. Fletcher and Massinger, *The Sea Voyage,* act 1, scene 4, line 148.

56. Fletcher and Massinger, *The Sea Voyage,* act 1, scene 4, line 113, my italics.

57. Samuel Purchas, *Hakluytus posthumus; or, Purchas his pilgrimes,* vol. 4 (London, 1625), 1757.

58. John Smith, *The Complete Works of John Smith,* vol. 2, edited by Philip L. Barbour (North Carolina: University of North Carolina Press, 1986), 157.

59. Herman Pleij, *Dreaming of Cockaigne: Medieval Fantasies of the Perfect Life* (New York: Columbia University Press, 1997), 107.

60. Percy, *A True Relation of the Proceedings and Occurances of Moment,* 267.

61. Fletcher and Massinger, *The Sea Voyage,* act 3, scene 1, lines 52–54.

62. See *Oxford English Dictionary Online,* s.v. "wen, n."

63. Fletcher and Massinger, *The Sea Voyage,* act 3, scene 1, line 106 ("young and tydie"), lines 107–108 ("eate delicatly").

64. Fletcher and Massinger, *The Sea Voyage,* act 3, scene 1, line 99.

65. Fletcher and Massinger, *The Sea Voyage,* act 3, scene 1, lines 111–112.

66. See *Oxford English Dictionary Online,* s.v. "powder, n.," esp. def. 5b and 5e.

67. Appelbaum, *Aguecheek's Beef, Belch's Hiccup, and Other Gastronomic Interjections,* 274.

68. Purchas, *Hakluytus posthumus,* 1757.

69. Parr, "Introduction," 21.

70. Fletcher and Massinger, *The Sea Voyage,* act 3, scene 1, lines 88–91.

71. Fletcher and Massinger, *The Sea Voyage,* act 3, scene 1, lines 118–119 ("cut her throat"), lines 141–143 ("hinder parts").

72. Keith Wrightson, *Earthly Necessities: Economic Lives in Early Modern Britain* (New Haven, CT: Yale University Press, 2000), 179.

73. Christopher Hill, *Reformation to Industrial Revolution: A Social and Economic History of Britain, 1530–1780* (London: Weidenfeld & Nicolson, 1967), 57.

74. Fletcher and Massinger, *The Sea Voyage,* act 3, scene 1, line 99 ("read in"), lines 100–101 ("Of such restoring meates").

75. Parr, "Introduction," 31.

## Chapter 7

1. More recently, Sawney Bean has been the focus of modern feature films, including *The Hills Have Eyes,* directed by Wes Craven, Blood Relations Co., 1977; and *Sawney: Flesh of Man,* directed by Ricky Wood, TVP Film & Multimedia, 2013. The story has also featured in modern rock and folk music, including "Sawney Bean," recorded by Sol Invictus on *Trees in Winter* (Tursa, 1990) and "Sawney Bean/ Sawney's Death Dance," recorded by Snakefinger on *Night of Desirable Objects* (AIM Records, 1987).

2. "Sawney Bean," in A. Knapp and W. Baldwin, *The Newgate Calendar; Comprising Interesting Memoirs of the Most Notorious Characters Who Have*

*Been Convicted of Outrages on the Laws of England since the Commencement of the Eighteenth Century; with Anecdotes and Last Exclamations of Sufferers,* vol. 1 (London: J. Robins, 1824–1826).

3. The most significant study of the story remains R. Holmes, *The Legend of Sawney Bean* (London: Frederick Muller, 1975). More populist debunking of the myth appears in articles such as S. Thomas, "In Search of Sawney Bean," *Fortean Times,* April 2005.

4. B. Pardoe, *Sawney Bean: Dissecting the Legend of the Scottish Cannibal* (Oxford: Fonthill, 2015). See also R. H. J. Urquhart, "Sawney Bean: Myth or Myth?" *Ayrshire History,* accessed April 22, 2018, http://www.ayrshirehistory.org.uk/sawney/myth.htm.

5. The Sawney Bean ride remains a popular exhibit in the Edinburgh Dungeon.

6. Dr. Louise Yeoman quoted in S. Brocklehurst, "Who Was Sawney Bean?" *BBC Scotland News Website,* February 22, 2013, accessed October 12, 2016, http://tinyurl.com/argjamj.

7. Captain Charles Johnson, *A General and True History of the Lives and Actions of the Most Famous Highwaymen, Murderers, Street-Robbers, &c.* (London, 1734). There is debate among literary scholars over whether the name Captain Charles Johnson was a pseudonym for Daniel Defoe. See W. Roughead, *Rogues Walk Here* (London: Cassell, 1934) for the claim that Johnson was in fact Defoe. This has been disputed by prominent Defoe scholar J. R. Moore in *Defoe in the Pillory and Other Studies* (Bloomington: Indiana University Press, 1939). Pardoe incorrectly dates the first text by Johnson to include the story of Sawney Bean in 1724, but *A General History of the Lives and Actions of the Most Famous Highwaymen* was not published until 1734. Johnson's earlier text, *A General History of the Robberies and Murders of the most Notorious Pirates . . . &c.* (London, 1724) did not include an account of Bean. See Pardoe, *Sawney Bean,* 35.

8. J. Nicolson, *Historical and Traditional Tales Connected with the South of Scotland* (Kirkcudbright: J. Nicolson, 1843). Alexander Smith published a popular compilation of crime broadsheets in 1719 that did not include Sawney Bean. See A. Smith, *A Compleat History of the Lives and Robberies of the Most Notorious Highway-Men, Foot-Pad, Shop-Lifters, and Cheats of Both Sexes, in and about London and Westminster, and All Parts of Great Britain, for above an Hundred Years Past, Continued to the Present Time. The Fifth Edition (Adorn'd with Cuts)* (London, 1719).

9. F. Black, "A Taste of Scotland: Historical Fictions of Sawney Bean and his family," in *The Polar Twins,* edited by E. J. Cowan and D. Gifford (Edinburgh: John Donald, 2000), 158.

10. C. Zika, "Cannibalism and Witchcraft in Early Modern Europe: Reading the Visual Images," *History Workshop Journal* 44 (Autumn 1997), 77–105, esp. 81.

11. M. Pittock, *Celtic Identity and the British Image* (Manchester: Manchester University Press, 1999), 31.

12. L. Colley, *Britons: Forging the Nation, 1797–1837* (New Haven, CT: Yale University Press, 1992), 13.

13. Karen Cullen, *Famine in Scotland: The 'Ill Years' of the 1690s* (Edinburgh: Edinburgh University Press, 2010), 2.

14. Colley, *Britons,* 15.

15. S. Hobbs and D. Cornwell, "Sawney Bean, the Scottish Cannibal," *Folklore* 108, nos. 1–2 (1997): 49–54, esp. 50.

16. For a discussion of eighteenth-century "Scotophobia," see T. Curley, *Samuel Johnson, the Ossian Fraud, and the Celtic Revival in Great Britain and Ireland* (Cambridge: Cambridge University Press, 2009), 105–106.

17. *North Briton,* April 2, 1763.

18. M. J. Powell, "Scottophobia versus Jacobitism: Political Radicalism and the Press in Late Eighteenth-Century Ireland," in *Cultures of Radicalism in Britain and Ireland,* edited by J. Kirk, M. Brown, and A. Noble (Oxford: Routledge, 2016), 49–62, 53.

19. *Oxford English Dictionary Online,* s.v. "Sawney, n."

20. Joy Fraser examines the link between the Scottish and culinary satire in J. Fraser, "Sawney's Kitchen Nightmares. Culinary Expressions of Scottophobia in late Eighteenth-Century England," *Appetite* 56, no. 2 (2011): 529.

21. Nichol Brown (1754) in Knapp and Baldwin, *The Newgate Calendar.* (The Calendar records the execution of Brown as taking place in August 1754, whereas the English newspapers refer to the murder as happening in November 1754, the trial in January 1755, and the execution in April 1755).

22. The *London Evening Post,* the *Whitehall Evening Post,* the *Public Advertiser,* and *Read's Weekly Journal* all record Brown's arrest, trial and sentencing in late 1754 and early 1755 but provide very few details of his crime other than the burning of his wife and her death.

23. R. Holinshed, *The First and Second Volumes of Chronicles Comprising 1 The Description and History of England, 2 The Description and History of Ireland, 3 The Description and History of Scotland* (London: Henry Denham, 1587).

24. D. Diehl and M. F. Donnelly, *Eat Thy Neighbour: A History of Cannibalism* (Stroud: Sutton, 2006).

25. Anonymous, *De Situ Britanniae* (London, 1757) mentions the Attacotti as cannibals. This text is now recognized as a fictitious account of Roman Britain but continues to be cited for "evidence" of the link between ancient Celtic tribes and cannibalism. See, for example, R. Tannahill, *Flesh and Blood: A History of the Cannibal Complex* (London: Hamilton, 1975), 104.

26. *The Horrid Life of Sawney Beane* (Carlisle: F. Jollie and Sons, 1815).

27. Annette Harrower-Gray, "That brawling, boisterous Scottish wench," *Scotland Magazine* 43 (February 2009): 21.

28. *English Post,* January 31–February 3, 1701.

29. Black, "A Taste of Scotland," 176.

30. See, for example, J. Goodacre, L. Martin, and J. Miller, eds., *Witchcraft and Belief in Early Modern Scotland* (Basingstoke: Palgrave, 2008).

31. *British Journal,* April 18, 1724.

32. T. Fitzpatrick, *The Bloody Bridge and Other Papers Relating to the Insurrection of 1641* (Dublin, 1903), 89, 138, quoted in C. Tait, *Death, Burial and Commemoration in Ireland, 1550–1650* (Basingstoke: Palgrave, 2002), 22, 171n99.

33. M. Powell, *The Politics of Consumption in Eighteenth-Century Ireland* (Basingstoke: Palgrave, 2005), 37.

34. J. Swift, *A Modest Proposal for Preventing the Children of Poor People from Being a Burthen to Their Parents or Country, and for Making Them Beneficial to the Publick* (London, 1729).

35. See J. K. O'Doherty, "Sir Cahir O'Doherty's Rebellion: Its Causes and Consequences," *IER*, 4th ser. 8 (1900), 325–6, quoted in C. Tait, *Death, Burial and Commemoration in Ireland*, 171n99.

36. *The Times*, July 11, 1798, quoted in M. De Nie, *The Eternal Paddy: Irish Identity and the British Press, 1798–1882* (Madison: University of Wisconsin Press, 2004), 61. The same sentiments were repeated in six other English newspapers.

37. See Kelly L. Watson, *Insatiable Appetites: Imperial Encounters with Cannibals in the North Atlantic World* (New York: New York University Press, 2015), 165.

38. Gananath Obeyesekere, *Cannibal Talk: The Man-Eating Myth and Human Sacrifice in the South Seas* (Berkeley: University of California Press, 2005), 29.

39. See for example ballads such as *The Oxfordshire Garland. In Four Parts* (London, 1736–1763); and *The Mournful Tragedy* (London, 1740–1760).

40. T. Potts, *The Wonderfull Discoverie of Witches* (London, 1612), sig. L.2.r.

41. See H. Pierce, "Anti-Episcopacy and Graphic Satire in England, 1640–1645," *Historical Journal* 47, no. 4 (2004): 809–848; M. Stoyle, "The Cannibal Cavalier: Sir Thomas Lunsford and the Fashioning of the Royalist Archetype," *Historical Journal* 59, no. 2 (2016): 293–317. Many thanks to Mark Stoyle for sharing his ideas about cannibal narratives and the Civil Wars with me.

42. Stoyle, "The Cannibal Cavalier," 317.

43. See, for example, *Gazetteer and New Daily Advertiser*, August 22, 1772.

44. Morning Chronicle and London Advertiser, January 15, 1783.

45. R. S. Charnock, "Cannibalism in Europe," *Journal of the Anthropological Society of London* 4 (1866): xxvi.

46. A. Salmond, *The Trial of the Cannibal Dog: The Remarkable Story of Captain Cook's Encounters in the South Seas* (New Haven, CT: Yale University Press, 2003), 7.

47. See, for example, *Penny London Morning Advertiser*, August 3–6, 1744; and *Argus*, January 13, 1790. For a discussion of the killing of cats in 1730s Paris as a workers' protest, see R. Darnton, *The Great Cat Massacre and Other Episodes in French Cultural History* (London: Allen Lane, 1984), 75–106.

48. Souden provides the example of John Breads, whose gibbeted corpse disappeared in Rye in 1743, possibly so his bones could be used to make a cure for rheumatism, but the anecdote is unreferenced. D. Souden, *Short Breaks in Historic Country Towns* (London: George Phillip, 1991), 114, cited in H. L. Malchow, *Gothic Images of Race in Nineteenth-Century Britain* (Stanford, CA: Stanford University Press, 1996), 56.

49. *London Evening Post*, August 26–28, 1746.

50. *The Lady Isabella's Tragedy; or, the Step-Mother's Cruelty* (Newcastle-upon-Tyne, ca. 1711).

51. R. Crone, "From Sawney Beane to Sweeney Todd: Murder Machines in the Mid-Nineteenth-Century Metropolis," *Cultural and Social History* 7, no. 1 (2010): 59–85.

52. *A Shocking Discovery, of Human Cannibals, Who Resided Near the Turnpike at Mile End, and Were Apprehended on Monday Last, When Searching the House, Two Hundred Skeletons Were Found, and Coppers Boiling with Human Flesh in Them. Also, a Skull Made into a Saltcellar, with the Handles of Knives and Forks Made of Human Bones* (London, 1725).

53. *The Weekly Journal, or, Saturday Post,* May 6, 1721.

54. *Applebee's Original Weekly Journal,* December 1, 1721.

55. *The Weekly Journal,* January 14, 1727.

56. *London Evening Post,* January 13, 1736.

57. D. R. Mandell, "'The Indian's Pedigree' (1794): Indians, Folklore and Race in Southern New England," *William and Mary Quarterly* 61, no. 3 (2004): 521–538, esp. 531–532.

58. M. Pittock, *The Myth of the Jacobite Clans* (Edinburgh: Edinburgh University Press, 1995), 10.

59. See discussion in Ian Maxted, "A History of the Book in Devon," *Exeter Working Papers in British Book Trade History* 12, 48 (2001), accessed May 20, 2018, https://tinyurl.com/yc8la79w.

60. *The Dreadful History of John M'Claud, and His Crew of Thieves, Robbers, and Murderers Who Were All Taken in a Cave, near by the Sea Side, in Devonshire* (Glasgow: Printed at the desire of several gentlemen, 1800). See the discussion of the similarities and differences between the texts in Pardoe, *Sawney Bean,* 66–68.

61. There are few similarities between the account of Joseph Franks and the reports of Hungarian cannibals in the English press in the 1780s (see note 42 above), which suggests that the stories of M'Claud and Franks are fictions.

62. R. Ward and P. King, "Rethinking the Bloody Code in Eighteenth-Century Britain: Capital Punishment at the Centre and on the Periphery," *Past and Present* 228, no. 1 (2015): 159–228, esp. 168.

63. F. McLynn, *Crime and Punishment in Eighteenth-Century England* (London: Routledge, 1989), 173.

64. Johnson's text was not published in Scotland until 1814.

65. K. Baston, "Harlequin Highlander: Spectacular geographies at the Edinburgh Equestrian Circus, 1790–1800," *Early Popular Visual Culture* 12, no. 3 (2014): 283–303.

## Chapter 8

1. Frank Lestringant, *Cannibals: The Discovery and Representation of the Cannibal from Columbus to Jules Verne,* translated by Rosemary Morris (Berkeley: University of California Press, 1997); Michel de Certeau, *Heterologies: Discourse on the Other,* translated by Brian Massumi (Minneapolis: University of Minnesota Press, 1986), esp. 67–79.

2. See Terry Jay Ellingson, *The Myth of The Noble Savage* (Berkeley: University of California Press, 2001). Ellingson is alert to the complications and contradictions in the myth but spends too much time worrying whether writers actually use the word "noble" when describing admirable savages.

3. Quoted in Bruce E. Johansen, *Forgotten Founders: Benjamin Franklin, the Iroquois, and the Rationale for the American Revolution* (Ipswich, MA: Gambit, 1982), ch. 5, accessed September 1, 2016, http://tinyurl.com/hxxwvmd.

4. Claude Lévi-Strauss, *Tristes Tropiques: An Anthropological Study of Primitive Societies in Brazil,* translated by John Russell (New York: Atheneum, 1970), 308.

5. On the state of the controversy over the existence of Tupí cannibalism, at least up to 2005, see Derek Petrey, "Write about All of This: Concerning Cannibalism Revisionism," *Chasqui* 34, special issue no. 1 (2005): 113–123. Petrey asserts: "There is

now conclusive evidence that nonstarvation cannibalism has been intrinsic to many groups of humans throughout history, including Cro-Magnons, the Anasazi, the Aztecs, the Tupinambá, and Europeans practicing Paracelsian medicine up to the 18th century" (120).

6. Lestringant, *Cannibals,* 22.

7. Lestringant, *Cannibals,* 3.

8. Jennifer Brown, *Cannibalism in Literature and Film* (London: Palgrave Macmillan, 2013). Also see Cătălin Avramescu's work, which makes many of the same arguments, covering the same materials, as Lestringant's. Cătălin Avramescu, *An Intellectual History of Cannibalism,* translated by Alistair Ian Blyth (Princeton, NJ: Princeton University Press, 2009).

9. Philippe Desan, *Les commerces de Montaigne: Le discours économique des "Essais"* (Paris: A.-G. Nizet, 1992).

10. Lestringant, *Cannibals,* 216n33.

11. Michel de Montaigne, *Michel de Montaigne: The Complete Works,* translated by Donald M. Frame (London: Everyman's Library), 186. (Hereafter *Complete Works.*) I find this translation accurate enough that I don't feel a need also to cite the original French.

12. Montaigne, *Complete Works,* 189.

13. Montaigne, *Complete Works,* 188.

14. See Jacob Vance, "Force and Fraud in Michel de Montaigne's Essays," *MLN* 127, no. 5 (2012): 267–293.

15. Montaigne, *Complete Works,* 188.

16. Montaigne, *Complete Works,* 189.

17. On the Eucharist, see Rebecca Earle's chapter in this volume.

18. Léry devotes a good part of his narrative to his disputes with the colony leader over the nature of the Eucharist. Jean de Léry, *Histoire d'un voyage fait en la terre du Brésil* (Lausanne: Bibliothèque Rumande, 1972). See Frank Lestringant, *L'huguenot et le sauvage* (Paris: Aux Amateurs, 1900); Andrea Frisch, "In a Sacramental Mode: Jean de Léry's Calvinist Ethnography," *Representations* 77, no. 1 (2002): 82–106.

19. For an overview of the early development of the theory, see Peter Singelman, "Exchange as Symbolic Interaction: Convergences between Two Theoretical Perspectives," *American Sociological Review* 37, no. 4 (1972): 414–424. A more up-to-date review of the theory is Seth Mallios, *The Deadly Politics of Giving: Exchange and Violence at Ajacan, Roanoke, and Jamestown* (Tuscaloosa: University of Alabama Press, 2006), 25–37.

20. Jean Baudrillard, *Symbolic Exchange and Death,* translated by Iain Hamilton Grant (Los Angeles: Sage, 1993), esp. 9–30.

21. Jean Baudrillard, *The Mirror of Production,* translated by Mark Poster (St. Louis: Telos Press, 1975), 78–79, all italics Baudrillard's.

22. Marcel Mauss, *The Gift: The Form and Reason for Exchange in Archaic Societies,* translated by W. D. Halls (London: Routledge, 1990).

23. C. A. Gregory, *Gifts and Commodities* (London: Academic Press, 1982), 46. I owe my awareness of this text to Charles Piot, who has also written perceptively on this subject. Charles Piot, *Remotely Global: Village Modernity in West Africa* (Chicago: University of Chicago Press, 1999), 52–75.

24. Mauss, *The Gift.*

25. Mallios, *The Deadly Politics of Giving.*

26. George Bataille, *Consumption,* vol. 1 of *The Accursed Share: An Essay on General Economy,* translated by Robert Huley (New York: Zone Books, 1991). Bataille and Baudrillard's idealization of gift economy may owe something to Raoul Vanetgem, *The Revolution of Everyday Life,* 2nd rev. ed., translated by Donald Nicholson-Smith (London: Rebel Press, 1994), esp. 67–82.

27. Mauss, *The Gift,* 1.

28. Mauss, *The Gift,* 89.

29. Henri Hubert and Marcel Mauss, *Sacrifice: Its Nature and Functions,* translated by W. D. Halls (Chicago: University of Chicago Press, 1964).

30. In ancient Hebrew law, sacrificing a stranger would be an abomination.

31. Lawrence H. Keeley, *War before Civilization* (New York: Oxford University Press, 1996); Azar Gat, *War in Human Civilization* (Oxford: Oxford University Press, 2006). In the essays Laurence R. Goldman has collected, the majority of plausible cases of cannibalism in preliterate society are linked to homicidal aggression and often to warfare. Laurence R. Goldman, ed., *The Anthropology of Cannibalism* (Westport: Praeger, 1999).

32. Hubert and Mauss. *Sacrifice,* 13. Also see J. H. M. Beattie, "On Understanding Sacrifice," in *Sacrifice,* edited by M. F. C. Bourdillon and Meyer Fortes (London: Academic Press, 1980), 29–44; and Terry Eagleton, *Holy Terror* (New York: Oxford University Press, 2005), 128–140.

33. Jacques Derrida, "Plato's Pharmacy," in *Dissemination,* translated by Barbara Johnson (London: Athlone Press, 1981), 61–172.

34. René Girard, *Violence and the Sacred,* translated by Patrick Gregory (London: Continuum, 2005).

35. For supplementary evidence from Europeans, especially Portuguese observers, see Donald W. Forsyth, "The Beginnings of Brazilian Anthropology: Jesuits and Tupinamba Cannibalism," *Journal of Anthropological Research* 39, no. 2 (1983): 147–178.

36. René Girard, *A Theater of Envy: William Shakespeare* (South Bend, IN: St. Augustine's Press, 2004).

37. Montaigne, *Complete Works,* 190.

38. Montaigne, *Complete Works,* 188.

39. For a summary of the evidence, see D. W. Forsyth, "The Beginnings of Brazilian Anthropology: The Jesuits and Tupinamba Cannibalism," *Journal of Anthropological Research* 39, no. 2 (1983): 147–148. Also see Georges Guille-Escuret, "Épistémologie du témoignage: Le cannibalisme ni vu ni connuurce," *L'Homme* 153 (2000): 183–205; and Adone Agnolin, "Antropofagia ritual e identidade cultural entre os Tupinambá," *Revista de Antropologia* 45, no. 1 (2002): 131–185. The latter two authors anticipate my own conclusions.

40. Gilles-Escuret nevertheless suggests that Tupì cannibalism served a political purpose: the confirmation of patriarchal authority and patrilineal descent. Gilles-Escuret, "Épistémologie du témoignage." Agnolin suggests that sacrifice, as here discussed, was a primordial value among the Tupì. Agnolin, "Antropofagia ritual e identidade cultural entre os Tupinambá." In both cases, the assimilation of the victim into tribal society before his killing is key.

## Chapter 9

1. Samuel Purchas, *Purchas His Pilgrimage. Or Relations of the World and the Religions Observed in All Ages and Places Discouered, from the Creation unto This Present in Foure Partes* (London: William Stansby for Henrie Fetherstone, 1613).

2. Samuel Purchas, *Purchas His Pilgrimes In Five Bookes,* 4 vols. (London: William Stansby for Henrie Fetherstone, 1625).

3. Following scholarly custom, I will quote from the 1901 edition by Ravenstein, which is accessible online through Google Books. E. G. Ravenstein, ed., *The Strange Adventures of Andrew Battell of Leigh, in Angola and the Adjoining Regions,* 2nd series, no. 6 (London: The Hakluyt Society, 1901).

4. John Thornton, "Cannibals, Witches, and Slave Traders in the Atlantic World," *William and Mary Quarterly* 60, no. 2 (2003): 273–294, quote on 289.

5. Thorstein Veblen, *Theory of the Leisure Class: An Economic Study in the Evolution of Institutions* (New York: Macmillan, 1899).

6. Atlanticists are increasingly interested in analyses of fear and anxiety. Two examples that have shaped my thinking are Tobias Green, "Fear and Atlantic History: Some Observations Derived from the Cape Verde Islands and the African Atlantic," *Atlantic Studies* 3, no. 1 (2006): 25–42; and Jason Sharples, "Discovering Slave Conspiracies: New Fears of Rebellion and Old Paradigms of Plotting in Seventeenth-Century Barbados," *American Historical Review* 120, no. 3 (June 2015): 811–843.

7. Jan Vansina, "On Ravenstein's Edition of Battell's Adventures in Angola and Loango," *History in Africa* 34 (2007): 321–347.

8. Jared Staller, "Rivalry and Reformation Politics: Reflections on Andrew Battell's Jaga Materials Printed by Samuel Purchas from 1613 to 1625," *History in Africa* 43 (2016): 7–28.

9. Richard Hitchcock, "Samuel Purchas as Editor: A Case Study: Anthony Knyvett's Journal," *Modern Language Review* 99, no. 2 (2004): 301–312.

10. Clues about Battell's upbringing as either common or privileged are also critical for determining whether he was literate and could write "Strange Adventures." Staller, "Rivalry and Reformation Politics," 14n28.

11. Ravenstein, *Strange Adventures,* 3.

12. I recall seeing a waterfall while traveling in a boat from Rolas toward São Tomé Island.

13. Ravenstein, *Strange Adventures,* 5. The island's name is now, of course, Spanish: Isla de Lobos.

14. Ravenstein, *Strange Adventures,* 5.

15. Mary Black-Rogers, "Varieties of 'Starving': Semantics and Survival in the Subarctic Fur Trade, 1750–1850," *Ethnohistory* 33, no. 4 (1986): 353–383.

16. Ravenstein, *Strange Adventures,* 6.

17. Battell does not explain why the Amerindians would carry them to Rio de Janeiro instead of São Paulo, which was about eighty miles closer.

18. Ravenstein, *Strange Adventures,* 7.

19. Battell's dating of his adventures is frequently incorrect. Governor Furtado de Mendonça did not arrive in Luanda until 1594, but Battell's narrative makes it

seem as if the year was 1590 or 1591. Ravenstein first noted the problem of this date. Ravenstein, *Strange Adventures,* 7.

20. Ravenstein, *Strange Adventures,* 10.

21. Ravenstein, *Strange Adventures,* 11.

22. Ravenstein, *Strange Adventures,* 13.

23. Ravenstein, *Strange Adventures,* 13.

24. Ravenstein, *Strange Adventures,* 39–40.

25. Note that this is the third time Battell claimed that a difficult episode in his life lasted for a month, just as on the journey from Ilha Grande to Seal Island and again on Seal Island. Perhaps these separate events did each last for about thirty days or perhaps the month time period that Battell recalled operates as a category for a lengthy but not too extensive period of discomfort.

26. Battell said the locals called this fish "Sombo," which Ravenstein claims is an African electric catfish ("electric silurus"). However, the fish was probably the modern *nzombó,* which is an eel-like African lungfish (one of the four varieties of African *Protopterus*). Ravenstein, *Strange Adventures,* 40n4.

27. Ravenstein, *Strange Adventures,* 40.

28. Ravenstein, *Strange Adventures,* 21. The Eurocentric commentary about the superfluity of these alleged anthropophagites, glossed hyperbolically as the greatest cannibals in the world, is, in my opinion, an addition by one of the Purchases.

29. Joseph C. Miller's *Kings and Kinsmen* is still the standard text on Imbangala history. Joseph C. Miller, *Kings and Kinsmen: Early Mbundu States in Angola* (Oxford: Clarendon Press, 1976), 176–257.

30. Joseph C. Miller, "The Significance of Drought, Disease and Famine in the Agriculturally Marginal Zones of West-Central Africa," *Journal of African History* 23, no. 1 (1982): 17–61.

31. Jane I. Guyer and Samuel M. Eno Belinga, "Wealth in People as Wealth in Knowledge: Accumulation and Composition in Equatorial Africa," *Journal of African History* 36, no. 1 (1995): 91–120.

32. Ravenstein, *Strange Adventures,* 22.

33. Miller, "The Significance of Drought, Disease, and Famine," 26.

34. Ravenstein, *Strange Adventures,* 30.

35. Ravenstein, *Strange Adventures,* 25.

36. Ravenstein, *Strange Adventures,* 26.

37. Ravenstein, *Strange Adventures,* 28.

38. Ravenstein, *Strange Adventures,* 30–31. This strategic terrorizing seemed to work because Battell explicitly remarks on the powerful lord Mafrigosat's fear of Imbe Calundula's army. Ravenstein, *Strange Adventures,* 22.

39. Ravenstein, *Strange Adventures,* 34.

40. Ravenstein, *Strange Adventures,* 32–33.

41. Sandra Young, "Early Modern Geography and the Construction of a Knowable Africa," *Atlantic Studies* 12, no. 4 (2015): 412–434.

42. See Fitzgerald's analysis of Purchas's rather early attempts at ethnography in Timothy Fitzgerald, *Discourse on Civility and Barbarity: A Critical History of Religion and Related Categories* (New York: Oxford University Press, 2007), 193–230.

43. Marcus Rediker, "History from below the Water Line: Sharks and the Atlantic Slave Trade," *Atlantic Studies* 5, no. 2 (2008): 285–297.

## Chapter 10

I am grateful to Christer Petley and Mark Stoyle for their comments on this chapter.

1. This essay generally refers to people as "enslaved" first rather than as "slaves" to indicate the lack of choice they had in the matter. Nevertheless, I sometimes use the term "slaves" here for reasons of intelligibility.

2. For an assessment of the field, see April Langley, "Early American Slave Narratives," in *The Oxford Handbook of Early American Literature,* edited by Kevin J. Hayes (New York: Oxford University Press, 2008), 416–430. The debate about Equiano's identity is discussed below.

3. W. Jeffrey Bolster, *Black Jacks: African American Seamen in the Age of Sail* (Cambridge, MA: Harvard University Press, 1997), 5–6.

4. Mimi Sheller, *Consuming the Caribbean: From Arawaks to Zombies* (New York: Routledge, 2003); Vincent Woodard, *The Delectable Negro: Human Consumption and Homoeroticism within US Slave Culture,* edited by Justin A. Joyce and Dwight A. McBride (New York: New York University Press, 2014).

5. For discussions of hunger topoi, see essays by Hower and Williamson in this volume.

6. Amy Mitchell-Cook, *A Sea of Misadventures: Shipwreck and Survival in Early America* (Columbia: University of South Carolina Press, 2013), 117. See also Peter Thompson's discussion of the *Peggy*'s voyage from the Azores back to New York in 1765; a slave was also first to be cannibalized in this instance. Peter Thompson, "No Chance in Nature: Cannibalism as a Solution to Maritime Famine c. 1750–1800," in *American Bodies: Cultural Histories of the Physique,* edited by Tim Armstrong (New York: New York University Press, 1996), 32–44, esp. 34–35.

7. Woodard, *The Delectable Negro,* 5, 71.

8. Woodard, *The Delectable Negro,* 4, 15–16. Woodard's provocative text is a challenging one to engage with because the author died in the midst of preparing his manuscript. Although editors Justin Joyce and Dwight McBride subsequently completed it, they acknowledge that some of Woodard's claims are not as well substantiated by textual evidence as they might have preferred.

9. Lynn R. Johnson, "Narrating an Indigestible Trauma: The Alimentary Grammar of Boyrereau Brinch's Middle Passage," in *Journeys of the Slave Narrative in the Early Americas,* edited by Nicole N. Aljoe and Ian Frederick Finseth (Charlottesville: University of Virginia Press, 2014), 127–142, esp. 128–129.

10. Vincent Carretta, *Equiano, the African: Biography of a Self-Made Man* (New York: Penguin Books, 2005), 238–239.

11. Woodard, *The Delectable Negro,* 17.

12. Shirley Lindenbaum, "Thinking about Cannibalism," *Annual Review of Anthropology* 33 (2004): 475–498; Woodard, *The Delectable Negro,* 31.

13. *The Royal African: or, Memoirs of the Young Prince of Annamaboe. Comprehending a Distinct Account of His Country and Family; His Elder Brother's Voyage to France, and Reception There; the Manner in Which Himself Was Confided by His Father to the Captain Who Sold Him; His Condition While a Slave in Barbadoes; the True Cause of His Being Redeemed; His Voyage from Thence; and Reception Here in England. Interspers'd throughout with Several Historical Remarks on the Commerce of the European Nations, Whose Subjects Frequent the Coast of Guinea. To Which Is Prefixed a Letter from the Author to*

*a Person of Distinction, in Reference to Some Natural Curiosities in Africa; As Well As Explaining the Motives Which Induced Him to Compose These Memoirs*, 2nd ed. (London: Printed for W. Reeve, 1750); *Narrative of the Uncommon Sufferings and Surprizing Deliverance of Britton Hammon, A Negro Man,—Servant to General Winslow, of Marshfield, in New-England; Who Returned to Boston after Having Been Absent Almost Thirteen Years. Containing An Account of the Many Hardships he Underwent from the Time He Left His Master's House, in the Year 1747, to the Time of His Return to Boston.—How He Was Cast Away in the Capes of Florida;—The Horrid Cruelty and Inhuman Barbarity of the Indians in Murdering the Whole Ship's Crew;—the Manner of His Being Carry'd by Them into Captivity. Also, an Account of His Being Confined Four Years and Seven Months in a Close Dungeon,—And the Remarkable Manner in Which He Met with His Good Old Master in London; who returned to New-England, a Passenger, in the Same Ship* (Boston: [John] Green & [Joseph] Russell, 1760), in *Unchained Voices: An Anthology of Black Authors in the English-Speaking World of the Eighteenth Century*, edited by Vincent Carretta (Lexington: the University Press of Kentucky, 1996); Ottobah Cugoano, "Narrative of the Enslavement of Ottabah Cugoano, a Native of Africa; Published by Himself in the Year 1787," in *The Negro's Memorial; or, Abolitionist's Catechism; by an Abolitionist, edited by Thomas Fisher* (London: Hatchard and Co., 1825), *Documenting the American South*, accessed April 7, 2016, http://tinyurl.com/zjeub5z; Olaudah Equiano, *The Interesting Narrative of the Life of Olaudah Equiano, or Gustavus Vassa, the African. Written by Himself*, 2 vols. (London: Printed for and sold by the author, 1789); Venture Smith, *A Narrative of the Life and Adventures of Venture, a Native of Africa: But Resident Above Sixty Years in the United States of America. Related by Himself* (New London: C. Hold, 1798); Benjamin F. Prentiss, *The Blind African Slave, or Memoirs of Boyrereau Brinch, Nick-Named Jeffrey Brace. Containing an Account of the Kingdom of Bow-Woo, in the Interior of Africa; with the Climate and Natural Productions, Laws, and Customs Peculiar to That Place. With an Account of His Captivity, Sufferings, Sales, Travels, Emancipation, Conversion to the Christian Religion, Knowledge of the Scriptures, &c. Interspersed with Strictures on Slavery, Speculative Observations on the Qualities of Human Nature, with Quotation from Scripture* (St. Albans, VT: Harry Whitney, 1810); Omar Ibn Said, *A Muslim American Slave: The Life of Omar Ibn Said*, edited and translated by Ala Alryyes (Madison: University of Wisconsin Press, 2011).

14. Thomas Clarkson, *The Substance of the Evidence of Sundry Persons on the Slave-Trade, Collected in the Course of a Tour Made in the Autumn of the Year 1788* (London: James Phillips, 1789); Alexander Falconbridge, *An Account of the Slave Trade on the Coast of Africa, by Alexander Falconbridge, Late Surgeon in the African Trade*, 2nd ed. (London: James Phillips, 1788).

15. On silences about the Middle Passage, see Jerome S. Handler, "Survivors of the Middle Passage: Life Histories of Enslaved Africans in British America," *Slavery & Abolition* 23, no. 1 (2003): 25–56, esp. 27.

16. James Sidbury, *Becoming African in America: Race and Nation in the Early Black Atlantic, 1760–1830* (New York: Oxford University Press, 2007), 40.

17. Woodard, *The Delectable Negro*, 35. See also Ronald Paul, "'I Whitened My Face, That They Might Not Know Me': Race and Identity in Olaudah Equiano's Slave Narrative," *Journal of Black Studies* 39, no. 6 (2009): 848–864, esp. 849.

18. I follow Carretta in calling him Equiano rather than Gustavus Vassa because this is the name with which scholars are most familiar.

19. Carretta, *Equiano, the African,* xiv–xv, 33; John Thornton, "Cannibals, Witches, and Slave Traders in the Atlantic World," *William and Mary Quarterly* 60, no. 2 (2003): 273–294, esp. 274. For Equiano's passage on a ship of a different name, see Woodard, *The Delectable Negro,* 36. For disagreements with Carretta's conclusions, see Paul E. Lovejoy, "Autobiography and Memory: Gustavus Vassa, alias Olaudah Equiano, the African," *Slavery & Abolition* 27, no. 3 (2006): 317–347. James Sweet concludes that pinning down Equiano's place of birth is less important than figuring out why the South Carolinian interpretation predominated more than the African one during some moments in Equiano's life. See James H. Sweet, "Mistaken Identities? Olaudah Equiano, Domingos Álvares, and the Methodological Challenges of Studying the African Diaspora," *American Historical Review* 114, no. 2 (2009): 279–306, esp. 301.

20. Carretta, *Equiano, the African,* xvi.

21. Rachel B. Herrmann, "The 'tragicall historie': Cannibalism and Abundance in Colonial Jamestown," *William and Mary Quarterly* 68, no. 1 (2011): 47–74, esp. 73. See also the introduction to this volume.

22. Peter Hulme, Colonial Encounters: Europe and the Native Caribbean, 1492–1797 (London: Methuen, 1986), 12.

23. Quobna Ottobah Cugoano, *Thoughts and Sentiments on the Evil of Slavery,* edited by Vincent Carretta (New York: Penguin Books, 1999), x.

24. Cugoano, "Narrative of the Enslavement of Ottabah Cugoano," 122.

25. Thornton, "Cannibals, Witches, and Slave Traders in the Atlantic World," 275.

26. Lindenbaum, "Thinking about Cannibalism," 486. See also Ty M. Reese, "'Eating' Luxury: Fante Middlemen, British Goods, and Changing Dependencies on the Gold Coast, 1750–1821," *William and Mary Quarterly* 66, no. 4 (2009): 851–872.

27. Woodard, *The Delectable Negro,* 56.

28. Thornton, "Cannibals, Witches, and Slave Traders in the Atlantic World," 277.

29. Woodard, *The Delectable Negro,* 9.

30. Cugoano, "Narrative of the Enslavement of Ottabah Cugoano," 123. On fears of European cannibals in the interior, see William D. Piersen, "White Cannibals, Black Martyrs: Fear, Depression, and Religious Faith as Causes of Suicide among New Slaves," *Journal of Negro History* 62, no. 2 (1977): 147–159, esp. 148.

31. Equiano, *The Interesting Narrative,* 70 ("was carried" and "immediately handled"), 71 ("a large furnace" and "no longer doubted"), 72 ("if we were not").

32. Equiano, *The Interesting Narrative,* 84.

33. For enslaved people reassuring Equiano he would not be eaten, see Equiano, *The Interesting Narrative,* 72, 85.

34. Carretta, *Equiano, the African,* xvi. For recent work on the Royal Navy see John McAleer and Christer Petley, *The Royal Navy and the British Atlantic World, c. 1750–1820* (London: Palgrave Macmillan, 2016).

35. Equiano, *The Interesting Narrative,* 97.

36. On the homoerotic relationship between Equiano and Baker, see Woodard, *The Delectable Negro,* 41–42.

37. Equiano, *The Interesting Narrative,* 98–99.

38. Woodard, *The Delectable Negro,* 31, 40 (quote).

39. Prentiss, *The Blind African Slave,* 82.

40. Johnson, "Narrating an Indigestible Trauma," 134–135.

41. On foodstuffs being good and bad to eat, see Marvin Harris, *Good to Eat: Riddles of Food and Culture* (Long Grove, IL: Waveland Press, Inc., 1998).

42. Carl Plasa, "'Stained with Spots of Human blood': Sugar, Abolition and Cannibalism," *Atlantic Studies* 4, no. 2 (2007): 225–243, esp. 226, 230–231.

43. Clarkson, *The Substance of the Evidence of Sundry Persons on the Slave-Trade,* v; Falconbridge, *An Account of the Slave Trade on the Coast of Africa.*

44. Clarkson, *The Substance of the Evidence of Sundry Persons on the Slave-Trade,* 84.

45. Marcus Rediker, "History from below the Water Line: Sharks and the Atlantic Slave Trade," *Atlantic Studies,* 5, no. 2 (2008): 285–297, esp. 287, 289, 292.

46. Rediker, "History from below the Water Line," 285 (for terror), 291 (for slave corpses), 293–4 (for desertion and suicide).

47. Rediker, "History from below the Water line," 292; Carretta, *Equiano, the African,* 43.

48. Clarkson, *The Substance of the Evidence of Sundry Persons on the Slave-Trade,* 40.

49. Falconbridge, *An Account of the Slave Trade on the Coast of Africa,* 40.

50. Falconbridge, *An Account of the Slave Trade on the Coast of Africa,* 39.

51. Equiano, *The Interesting Narrative,* 97.

52. Carretta, *Equiano, the African,* 43.

53. Rediker, "History from below the Water Line," 290.

54. For a thorough discussion of types of provisions on eighteenth-century slave ships and their relationship to enslaved peoples' health and mortality, see Sowande' Mustakeem, "'I Never Have Such a Sickly Ship Before': Diet, Disease, and Mortality in 18th-Century Atlantic Slaving Voyages," *Journal of African American History* 93, no. 4 (2008): 474–496, esp. 480; Sowande' Mustakeem, *Slavery at Sea: Terror, Sex, and Sickness in the Middle Passage* (Urbana: University of Illinois Press, 2016), 64–72.

55. Clarkson, *The Substance of the Evidence of Sundry Persons on the Slave-Trade,* 27.

56. *Oxford English Dictionary Online,* s.v. "horse-bean, n."

57. Clarkson, *The Substance of the Evidence of Sundry Persons on the Slave-Trade,* 31.

58. Falconbridge, *An Account of the Slave Trade on the Coast of Africa,* 28.

59. Johnson, "Narrating an Indigestible Trauma," 128–129, quote on 129.

60. Prentiss, *The Blind African Slave,* 90.

61. Equiano, *The Interesting Narrative,* 90. It is unclear whether the slaves on this ship were eating fruit from the Caribbean fat pork tree or fatty pork.

62. Equiano, *The Interesting Narrative,* 95.

63. On the Somerset decision and its limits, see Patricia Hagler Minter, "'The State of Slavery': Somerset, The Slave, Grace, and the Rise of Pro-Slavery and Anti-Slavery Constitutionalism in the Nineteenth Century Atlantic World," *Slavery & Abolition* 36, no. 4 (2015): 603–617.

64. Equiano, *The Interesting Narrative,* 103.

65. Clarkson, *The Substance of the Evidence of Sundry Persons on the Slave-Trade,* 3.

66. Clarkson, *The Substance of the Evidence of Sundry Persons on the Slave-Trade,* 31.

67. Equiano, *The Interesting Narrative,* 80–81.

68. Clarkson, *The Substance of the Evidence of Sundry Persons on the Slave-Trade,* 66.

69. For different types of cannibalism, see Arens, *The Man-Eating Myth,* 17–18.

70. Woodard, *The Delectable Negro,* 4–5, 47.

71. Clarkson, *The Substance of the Evidence of Sundry Persons on the Slave-Trade,* 23, 65, 76.

72. Falconbridge, *An Account of the Slave Trade on the Coast of Africa,* 29.

73. Equiano, *The Interesting Narrative,* 49–51, quote on 51.

74. Clarkson, *The Substance of the Evidence of Sundry Persons on the Slave-Trade,* 23, 65.

75. Kyla Wazana Tompkins, *Racial Indigestion: Eating Bodies in the 19th Century* (New York: New York University Press, 2012), 4–5.

76. For early works, see Piersen, "White Cannibals, Black Martyrs," 147–159, esp. 150. See also Terri L. Snyder, *The Power to Die: Slavery and Suicide in British North America* (Chicago: University of Chicago Press, 2015).

77. Johnson, "Narrating an Indigestible Trauma," 128.

78. Equiano, *The Interesting Narrative,* 50.

79. Equiano, *The Interesting Narrative,* 73.

80. Cugoano, "Narrative of the Enslavement of Ottobah Cugoano," 123.

81. Equiano, *The Interesting Narrative,* 80–81.

82. Clarkson, *The Substance of the Evidence of Sundry Persons on the Slave-Trade,* 20.

83. Marcus Rediker, *Between the Devil and the Deep Blue Sea: Merchant Seamen, Pirates, and the Anglo-American Maritime World, 1700–1750* (Cambridge: Cambridge University Press, 1987), 127, 222, 224.

84. Carretta, *Equiano, the African,* 32.

85. Falconbridge, *An Account of the Slave Trade on the Coast of Africa,* 27 (quote), 48.

86. Clarkson, *The Substance of the Evidence of Sundry Persons on the Slave-Trade,* 24.

# CONTRIBUTORS

**Robert Appelbaum** is a professor of English literature at Uppsala University in Sweden. His research focuses on early modern studies, food studies, and terrorism studies. In 2007 he received the Roland H. Bainton Prize for *Aguecheek's Beef*, a discussion of the culture of food and writing in the Renaissance. His most recent books are *Dishing It Out: In Search of the Restaurant Experience* (2011), *Working the Aisles: A Life in Consumption* (2014), *Terrorism before the Letter: Mythography and Political Violence in England, Scotland and France 1559–1642* (2015), and *The Aesthetics of Violence: Art, Fiction, Drama and Film* (2017).

**Elena Daniele** is a professor of practice in Italian at Tulane University in New Orleans. She pursues research in early modern ethnographic travel writing, particularly the Italian contribution to the early exploration of the Americas.

**Rebecca Earle** is a professor of history at the University of Warwick in Coventry. She is the author of several books on Spanish American cultural and political history. Her current research explores the cultural significance of food and eating and the impact of New World foods on early modern European mentalities and political culture.

**Julie Gammon** is an associate professor of history at the University of Southampton in Southampton. Her work on sexual violence against women in the long eighteenth century is forthcoming from Manchester University Press. She is also interested in histories of sodomy and in portrayals of gypsies as criminals in eighteenth-century England.

**Rachel B. Herrmann** is a lecturer in modern American history at Cardiff University in Cardiff. She is currently completing a manuscript titled *No Useless Mouth: How Native American and Black Revolutionaries Lost the Fight against Hunger* for Cornell University Press. Her previous research has appeared in *Diplomatic History, Labor: Studies in Working-Class History of the Americas, The Routledge History of American Foodways, The Routledge History of Food, Slavery & Abolition,* and the *William and Mary Quarterly.* She blogs regularly for *The Junto: A Group Blog on Early American History.*

**Jessica S. Hower** is an assistant professor of history at Southwestern University in Georgetown, Texas. Her research focuses on the significance of the Tudor century to the formation and development of Britain and its empire. Her monograph *Tudor Empire: The Making of Britain and the British Atlantic World, 1485–1603* is forthcoming from Palgrave Macmillan.

**Gregory D. Smithers** is a professor at Virginia Commonwealth University in Richmond. He is the author of numerous books and articles about Native American and African American history, his latest being *The Cherokee Diaspora: An Indigenous History of Migration, Resettlement, and Identity* (2015).

**Jared Staller** is a faculty member and history department coordinator at St. Francis Episcopal School in Houston, Texas. His monograph *Converging on Cannibals: Terrors of Slaving in Atlantic Africa, 1509–1670* is forthcoming from Ohio University Press.

**Kelly L. Watson** is an associate professor of history and a member of the faculty of women's and gender studies at Avila University in Kansas City, Missouri. She is the author of *Insatiable Appetites: Imperial Encounters with Cannibals in the North Atlantic World* (2015).

**Matt Williamson** is a senior lecturer in British literature at the University of Oslo in Norway. He specializes in the study of food in the drama of the early modern period. His PhD thesis at Queen's University Belfast was entitled "Hunger, Appetite and the Politics of the Renaissance Stage."

# INDEX